NEW DIRECTION

BIBLE READING GUIDE
with David Mainse

Crossroads Christian Communications Inc.
100 Huntley Street, Toronto, Ont. M4Y 2L1

ISBN-0-919463-15-0

Published by CROSSROADS CHRISTIAN COMMUNICATIONS INC.
100 Huntley Street, Toronto, Ontario

Printed in Canada by Harmony Printing Limited, Toronto, Ontario.

NEW DIRECTION

BIBLE READING GUIDE
with David Mainse

VOLUME II

Edited by Doug Burke
and
Paul Knowles

Photography by David Helsdon
Cover photo by Miller Services Ltd.

FOREWORD

Daily Bible reading requires "stick-to-it-iveness". It's a shame that well-meaning Christians often fail in this area. However, you who hold this book in your hands have a leg up to "overcoming" the lethargy and lack of discipline that often plague us.

This is the second volume in a "Through the Bible in Two Years" program. We've experimented in the lofty goal of a "One Year" program, but I received too many reports of discouraged readers who quit, or readers who hung on but didn't really understand what they had read because the readings were too long and involved.

Of course, Volume I has been in use all this past year and will again serve the year after this. You can write for your copy of Volume I at any time so as to have both books in the set.

I want to thank God, from my heart, for the wonderful gift of the loving and faithful people who had direct written input into these commentaries: Rev. Bill Absolom, Doug Burke, Rev. George Elsasser, Paul Knowles, Rev. Ron Orr, Doug Pearson, Rev. Art Rader and Rev. John Summers. I am also very grateful to those writers who have graciously contributed their poetry to this volume, and to David Helsdon, whose photographs illustrate both volumes of the New Direction Bible Reading Guide.

I want to give special mention to the efforts in editing and general preparation of Doug Burke and Paul Knowles.

As you use the New Direction Bible Reading Guide daily, I pray that God will open His Book to you, leading you in the green pastures and beside the still waters of His Word.

In Christ's Love and Service,

David Mainse

David Mainse
President and Host
of 100 Huntley Street

A New Year

The years with Thee, O Lord, we've spent—
The years Thy precious love hath lent.
For all the mercies Thou hast sent,
O Lord, accept our praise.

For all the joys that we could share,
E'en for the load so hard to bear
That sent us to Thy throne in prayer,
O Lord, accept our praise.

A year, O Lord, we face just now,
And fresh allegiance to Thee vow.
O may we all Thy will allow;
May we show forth Thy praise.

May self with Thee be crucified,
Thy Spirit in our hearts abide.
No matter what the future hide,
May we show forth Thy praise.

Our hands in Thine we place once more,
Knowing Thy faithfulness of yore.
Help us to worship and adore
And live, O Lord, for Thee.

— Marion Poynter

Genesis, the first book of Moses, is Act One of the cosmic drama of God and His creation. In this book, we meet the eternal God. We watch as He speaks and shapes His complete creation, "and it was good."

The pinnacle of that creation was a special creature named "man". This creature was special because, unlike anything else created by God, man was declared to be made "in the image of God." This meant that he was spiritual, capable of communing with, and loving, God. But it also created the possibility of choice: if man could choose to love, he could also choose to disobey. The curtain comes crashing down after Scene One, with the stage in total disarray—Adam and Eve have sinned, and brought upon themselves the ultimate penalty: death and isolation from their Creator.

But Scene Two reveals God knew full well that man would fall. He had already prepared the plan for man's salvation (See I Peter 1:18-20; Revelation 13:8). We do not see that full picture until the New Testament, where we read of the death, resurrection and ascension of the God-Man, the Anointed One, Jesus Christ. But much of the rest of Genesis is direct prophecy pointing to that coming One who will deliver His people from their sins.

We see pictures of Christ in the very first sacrifices of Abel and then of Noah, Abraham and other early men of faith. We see Him depicted in the Ark built by Noah to save himself and his family, a deliverance completely blueprinted by God. We see Him in the highly symbolic substitution of a ram for Isaac after Abraham has been comanded to sacrifice his son of promise. And we see Him in the life of Joseph.

January 1: Read Genesis 1,2

Key verse: "So God created man in His own image; in the image of God He created him; male and female He created them" (Genesis 1:27 NKJV).

You are made in the image of God. In very special ways, the Lord created you to be like Himself.

The Bible makes no such claim about any other creature. The animals, birds and fish are marvellous creations, but they are not made in God's image. That is not even claimed for the angels—only for men and women.

What does it mean, that you are an image-bearer?

First, it means that you are a spiritual being. Unlike animals, we have the capacity for life beyond the mere realm of the physical.

Our spiritual nature has made it possible for us to communicate with other spiritual beings. We can hear the voice of God—and we can hear the voice of Satan. Our choice concerning whom we listen to and obey will govern the nature of our spiritual life—or our spiritual death.

This leads us to another similarity between ourselves and our Creator. Like Him, we are intended to live forever, to share eternal life with Him. The choice of spiritual lord, God or Satan—which we mentioned earlier—will govern whether or not that potential is realized.

Because we are made in God's image, we can know God. But, also because we are in His image, we have the freedom to choose. That freedom allows us even to ignore and reject Him, though such a choice would lead to eternal condemnation.

Direction for today: Come to the Creator, the One whose image you carry.

Prayer for today: "Father, thank you for creating me with the capacity for everlasting life!"

January 2: Read Genesis 3,4

Key verse: "Then the man said, 'The woman whom You gave to be with me, she gave me of the tree, and I ate'" (Genesis 3:12 NKJV).

For the first time in the history of humanity—although certainly not for the last—man and woman had been caught in sin. Lured on by the lies of the serpent, Eve and Adam had chosen to disobey the commandment of their Lord and Creator, with disastrous results.

In eating from the tree of the knowledge of good and evil, the first people doomed themselves and their descendants, through all time, to a life of pain and hardship, and to eventual death.

Praise the Lord, Jesus has rescued us from this eternal fate. Through His death and resurrection, He both defeated sin and death and ransomed us from the penalty of death that we deserve.

But to know the life that Jesus gives, we must repent—turn from—our sin, our disobedience to God. Adam and Eve give us excellent examples of what repentance is not! Both of them attempted to blame someone else for their sin. Adam blamed both God and Eve (see our key verse); Eve blamed the serpent.

But if we are to know the freedom Jesus gives, we must first acknowledge our own disobedience and turn from it. We must say, "No one made me sin, Lord. I did it, and I'm responsible." That is the first step to freedom from sin, death and hell.

Direction for today: Be honest with God about your own sin.

Prayer for today: "Lord, I confess my sins to You and ask for Your forgiveness and cleansing, in the name of Jesus."

January 3: Read Genesis 5,6

Key verse: *"Enoch walked with God; then he was no more, because God took him away" (Genesis 5:24 NIV).*

What do you have to do to please God? Must you win hundreds of people to Him—or write great spiritual books or preach to thousands? Not at all.

God asks us to do only one thing: to walk with Him. Our key verse tells us that Enoch walked with God. And in Hebrews 11:5, one of the few verses in the Bible about this man, we learn that Enoch "was commended as one who pleased God."

How do we walk with God? We must walk in obedience to Him; Adam and Eve, once they had sinned, ceased to walk with God and, instead, hid in the garden (Genesis 3:8). If we are disobedient to the Lord, we cease to walk with Him and need to repent of our sins and return to loving obedience.

The New Testament tells us that walking with God is "walking in the Spirit" (Galatians 5:16). If you desire to please God, to walk with Him as did Enoch, why not ask God to fill you with His Spirit, as you surrender in obedience, so that you may truly walk with Him?

Direction for today: The only way to please God is to walk with Him in obedience. Do so!

Prayer for today: "Father, fill me with Your Spirit, that I may walk with You."

Memory Verse

"Know that the Lord, He is God; it is He who has made us, and not we ourselves; we are His people and the sheep of His pasture" (Psalm 100:3 NKJV).

January 4: Read Genesis 7,8

Key verse: *"So He destroyed all living things which were on the face of the ground: both man and cattle, creeping thing and bird of the air. They were destroyed from the earth. Only Noah and those who were with him in the ark remained alive" (Genesis 7:23 NKJV).*

The story of Noah and the great flood is a wonderful account of deliverance and salvation. We look to Noah and his family as examples of the "saved", and we identify with them.

But it is also important to remember the multitude of lives which were lost in the flood. As God's judgment was poured out, all who were unrighteous were destroyed.

History will come to an end with another, even more final, judgment as Christ returns, and all who have denied Him will be cast into eternal death. But this time, the ark is big enough to hold many more than eight people. God has provided a way, through Jesus, whereby all who will accept Him as Saviour and Lord will be saved.

Noah must have wept as he considered the fate of his lost neighbours; but there was nothing he could do. We should weep, also, when we consider our relatives and friends who will be lost for eternity if they do not repent. But there is much that we can do! It is our job to invite them into the ark, to tell them of the wonderful salvation that can be theirs in Christ.

Direction for today: Tell your relatives and friends about the importance of accepting salvation in Christ.

Prayer for today: "Lord, give me a deep, heart felt concern for the lost."

January 5: Read Genesis 9,10

Key verse: "So God blessed Noah and his sons, and said to them: 'Be fruitful and multiply, and fill the earth'" (Genesis 9:1 NKJV).

Our God is a God of second chances and forgiveness. The sin of man had grown so great that God had no choice but to destroy almost every member of the race. Instead of giving up on human beings, however, the Lord saved Noah, giving to mankind a second chance.

He gave Noah the same command that He had given to Adam: "Be fruitful and multiply." The Lord knew that some would turn to Him in love.

In this we see God's great love for His creation. Although the people He created had done almost everything imaginable to reject God, the Lord saved the race. And although those since Noah have followed the same pattern, or worse, the Lord's compassion continues.

Here in chapter nine, we also see God's love for mankind in His commands about the sanctity of human life. No one is to take another life; one who does so must give "a reckoning" (verse 5) to the Lord. This certainly tells us much about the responsibility of those who daily take human lives through abortion. If they do not repent, they fall under the judgment of God.

Direction for today: Remember that human life is a precious, God-given gift. Be thankful for your life, and work to save others.

Prayer for today: "Lord, thank You that You are a God of forgiveness and second chances!"

January 6: Read Genesis 11-13

Key verse: "And the Lord said unto Abram, . . . lift up thine eyes and look from the place where thou art." (Genesis 13:14 KJV).

We serve a faithful God, who is concerned about every detail of our lives. The cares and concerns that we carry are known to Him. It seems so easy for us to get our eyes on circumstances and let them control us, rather than putting our trust in the Lord.

"Lift up thine eyes and look from the place where thou art . . ." is a message that should strengthen us today. It was quite possible for Abram to look at the circumstances of the transaction and become discouraged. In his unselfishness he gave Lot the choice of where he was to go with his family and herdsmen. Lot chose that which looked lush and plentiful. God's immediate response to Abram was for him to get his eyes off the circumstances and look elsewhere. Was he not in a sense saying, "Get your eyes on Me"?

As Abram did that, the Lord gave him much more than he would have had in what Lot had chosen. Ephesians 3:20 tells us that He is able to "do exceedingly abundantly above all we ask or think . . .". In His covenant with Abram, God did exactly that. As Abram lifted his eyes off the situation at hand and trusted the Lord, the Lord made a covenant with him that affected not only him but all his seed as well. Abram's response was to build an altar onto the Lord. This became a time of thanksgiving and praise. In obedience, do the same in your life today.

Direction for today: Remember that, though you are in this world, you are not of this world.

Prayer for today: "Help us, Lord, to have enough faith to be obedient to You."

January 7: Read Genesis 14,15

Key verse: "And he believed the Lord; and He counted it to him for righteousness." (Genesis 15:6 KJV).

Abram's belief in God was not merely convenience. But his belief caused him to make decisions in a manner he would not ordinarily have done. His decisions perhaps to the natural man were foolish, but to the spiritual man were wise.

Belief to the Jewish mind was not simply an acknowledgement of a historical or scientific fact. But belief was of such consequence that entire lifestyles could, and often would be, altered based on belief "on" something or someone as opposed to their belief "in" it. Paul says in Romans 4:1—3, "What shall we say then that Abraham our father, as pertaining to the flesh, hath found? For if Abraham were justified by works, he hath whereof to glory; but not before God. For what saith the scripture? Abraham believed God, and it was counted unto him as righteousness."

Abram did not depend on his works to establish a right relationship with God. But he depended upon his faith and trust to open the door into God's presence. Our works will never gain us a place in heaven or even its doorstep. It is God's gift of grace and mercy manifested in the supreme and eternal sacrifice of the Lord Jesus Christ. Only through faith and trust in Him will we be admitted to God's eternal kingdom.

James 2:20 says that "faith without works is dead." However the works are only to provide an outward and tangible confirmation of the motivating force behind them, belief and trust in God.

Direction for today: Let all of your service for God today be motivated by belief and trust in God.

Prayer for today: "Father, thank You for Your unconditional love. Help me to practise this same quality in my life."

January 8: Read Genesis 16,17

Key verse: "When Abram was ninety-nine years old, the Lord appeared to him and said, 'I am God Almighty; walk before Me and be blameless,' " (Genesis 17:1 NIV).

Chapter 17 contains the articles of the covenant agreement between our Heavenly Father, on the one part, and Abram, our spiritual father, on the other. Abram was ninety-nine years old when God made this gracious visit, a full thirteen years after the birth of Ishmael.

This first verse provides the general scope and summary of the covenant that is the foundation on which all the rest was built. It is the covenant of God's grace, which He continues to make with all those who believe in Jesus Christ.

In making Himself known to Abram as the "Almighty God," we are told what we may expect God to be to us; namely, a God who is enough: an all-sufficient God.

What God requires is that we walk before Him in integrity. The covenant is mutual: if we honour God, He will honour us (1 Samuel 2:30).

Direction for today: Remember, "No good thing does He withhold from those whose walk is blameless" (Psalm 84:11 NIV).

Prayer for today: "Thank you, Lord, for the grace by which we are saved."

January 9: Read Genesis 18,19

Key verse: "Then the Lord said, 'Shall I hide from Abraham what I am about to do?'" (Genesis 18:17 NIV).

In Chapter 18, verses 16 to 22, we have a perfect example showing that God honours those who honour Him.

Abraham had honoured his guests, the three messengers from heaven, by showing them hospitality and graciously entertaining them. When they left, he "walked along with them to see them on their way", thereby paying his utmost respect. God returned the honour by informing Abraham of His purpose to destroy Sodom.

But why must Abraham be so informed? First, he must know because God promised to bless the earth through him (verse 18), and those who, by faith, live a life of communion with God cannot help but know more of His mind than others. They have better insight as to what is happening now and in the future.

Second, Abraham must know so that he will direct his children and his household (verse 19). He taught them to "keep the way of the Lord by doing what is right and just"; that is, to be serious in the worship of God and honest in their dealings with all people.

But Abraham also was told in order that he might be aware of what was about to happen to his relative, Lot. God tells Abraham of the evidence against Sodom so that he may know that His judgments are never the result of rash or sudden decisions.

Direction for today: Reach out to others in kindness and compassion, and thus honour God.

Prayer for today: "Help me to honour all people and to show kindness accordingly."

January 10: Read Genesis 20,21

Key verse: "Sarah became pregnant and bore a son to Abraham in his old age, at the very time God had promised him" (Genesis 21:2 NIV).

In Chapter 21 we see the fulfilling of God's promise in the conception and birth of Isaac.

As God had commanded him, Abraham named the boy Isaac, meaning laughter. There was good reason for the name because: (1) when Abraham received the promise of him, he laughed for joy (Genesis 17:17); (2) when Sarah received the promise, she laughed with disbelief (Genesis 18:12); (3) the promise, of which Isaac was the heir, became the joy of the saints of all ages.

Isaac was born according to the promise of God, "at the very time God had promised". God is always punctual, although His promised mercies may not come at the time we set. We can be sure they will come at the time He determines, and that is always the best time.

Direction for today: Trust in the Lord always.

Prayer for today: "Thank you, Lord, for being the source of my joy."

Memory Verse

"And be kind to one another, tenderhearted, forgiving one another, just as God in Christ also forgave you" (Ephesians 4:32 NKJV).

January 11: Read Genesis 22,23

Key verse: "'I will indeed bless you, and I will multiply your descendants as the stars of heaven and as the sand which is on the seashore. And your descendants shall possess the gate of their enemies" (Genesis 22:17 RSV).

After a long period of testing, Abraham and Sarah finally had their own little son. How they rejoiced! How they loved him! But now a new test confronted them. God told Abraham to offer his son as a sacrifice to Him. Abraham probably spent the night in tears, wrestling in prayer. Would God really make such a request? How could he give up his son?

Finally, as the sun began to rise, Abraham obeyed, took Isaac up to the mountain and placed him on the altar.

And then God responded, giving Isaac back and promising great blessing. He is faithful! He will do far above what we can ask or think! He has "provided Himself a Lamb"!

"Behold the Lamb of God which taketh away the sin of the world" (John 1:29).

Direction for today: Trust Jesus, with whom all things are possible.

Prayer for today: "Father, thank You for the Lamb, Your Son who died in my place".

January 12: Read Genesis 24

Key verse: "Come in, O blessed of the Lord; why do you stand outside?" (Genesis 24:31a RSV).

Can one truly depend on God to guide one's life and meet every need? Isaac's mother Sarah has been dead for three years now. He is lonely and needs a wife. He has no circle of young men and women with which to fellowship.

But Isaac has a father who trusts God, and he has a servant who also trusts God and is obedient. God provides a wonderful wife. He fulfills His promises.

Isaac is a type or picture of Christ, who is seeking His bride today. The servant is a type of the Holy Spirit. Rebekah is a type of the Church, the Bride of Jesus Christ.

As each person hears the gospel and opens his heart to Jesus, he begins to live in the kingdom of Heaven and to be part of God's promise that His people will carry out His great plan in history. And, just as Isaac received Rebekah and she became his wife, so will Jesus Christ come again and receive every believer to Himself for all eternity.

Direction for today: Be ready to move when God calls you.

Prayer for today: "Lord, I am Yours. Whatever You ask of me, I will do. Wherever You send me, I will go."

January 13: Read Genesis 25,26

Key verse: *"Now Isaac pleaded with the Lord for his wife, because she was barren; and the Lord granted his plea, and Rebekah his wife conceived" (Genesis 25:21 NKJV).*

Isaac and Rebekah had been married for nineteen years. Rebekah was barren, but God had made a promise. Isaac believed the promise—he prayed, and Rebekah became pregnant. He asked, and they received double from God—twins!

Fearful of the violent movement within her, Rebekah prayed, and she received (verse 23). But Isaac favored Esau; Rebekah favored Jacob. Unfortunately, Rebekah also took personal responsibility to try to work out God's calling in Jacob's life.

Isn't it great when God answers prayer? Shouldn't it make you pray all the more, with greater expectation? Unfortunately, in most circumstances, this doesn't happen. We revert to trying to achieve through human effort alone, rather than doing our part diligently and trusting God for His will to be done.

Let us learn to pray more and more. Let us believe God for greater and greater expressions of His miracle-working power. Let us reject—yes, let us crucify—the flesh, that we may enjoy resurrection life.

Direction for today: Find God's promise for your need, then fervently ask God to meet that need.

Prayer for today: "Lord, teach me to pray."

January 14: Read Genesis 27

Key verse: *"And Jacob said to his father, 'I am Esau'" (Genesis 27:19 NKJV).*

How many family problems would be solved if husband and wife would develop the art of honest communication. This whole unfortunate experience with father and mother and their twin sons would have been averted if Isaac and Rebekah had been sharing everything with each other.

Look at the mistakes: Rebekah listens in on private communication; she plots dishonestly; she encourages Jacob to deceive and lie. As a result, Esau is filled with hatred and murder, and Jacob is forced to run away from home. Jacob's character is twisted and bent so badly that he spends years in deception and deceit.

Dear ones, are you communicating in Christian love and understanding? Are you working together with the Holy Spirit to make your family truly blessed?

Direction for today: Mom, Dad, love each other and communicate with each other!

Prayer for today: "God, may our family reflect Your presence in us."

January 15: Read Genesis 28,29

Key verse: "Behold I am with you and will keep you wherever you go, and will bring you back to this land for I will not leave you until I have done that of which I have spoken to you" (Genesis 28:15 RSV).

Jacob caught a glimpse of God. Unfortunately, this was not sufficient to change his twisted character as he went hunting for a wife. If only people would get right with God; if only they would commit themselves completely to Jesus for salvation and direction before looking for a lifetime partner in marriage!

God wants the best for us. He has a plan for our lives, and will give us the power and ability to carry it out if we will trust Him. Many people are living defeated, frustrated lives because they put their desires ahead of God's plan.

Will you let Jesus Christ have complete control of your life today? He will give you joy and victory.

Direction for today: Let the Spirit of God have the reins of your life.

Prayer for today: "Holy Spirit, please guide me in all I do or say or think."

January 16: Read Genesis 30

Key verse: "Then God remembered Rachel; He listened to her and opened her womb" (Genesis 30:22 NIV).

Here we have the tragic story of two women living in the same household, vying for the affection and approval of the same man. They allowed jealousy to drive them to vindictiveness, which would cause family problems for years to come.

Jacob found it very difficult—in fact, impossible—to please both women, and it seems he surrendered all his authority to others. In doing so, he played into the hands of the women, and this led to endless heartache.

In the beginning, Jacob loved Rachel and paid a great price to receive her. It is heartwarming to see God answer Rachel's prayer by opening her womb. Had she been patient earlier in life, I'm sure God would have answered her prayer sooner, and many problems would never have occurred. But, in the end, God gave Rachel and Jacob a most beautiful gift in the birth of Joseph, who was to become one of the great men of the Bible.

God continued to bless Jacob with a great fortune because of his dedication to Him and his hard work for his father-in-law, Jethro.

Direction for today: Live and work within God's plan and His timetable rather than trying to do it all by yourself.

Prayer for today: "Lord, may Your will be mine. Please make me patient and willing to wait for Your timing, as You deal with my situation."

January 17: Read Genesis 31

Key verse: "Then the Lord said to Jacob, 'Go back to the land of your fathers and to your relatives, and I will be with you'" (Genesis 31:3 NIV).

In this story, Jacob hears from God and sets out to return to his homeland. But fear of a man dictates wrong action. Knowing the character of Laban leads Jacob to leave secretly. God was about to teach a great lesson.

Throughout the Bible, we repeatedly read of God placing a divine call upon someone. The call is heeded, but acted upon in a human manner. When we follow after God, He makes the way possible.

Jacob's human schemes did not save him; they only delayed the outcome. It is when we come to our wits' end that God intervenes. God's coming to Laban in a dream changed the outcome of the following day, and of history.

When God took over the job of protecting, Jacob learned that, ". . . in all things God works for the good of those who love Him, who have been called according to His purpose" (Romans 8:28 NIV). Through this intervention, God was able to bring enemies to peace. For years to come, a heap of stones stood as a monument to the treaty God arranged.

Direction for today: Allow God to have His way, rather than following your own devices.

Prayer for today: "Lord, I will follow You to the land to which You have called me. Lead me step by step with Your protecting hand."

"The Lord your God is a consuming fire, a jealous God"
(Deuteronomy 4:24 NKJV).

January 18: Read Genesis 32,33

Key verse: "Then the man said, 'Your name will no longer be Jacob, but Israel, because you have struggled with God and with men and have overcome'" (Genesis 32:28 NIV).

In life we need to experience two encounters: first with God, then with man.

Jacob had a great fear of his brother because of the deceit practised by his mother and himself years earlier, when Rebekah attempted to help God fulfill His plan. That deceit brought tremendous fear into the heart of Jacob, as he approached his homeland and his brother.

Before he could handle the fear of meeting his brother, it was necessary that Jacob first have a more important meeting. That encounter was with God. In his desperate state, he fought all night and would not let God go until he received a blessing.

When we have an encounter with God, face to face, not only can we confront the struggles at hand, but our very lives are changed. It was through this encounter that Jacob's name was changed to Israel. We, too, need that same determination to be blessed of God.

The encounter with God made it possible for Jacob to have a beautiful reunion with his brother, Esau, because God had prepared them both for reconciliation.

Direction for today: It's not easy to face the music, but it is something you must do. If there is a situation or a relationship which needs to be put right, do it now.

Prayer for today: "Lord, help me always to meet with You before I face the struggles of the world."

January 19: Read Genesis 34,35

Key verse: "Then Jacob said to Simeon and Levi, 'You have brought trouble on me, by making me odious among the inhabitants of the land' " (Genesis 34:30 NAS)

These chapters tell us of the treachery of Simeon and Levi, and the immoral betrayal by Reuben. From these accounts, and the continuing stories regarding these men and their descendants, we can learn two important lessons concerning sin and rebellion against God.

Simeon and Levi had a responsibility to deal with the sin against their sister Dinah perpetrated by Shechem (Genesis 34:2), but they went far beyond justice in attacking and killing many innocent people, lying and deceiving those who had made peace with their father, and in fact carrying out the same sin they charged Sechem with (34:29b).

Reuben's sin (35:22) is also obvious—he had sexual intercourse with his father's wife. It is important to note that, although no consequences of this sin are recorded here, we find that Reuben suffered for his action. His punishment is recorded in Genesis 49:4, as Israel revokes Reuben's rights as first-born, and bestows them on Judah.

In this same passage (see Genesis 49:5-7), Simeon and Levi are cursed by their father, and deprived of inheritance in the promised land. We find this actually took place—when the land was divided among the tribes (Joshua 19:19), Simeon was scattered among the tribe of Judah, with no inheritance for themselves.

The Levites met another end, however. The tribe, carrying the disgrace they shared with Simeon, continued nonetheless obedient to the Lord. In Exodus 32, as the entire nation turned to the worship of Aaron's golden calf, the Levites remained true, and stood with Moses on the side of the Lord. That loyalty to God resulted in a remarkable alteration of their punishment.

They still remained scattered throughout the land . . . not as punishment, but with a purpose. The Levites were appointed priests and tabernacle attendants (Numbers 3), and judges of the people (Deuteronomy 21:5). And they received the wonderful promise that they needed no earthly inheritance because "the Lord, the God of Israel, is their inheritance." (Joshua 13:33).

The Levites are a beautiful picture of God's mercy and forgiveness. As we stumble and fall, we can realize that while sin always carries consequences, the Lord is Almighty and can turn even the consequences of sin into blessing for a repentant, obedient believer.

Direction for today: Be sure that, within the innermost recesses of your heart, you constantly meet with God.

Prayer for today: "Still my heart, Lord, that I might hear from You and be directed in Your ways."

January 20: Read Genesis 36,37

Key verse: "So when the Midianite merchants came by, his brothers pulled Joseph up out of the cistern and sold him for twenty shekels of silver to the Ishmaelites, who took him to Egypt" (Genesis 37:28 NIV).

Even though God's promise was upon Jacob before his birth, Esau apparently refused to waste his life in bitterness and self-pity. We see how enthusiastically he received his brother Jacob back home and how God richly rewarded his attitude and generosity. By reading the list of descendants and their accomplishments, we can see that God blessed the house of Esau.

In the next chapter, we read the famous story of the dreamer. Future events were to prove that God had truly revealed His plan to Joseph in this unusual dream.

When we hear from God, it is important that we do not boast of it. A heart-wrenching family feud instantly developed due to the revelation of the dream by Joseph.

The problem did not start with the dream, but because Jacob loved Joseph more than the others. Such seemingly little things in life have a tendency to cause great heartache if they go uncorrected. Joseph aggravated the situation by bringing to his father a bad report about his brothers. However, God was about to use this difficulty as a means of starting Joseph off on the road to Egypt, where God needed him to save many lives in the years that lay ahead. And, among the lives to be saved, were those of his father and brothers.

Direction for today: Remember, the road to fulfilling God's calling is not always easy, but it is life-saving.

Prayer for today: "Lord, give me discretion in my dealings with the ones I love. Let me bring unity rather than discord."

January 21: Read Genesis 38,39

Key verse: "How can I do this great wickedness, and sin against God?" (Genesis 39:9 NKJV).

It almost seems as though young Joseph was living in twentieth-century North America. The problems he faced are the sort that adorn the front pages of our newspapers, the TV listings, and the movie ads each day.

He faced hatred from members of his family. Has there ever been an age of less family love than our age?

He faced and and enforced relocation to a land and culture unfamiliar to him. How many North Americans are living in cities or neighbourhoods which are strange to them, and where they have no friends?

And finally, in these chapters, Joseph faced a temptation that is glorified in our age—the temptation of sexual sin.

Knowing that Joseph faced problems and temptations that we can identify with, it is important that we consider his response to those situations. His response was courageousand holy—he refused to "do this great evil, and sin against God."

It is indeed possible to stand firm with the Lord, even in the face of temptations as enormous as those faced by North Americans in the 1980's. Joseph is a good example for us; and the Man he prefigured, our Lord Jesus Christ, is the supreme example of how we should live.

Direction for today: Stand firm in your witness for Christ. Be sure that all you do is honouring to Him.

Prayer for today: "Father, give me strength and victory over sin to live for You."

January 22: Read Genesis 40-41:37

Key verse: *"And Joseph said unto them, 'Do not interpretations belong to God? Tell them to me, please' " (Genesis 40:8 NKJV).*

Those who have not experienced the salvation of God by putting their trust in Him are unable to see or understand the things of God.

Jesus said, "Most assuredly, I say to you, unless one is born again, he cannot see the kingdom of God" (John 3:3). It is through the new birth that we are given perception and understanding of spiritual things.

Joseph had a vital, living relationship with God; therefore, no matter what happened to him or where he found himself, he always had the consciousness of God's presence and His enabling. Thus, when the butler and baker came to him with their troubling dreams, he was able to say with confidence that God would reveal the answer through him.

Likewise, those who are truly born again of God's Holy Spirit have been given an understanding of spiritual things, and by daily communication with God, are able to give wise counsel and direction to those whose hearts are longing for and enquiring after God.

Direction for today: Ask Jesus to give you wisdom and understanding.

Prayer for today: "O Lord, please teach me to be more sensitive to Your Holy Spirit."

January 23: Read Genesis 41:38-42

Key verse: *"And Joseph remembered the dreams which he dreamed of them . . . " (Genesis 42:9 KJV).*

Years had passed since Joseph shared with his brothers and father his dream of being a ruler and them bowing down to him. This vision that God had given to Joseph was just a little glimpse of God's plan for Joseph's life. God knew that, in order for Joseph to be prepared to fill the role of a ruler, he would need to go through hardship, persecution and rejection.

Joseph did go through rough times. He was put into a pit and into jail but during all this, Joseph trusted God to be able to fulfill that which He had promised in his vision. Joseph's father had forgotten the vision. Joseph's brothers had forgotten the vision. But Genesis 42:9 states, ". . . Joseph remembered the dream which he dreamed of them . . . ". In those moments of hardship, Joseph remembered that God had not forgotten him.

God has a plan for your life. Though at times it seems that your life is out of control, without any sense of direction, remember that God has not forgotten you. He will cause, ". . . all things to work together for good to them that love God, to them who are the called according to His purpose." (Romans 8:28).

Direction for today: Be sure that others can see in you the difference that comes from knowing the Lord.

Prayer for today: "Lord, let the Spirit of Christ be seen in me."

January 24: Read Genesis 43,44

Key verse: "Now his heart yearned for his brother; so Joseph made haste and sought somewhere to weep. And he went into his chamber and wept there" (Genesis 43:30 NKJV).

Joseph is a type, or picture, of the Lord Jesus Christ.

He was rejected by his brothers, sold for the price of a slave, was considered to be dead, yet was later declared to be alive and became a saviour to the children of Israel in the time of famine.

His brothers treated Joseph cruelly when he was young. The temptation to be angry and bitter against them must have been very real to him. Many today who have been treated badly by others have allowed bitterness and anger to take root in their lives, and have lost their beautiful testimony of God's love. Joseph, on the other hand, retained a soft, trusting heart and God blessed and honoured him for it.

Instead of punishing his brothers when he had a chance for revenge, he felt sorry for them and forgave them. What an example this is for us!

Direction for today: Forgive those who wrong you.

Prayer for today: "Father, help me to forgive others who wrong me and to love them for Jesus' sake."

Memory Verse

"Let your light so shine before men, that they may see your good works and glorify your Father in heaven" (Matthew 5:16 NKJV).

January 25: Read Genesis 45,46

Key verse: "But now, do not therefore be grieved or angry with yourselves because you sold me here; for God sent me before you to preserve life" (Genesis 45:5 NKJV).

Joseph's love for his brothers was so great that he found he was able to freely forgive them for the awful things they had done to him. He had learned, long before, how to forgive others. He had also observed that unforgiveness can harm a man who, although forgiving others who had wronged him, had not forgiven himself.

God had forgiven Joseph's brothers and Joseph had himself forgiven them, but here, in verse five, he exhorts them to forgive themselves. Joseph knew that, unless they did so, they would never rise above the slave mentality which they had shown as they came before him.

Direction for today: Rejoice in the refuge of the full forgiveness of God.

Prayer for today: "Lord, I forgive myself, even as You have forgiven me. Help me to realize that I am not a slave, but Your child."

January 26: Read Genesis 47,48

Key verse: "So Jacob blessed Pharaoh, and went out from before Pharaoh" (Genesis 47:10 NKJV).

This is an unusual detail included in the midst of a larger story of God's deliverance of His people: Jacob blessed Pharaoh. In those days, the act of conferring a blessing was a very serious thing, and it implied that the one giving the blessing was superior to the one receiving it. In the next chapter, for example, Jacob blesses his sons.

One would expect that Pharaoh would be superior, and Jacob inferior; but he did not act that way. Jacob's attitude tells us something very important about authority.

Pharaoh held an earthly office and, though he may have been the most important ruler on the earth at that time, Jacob had a much more important commission. God had personally called him to possess a land, to be father to a nation, and to bless the entire world! (Genesis 28:13-15).

Jacob knew he could act on the authority of the Lord. Thus, it was right that he should confer a blessing on Pharaoh. We, too, are commissioned by God, and are heirs of all of His promises. We, too, stand in His authority, and can face earthly authority without fear, for we are children of the heavenly King.

Direction for today: Realize your authority in Christ and allow Him to teach you to stand in it.

Prayer for today: "Father, may everything I do honour Your name."

January 27: Read Genesis 49,50

Key verse: "The sceptre shall not depart from Judah, nor a lawgiver from between his feet, until Shiloh comes; and to him shall be the obedience of the people" (Genesis 49:10 NKJV).

Judah was not the first-born of Jacob's children; in fact, he was born fourth, after Reuben, Simeon and Levi. Yet, in Jacob's blessing, Judah is granted the most important privileges including, as we know, the position as ancestor to Jesus. This was because his elder brothers had all failed in their responsibilities.

But Judah, from whose line came Christ, is granted a wonderful prophetic blessing through his father. He is told that his brothers will praise him, and we know that every tongue will declare that Jesus is

Lord. He is assigned the apparently contradictory names of "Lion" and "Shiloh" (Peace). Only in Christ is that possible, as Jesus both wins victory over all enemies of God and establishes peace.

Judah is told that others will bow to him; this prefigures the worship due to Jesus Christ. He is ruler and lawgiver, and we await His coming as King of kings and Lord of lords. Then Jacob says that Judah will wash his garments in wine; this picture is picked up again in the book of Revelation, as Jesus comes in garments washed in blood and the saints are cleansed by the blood of the Lamb. Judah could not have understood everything predicted of him, but every word was fulfilled centuries later in Jesus.

Direction for today: Remember that God always fulfills His promises.

Prayer for today: "Lord, have victory in my life and grant me peace."

Matthew

Although the book of Matthew does not name its own author, longstanding Christian tradition attributes the book to Matthew the disciple of Christ. (See Matthew 9:9).

A major purpose of the book is to show that Jesus was, and is, truly the Messiah, the descendant of David who is the eternal King of Israel. Matthew knows and demonstrates that the entire Old Testament is a prelude to the coming of Jesus the Christ, the anointed one, the King of kings.

The book also contains a great deal of practical Christian instruction, despite its narrative form. We especially see this in the Sermon on the Mount (Matthew 5-7).

January 28: Read Matthew 1,2

Key verse: "Behold, a virgin shall be with child, and bear a Son, and they shall call His name Immanuel, which is translated, 'God with us'" (Matthew 1:23 NKJV).

It is good to know that God is "God-with-us". In these two chapters, there are at least three examples which show that He was God-with-His-people.

Immediately after our key verse, we read that Joseph was awakened by God-being-with-him, who commanded him to marry Mary. In Matthew 2:12, God was with the wise men and warned them to bypass Herod on the way home. In Matthew 2:13, an angel told Joseph to take Jesus to Egypt. Each instance came about because God was God-with-His-people.

When Moses was faced with a troublesome people, when Daniel was thrown into the den of lions, when Paul was locked in jail—they may have wondered if God was still with them. He was.

Immanuel is our God today too. It is easy to feel that God is with us when everything is going well. When we're being blessed, when everything to which we set our hand comes out well—then it's easy to say that God is with us.

It's another matter when things aren't going so well. When marriage is a struggle, when our unsaved loved ones do not appear any closer to the kingdom today than they did ten years ago, when there's trouble in the church—whenever and whatever—our God who reigns is also our "God-with-us", our Immanuel.

Direction for today: Stand fast in the knowledge that, no matter what the situation, God is your Immanuel.

Prayer for today: "I thank You that You are 'God-with-me' in every circumstance, O Lord."

January 29: Read Matthew 3,4

Key verse: "Then they immediately left their nets and followed Him" (Matthew 4:20 NKJV).

You may be impressed by the word "immediately" in this verse. Many of us can't conceive of responding immediately to anything or anyone, not even to Jesus.

We want always to know what it's going to cost, this full-hearted, open response. We want to know that to which we're responding. It is important to count the cost. But, as we consider this story, in comparison with the stories of the boy Samuel and the prophet Isaiah, we are struck by the fact that none of these men appeared to understand entirely the call on their lives. And yet, because they believed in a great God who had in times past been faithful, they dared to believe that He would be faithful again, that He would not fail to provide for them in the face of the task He would set before them.

We also find ourselves eager for an "immediate" response, a response which answers now, "Here I am, send me." We want to obey immediately, without excuse or begging for time. We want our children to obey quickly and without question. Be sure that our heavenly Father also wants us to do today what we know He asks of us.

Transoceanic travellers talk about jet lag, which occurs because too many time zones are crossed too quickly for body clocks to keep up. In a similar way, we may have an obedience lag, that which causes us to put off obeying until we are ready or until we trust God enough to obey. Be an "immediately" obedient person.

Direction for today: Determine that, whatever the Lord asks of you today, you will immediately do it.

Prayer for today: "Lord, give me the grace to obey immediately."

January 30: Read Matthew 5

Key verse: *"But I say to you, love your enemies, bless those who curse you, do good to those who hate you, and pray for those who spitefully use you and persecute you" (Matthew 5:44 NKJV).*

We live in a society in which there is less and less love for anyone— never mind our enemies. The principle today seems to be to get even with those who wrong us. Our society increasingly lives with a "sue and be sued" mentality. If someone wrongs me, I must get even with him and wrong him in return.

But that's a far cry from what Jesus would have us do! He tells us: "Blessed are you when men revile and persecute you . . . rejoice and be exceedingly glad, for great is your reward in heaven." He tells us not to resist an evil person but, rather, to turn the other cheek when we have been taken advantage of or hurt. Could He really have meant what He said? Could it be that He wants us to purpose in our hearts to act in a similar way to those who are our enemies?

Yes. Jesus wants us to do exactly what He did. He wants us to return good for evil, to bless and pray for those who mistreat us. Jesus wants our relationships with people to be as His were.

Direction for today: Let Jesus be your example today. Bless those who would be your enemies.

Prayer for today: "Lord, help me to love the unlovable, just as You loved me."

January 31: Read Matthew 6

Key verse: *"But seek ye first the kingdom of God, and His righteousness; and all of these things shall be added unto you" (Matthew 6:33 NKJV).*

The passage that includes Matthew 6:25-33, reminds us of Paul's words to the church at Philippi. Paul testifies, "I have learned, in whatsoever state I am, therewith to be content" (Philippians 4:11). Somehow that seems so idealistic and impossible for us today. After all, it seems we need so much more of this world's goods than did Jesus and His disciples, or Paul and his friends.

But being content has nothing to do with possessions or material gain. Instead, our Father wants us to understand His love and care for us. He desires us to be good stewards of that which He's given us, but He especially asks us to fix our eyes on Him, and to trust Him.

He desires to satisfy our needs, to give us good gifts, and to be our Father in every sense of the word. But we need to let Him do so.

Let's not be concerned today about the issues of tomorrow. Tomorrow will take care of itself. Count on it: the Word says so!

Direction for today: Trust the Lord. He will not fail you.

Prayer for today: "Lord, I resolve to trust You for my every need."

Stone In His Sandal

I remember the day He had a stone in His sandal.
He was talking and laughing
With Thomas and the others
And He didn't notice it for a bit,
Until He began to limp.

I remember too, that same day,
That we stopped for a bit along the way
And watched a funeral pass by.
How the women cried,
Especially the dead youth's mother.
First a widow, and now another death.
And Jesus stepped forward, still limping a bit.
He touched her hand, and dried her eyes,
And said to that body, "Young man, rise!"
And the boy sat up.
Why, I almost died!
Now new tears shone as his mother cried,
And we all spoke in whispers and watched in awe
The man with the limp: the Son of God.

— Paul Knowles

"The Spirit Himself bears witness with our spirit that we are children of God" (Romans 8:16 NKJV).

February 1: Read Matthew 7

Key verse: *"Therefore whosoever heareth these sayings of mine, and doeth them, I will liken him unto a wise man, which built his house upon a rock" (Matthew 7:24 KJV).*

The three words "and doeth them" are of utmost importance.

Many Christians go through life waiting for God to do something for them. They wonder why the God who gloriously saved them, who marvelously filled them with His Holy Spirit and who may have done any number of miraculous signs and wonders, doesn't seem to be filling them with a zest for life. Instead of going from "victory to victory" they seem to be going from "defeat to defeat". But the problem is not God; The problem is us.

It is God who saves us and fills us with the Spirit and heals us, but Scripture has some very specific commands directed to us. Someone once said that we cannot do what God must do, and God will not do what we can do. God wants us to obey His Word; there are so many promises for those who will be obedient to Him.

This is the last of the chapters which make up the Sermon on the Mount. Jesus completes the Sermon with this word about obedience. He wants His hearers to practise all they have heard Him teach.

Are there areas in which you've not been obedient?

Direction for today: Hear and obey.

Prayer for today: "Forgive me, Lord, for the areas in which I have failed to obey You."

February 2: Read Matthew 8

Key verse: *"And He touched her hand, and the fever left her. Then she arose and served them" (Matthew 8:15 NKJV).*

This story of the healing of Peter's mother-in-law is a beautiful example of how things work in God's plan. Here we see the healing touch of the Lord Jesus, but we also see the worshipful response of the one who was healed. The woman served Jesus and His companions.

God's will is that we should use His gifts to us to serve others in His name. How often do we receive a wonderful blessing from the Lord, and then treat such a gift selfishly? We are healed, but we do not give God the glory or use our new-found health to serve Him. We are financially blessed, but we spend our gain greedily, for ourselves and not for the kingdom. We are saved from sin and death, but we continue to live our lives as though they were our own, ignoring the truth that we are "bought with a price" at the cost of Jesus' life.

We should follow the example of Peter's mother-in-law. When Jesus healed her, she responded by serving Him.

How has Jesus blessed you? Has He given physical healing, spiritual life, financial blessings, family wholeness, emotional health? How should you respond to these great gifts from the Lord?

Direction for today: Rise up and serve Jesus!

Prayer for today: "Father, I thank You for Your great gifts to me. Help me to express my gratitude in deeds, as well as words."

February 3: Read Matthew 9

Key verse: "Then He said to His disciples, 'The harvest truly is plentiful, but the labourers are few. Therefore, pray the Lord of the harvest to send out labourers into His harvest'" (Matthew 9:37,38 NKJV).

Perhaps biblical promises should come with labels like many modern products do: "Caution, contents under pressure"; "Apply with care." These particular verses might carry the warning: "Application of this prayer may change your life!"

Jesus has commanded us to ask the Father to pray for labourers in His spiritual harvest fields. But as soon as we offer that prayer, we become part of the answer—we are, each one, called to be labourers for the Lord in His harvest.

The work is hard. It is never easy to bring home a harvest, but the rewards are very great.

There is no greater joy for a believer than to share in bringing a new brother or sister into the kingdom of God. There is no greater blessing than to see a ruined, broken life made whole again by the power of the Holy Spirit. There is no greater thrill than to be used by God for His work.

Our responsibility is not small. Our joy is full.

Do not pray this prayer lightly, for you are volunteering for active duty in the King's army. But do pray it joyfully and with great anticipation, for the Lord will do wonderful things in and through you as He answers your prayer.

Direction for today: Obey Jesus and be prepared to live life in obedience.

Prayer for today: "Lord, send labourers into the harvest . . . and I am available to do Your will."

February 4: Read Matthew 10

Key verse: "And when He had called His twelve disciples to Him, He gave them power over unclean spirits, to cast them out, and to heal all kinds of sickness and all kinds of disease" (Matthew 10:1 NKJV).

God has given enormous authority to every one of us who is a follower of Jesus Christ and who is indwelt by the Holy Spirit. Jesus prophesied that His followers would do even greater works than He did. This has certainly come to pass, for, while Jesus wrought miracles only in a small country, His disciples have carried the message and the miracles of God throughout the world!

Through the baptism of the Holy Ghost, each of us is given power over unclean spirits, over sickness and all the works of the Devil. We are called to carry the deliverance and healing of Christ to all who will receive Him.

But we must take note of the source of such power. Our key verse says that Jesus called His disciples and gave them power. It is only as we continually go to Him and keep filled with the Spirit of God that we have the power to win spiritual battles.

We cannot go out in our own strength. We cannot win on the basis of an experience with Christ that took place months or years ago. We will know this kind of victory only when we are continually coming to Him in obedience, love and, when necessary, repentance.

Direction for today: Draw close to Jesus at all times.

Prayer for today: "Lord, help me to experience Your presence, and then Your power."

February 5: Read Matthew 11

Key verse: "Jesus answered and said to them, 'Go and tell John the things which you hear and see: the blind receive their sight and the lame walk; the lepers are cleansed and the deaf hear; the dead are raised up and the poor have the gospel preached to them'" (Matthew 11:4,5 NKJV).

Too often, and for too long, Christianity has been proclaimed as a private faith, a belief that is hidden in the heart of the believer. Of course, Christian faith is rooted in our hearts, but Jesus never intended His followers to concern themselves only with the inner man. Christianity is a faith of miracles, of public demonstrations of God's power.

When John asked for proof of Christ's mission on earth, Jesus did not point only to inner changes in the hearts of His followers. No one except God knows of that miracle but the miracles of healing and deliverance are evident to all.

The Lord grants these external blessings for three reasons: to bless the one who is healed; to bless the one who is acting in the authority of Christ; and to draw to Himself others who see His power demonstrated in these ways.

Seek the Lord in this. Allow Him to use you in miraculous ways, that many may be blessed through the power of the Holy Spirit.

Direction for today: The gospel of Jesus Christ is good news for the whole person, a miraculous power that will draw others. Tell it, that others may be blessed.

Prayer for today: "Lord, please cause us to see Your miracles in our churches and everywhere."

February 6: Read Matthew 12

Key verse: "A good man out of the good treasure of his heart brings forth good things, and an evil man out of the evil treasure brings forth evil things" (Matthew 12:35 NKJV).

What are you storing up in your heart? Jesus told us that your heart has two treasure boxes—one spiritual, the other carnal. We may read our Bibles every day; we certainly listen to at least part of the sermon on Sunday morning; these go into our spiritual treasure boxes. Most of us are also storing up, in our carnal treasure chests, incredible garbage from television, music and literature.

The problem is, we cannot separate things that way. If we are storing up corrupt and evil treasure, that will bring corruption to our entire life. It's like the old parable about one bad apple spoiling a whole barrel.

We are constantly bombarded with opportunities to store up evil treasure. This comes at us in newspapers, magazines, on radio and television. We must keep our spiritual defenses strong. That will mean acting in the power of the Spirit to turn off the television if the program doesn't honour God, or turning the page of the newspaper or magazine, walking away from lewd jokes, or severing friendship which are dishonouring to God. We must go beyond a few minutes a day with God to walking with Him continually. We must allow the "mind of Christ" to develop in us.

Direction for today: Keep your treasure chest full of good things.

Prayer for today: "Lord, help me to clean out my store of treasures. May I treasure only that which honours You."

February 7: Read Matthew 13

Key verse: "Again, the kingdom of heaven is like a merchant seeking beautiful pearls, who, when he had found one pearl of great price, went and sold all that he had and bought it" (Matthew 13:45,46 NKJV).

The message of this parable is beautifully simple: there is nothing that can equal the worth of the kingdom of God. What could possibly be valued more highly than the love of Christ, the power of the Holy Spirit, fellowship with the Father, and membership in the family of God? The kingdom of God means salvation, healing, deliverance and freedom. Being a member of the kingdom sets you free from sin and death: it is the key to life, health, joy and peace.

And it is all free, offered to us a gift by our Saviour! But, in order to accept this wondrous gift, we must lay aside all of the things that are cluttering up our life. We must empty our hands and our hearts so that God may fill them.

What does He ask us to give up? Only sure death, pain, suffering, evil, corruption, deception and bitterness. Only those things that rot the living and torture the dead.

What a wonderful bargain! Satan would try to blind our eyes, but the Word of God expresses the wonderful truth so clearly and vividly: truly, life in Christ, membership in the kingdom of God, is a pearl of infinitely great value!

Direction for today: Nothing could possibly equal the worth of life in Jesus!

Prayer for today: "Thank You, Lord, for the gift of this pearl of great price."

Memory Verse

"But He was wounded for our transgressions, He was bruised for our iniquities; the chastisement for our peace was upon Him, and by His stripes we are healed" (Isaiah 53:5 NKJV).

February 8: Read Matthew 14

Key verse: "And immediately Jesus stretched out His hand and caught him, and said to him, 'Oh you of little faith, why did you doubt?'" (Matthew 14:31 NKJV).

Poor Peter. He was so often torn in two directions: between faith and doubt: between boldness and fear. In these verses, his faith carried him out of the boat, but his doubt immediately brought big problems! We should not be too hard on Peter, for isn't he exactly like you and me? We have occasional moments of great faith and many times of doubt and anxiety.

However, it is interesting to follow Peter's life after the day of Pentecost. The Peter of "The Acts of the Apostles" is a very different person. He is consistently courageous and faithful. Why? Because he was filled with the Holy Spirit, and because his memory improved.

That second reason may sound trivial, but is really important in understanding consistent faith. Peter, as we read of him in the book of Acts, could never forget the tremendous things Jesus had done. His messages, as recorded in that book, are full of the works of Jesus. He remembered, and his recollections gave him reason for faith. But here, as he began to sink, Peter might have taken heart had he recalled that, only hours before, Jesus had worked the great miracle of feeding the five thousand.

So, too, with us. Our faith will continue strong if we remember the great things Jesus has done for us. When we meet a situation that seems impossible, we should remember how He brought victory in the last impossible situation we faced. When we are sick, we should remember healing that has been given by Christ.

Direction for today: Remember that the miracles of former days are great foundations for your faith.

Prayer for today: "Thank You, Lord, for the miracles You have brought to my life. May my remembrance of them help my faith to grow ever stronger."

February 9: Read Matthew 15

Key verse: *"And in vain they worship Me, teaching as doctrines the commandments of men" (Matthew 15:9 NKJV).*

Recently, a pastor told his congregation that, if he ever says anything in a message which is not founded on the Word of God, they should completely ignore it.

He was right, and completely in line with this teaching of our Lord Jesus. Here, He warns His followers against the dangers of legalism and of egomania. Either of these may be the cause when the doctrines of men are substituted for the truth of God.

We must be vigilant against these things, just as the early church had to be. Often, in the history of the church, the freedom of the Holy Spirit has been lost in the bondage of legalism. It happened to the church at Galatia and it is happening today. Legalism occurs when the teachings or prejudices of man take precedence over the truths of God.

As well, our world is well-populated with cult leaders and false prophets who lead many astray, claiming that they have new truth or the only true understanding of the Scriptures. Again, cults occur when the teachings of man become more important than the truth of God, as revealed through His Son and His Word.

Direction for today: Truth is always founded on the Word of God. Use this as a test for all that you are told.

Prayer for today: "Lord, keep Your people safe from the dangers of legalism and false teaching."

February 10: Read Matthew 16,17

Key verse: *"And Simon Peter answered and said, 'You are the Christ, the Son of the living God'" (Matthew 16:16 NKJV).*

This brief confession spoken by Peter contains the entire, essential truth of the gospel. These words are so full of divine meaning that Jesus said Peter could not have come upon them on his own—only the Father could have revealed these things to him.

Peter declared, "You are the Christ." So much is wrapped up in that title: Christ, the anointed one. Jesus was anointed to be the ultimate prophet, the great high priest, the King of kings. He was anointed to reign and rule. But He was also anointed for death, to carry the iniquity of us all, that through Him we might be healed. Jesus is surely the anointed, "the Christ".

Not only was His commission a special one, but His very being was beyond human understanding. He was anointed to eternal tasks and roles, but He existed, and exists today, as "the Son of the living God". Of course, we immediately confess that we are incapable of understanding all that is meant by that phrase. But we know that, as a man's son is man, so also must this description mean that God's Son is God. This title points to the absolute divinity of Jesus. He was no mere man containing a divine spark: He was not only a great example, but fully God as truly as He was fully man.

Direction for today: Meditate on today's great proclamation of Christ.

Prayer for today: "Praise you, Jesus, that You are the Christ, the Son of the living God."

February 11: Read Matthew 18

Key verse: *"For where two or three are gathered together in My name, I am there in the midst of them" (Matthew 18:20 NKJV).*

What a wonderful promise! When we gather together to pray, to worship, to be taught or simply to share in Christian fellowship, Jesus has promised always to be with us! His promises are sure: each time we meet in His name, He is there!

Just think of what this means. When we pray, we are not stretching upward, hoping to communicate to a far-away God; instead, we are talking to a friend as close as if He were seated on the next chair. When we bring needs to Him, He is as close at hand as He was when He reached out to touch and heal those who came to Him in Galilee.

When we confront problems and difficulties, we are not alone in a terrible situation; rather, we are standing with the Lord, waiting for the victory! If we seek to minister to a brother or a sister, we again are not alone, for Jesus stands with us to heal and to bless.

Direction for today: Remember, when Christians meet, we meet with Jesus!

Prayer for today: "Lord, help me, and the Christians with whom I meet, to be continually aware of Your presence in our midst."

February 12: Read Matthew 19,20

Key verse: *"And whoever desires to be first among you, let him be your slave—just as the Son of Man did not come to be served, but to serve, and to give His life a ransom for many" (Matthew 20:27,28 NKJV).*

No business will ever thrive or grow unless it has an effective, efficient structure—good leaders and adequate organization. This is true of any group or institution, from a tire company to a university or hockey team.

It's also true of the church. The New Testament has much to say about the structure and organization of the church, especially in 1 Corinthians 12-14, and 1 Timothy and Titus.

However, there are several key differences between the structure and leadership of a company and that of the church. The first is apparent in our key verses. Usually, in any secular setting, a leader emerges who is hard-driving, ambitious, and sufficiently selfish to strive for the position. This is entirely the opposite of Christ's teaching regarding the church. In the body of Christ, only the humble should lead; they lead not from a place of pride, but from a position of serving.

Another difference between the church and secular organizations has to do with power. Eventually, in a secular company, someone emerges as the ultimate power, the president or chairman of the board. If he or she retires, someone else takes top place. In the church, top place is eternally occupied by the Chief Servant, and we seek to serve Him instead of ourselves.

Direction for today: Seek to serve.

Prayer for today: "Jesus, give me a heart like Yours—a servant's heart."

February 13: Read Matthew 21

Key verse: "And he answered and said, 'I go, sir,' but he did not go" (Matthew 21:30b NKJV).

How many times have you made a promise to God and broken it? How often, in the midst of an emotional moment, have you made a commitment to Jesus, and then, within a few days, forgotten all about it?

The message of this parable is very clear. Jesus judges the promise-breaker much more seriously than He does the one who was initially rebellious, but ultimately obedient.

Praise the Lord that both sons are in this story. Each of us who has broken a promise still has the choice of playing either role: we can go on ignoring our commitment to God and thus receive the harsher judgment, or we can repent of our rebellion and dishonesty, and turn and serve the Lord. For that one, Christ offers only forgiveness, never rebuke.

Which kind of child are you?

Direction for today: Keep the promises you make to the Lord.

Prayer for today: "Father, if I have failed to keep my word to You in the past, bring it to mind, that I may confess, repent, and be made right before You."

February 14: Read Matthew 22

Key verse: *"Jesus answered and said unto them, "You are mistaken, not knowing the Scriptures nor the power of God"'" (Matthew 22:29 NKJV).*

All around us, people are falling into terrible spiritual error. Cults and false teachings abound. Churches sometimes teach doctrines that have no basis in the Scriptures. Believers are being led into falsehood, joining groups that can destroy their peace, their families, their personalities and perhaps even their own souls.

How can we be protected and protect one another from false teaching and from error? In His answer to the Saducees, Jesus told us two important things: we will not err if we know the Scriptures and the power of God.

The power of God comes through our relationship with Jesus Christ and through the indwelling Holy Spirit. We have no power on our own, but we have all power in the name of Christ, with the fullness of the Holy Spirit.

But power is not enough. Too often, Christians who have a genuine encounter with the Holy Spirit are swept away by emotion and drawn into falsehood, which has great emotional power but no spiritual truth. Our second guard is the Scriptures. God, by His Spirit, is never going to tell us to believe or to do something that His Word does not teach.

Direction for today: Remain in the Word and in the Spirit.

Prayer for today: "Lord, through Your Spirit and the truth of Your Word, keep me from error."

Memory Verse

"Then Peter said to them, 'Repent and let every one of you be baptized in the name of Jesus Christ for the remission of sins; and you shall receive the gift of the Holy Spirit" (Acts 2:38 NKJV).

February 15: Read Matthew 23

Key verse: *"Blind Pharisee! First clean the inside of the cup and dish, and then the outside also will be clean" (Matthew 23:26 NIV).*

If only we could learn to see things in God's perspective! About 3,000 years ago, God told his prophet, "For the Lord does not see as man sees; for man looks at the outward appearance, but the Lord looks at the heart" (1 Samuel 16:7 NKJV).

In 3,000 years, we have learned very little. Do we not often judge another's spiritual state only by what we see on the outside? Is it not true that we tend to associate with the lovely, the outgoing, the intelligent and the well-spoken? And, in ourselves, we are perhaps more concerned to present a spiritual image to our friends and church family than we are to

grow spiritually. Yet everything that matters most happens inside of us, where no one can see.

It is good to remember that, even if we could fool all of the people all of the time, God knows our hearts. Just as Jesus could look at these religious men and accuse them of hypocrisy, spiritual blindness and wickedness, so, too, can He perceive what is in our hearts.

Direction for today: Don't be overly concerned with outward appearance of yourself or of others. Seek to see with the eyes of the Lord.

Prayer for today: "Father, help me to see myself and others with eyes anointed with sensitivity and discernment."

February 16: Read Matthew 24

Key verse: "Therefore keep watch, because you do not know on what day your Lord will come" (Matthew 24:42 NIV).

This chapter contains one of the most detailed descriptions of events that lead up to the second coming of Jesus. The ultimate truth underlying all of this is that Jesus will indeed return to reign and rule a kingdom comprised of all who have believed in Him.

The chapter is full of warnings that the love of Christ can grow cold and disappear under temptation or persecution. And we are confronted with the stark truth that only those who endure will be saved!

The final conclusion of these revelations by Jesus is our key verse: "Keep watch."

We must keep watch to ensure that we are not deceived by false prophets, who abound in our day. We must keep watch to be certain that our love for Christ does not grow cold. We must keep watch to be ready for the persecution and martyrdom that will come with the end times.

But, most of all, we are to keep watch on our lives so that we will be a pure and holy bride for Christ when He returns for us; for His return is sure, and our salvation, certain.

Direction for today: Live in the awareness that He may come at any time!

Prayer for today: "Maranatha! Come, Lord Jesus."

February 17: Read Matthew 25

Key verse: "His master replied, 'Well done, good and faithfuul servant! You have been faithful with a few things; I will put you in charge of many things. Come and share your master's happiness'" (Matthew 25:21 NIV).

God has given gifts and responsibilities to every believer. None of us is charged with the duty of saving the whole world or our whole city—instead, the Lord, who made us and, therefore, knows us best, has assigned specific tasks to each of us, tasks which are suited to our gifts and our abilities.

Too often, Christians believe that someone else—the pastor, the deacons, or the television ministry—should be doing all of the work. Perhaps we are insecure, unsure of ourselves, or simply lazy. Whatever the reason, Christians far too often abandon the duties the Lord has given to them.

Notice the terrible result of that response in the story Jesus is telling. And note, too, the tremendous promises that come to all who are obedient, including the best promise of all: "Come and share your master's happiness."

Direction for today: Be faithful with the gifts and responsibilities the Lord has given to you.

Prayer for today: "Lord, show me Your will for my life today, and I will obey."

February 18: Read Matthew 26

Key verse: "But after I have risen, I will go ahead of you into Galilee" (Matthew 26:32 NIV).

It really is impossible to choose one key verse from this dramatic chapter of Matthew. The entire chapter, like all of the events surrounding the death and resurrection of Christ, is crucial to Christians.

But these few words, spoken in great confidence by our Lord, tell us of the surety of God's plan and His promises. When Jesus said these things, He had not yet faced the agony of Gethsemane, the betrayal of

Judas, the denial of His friends, the punishments, tortures and ultimate death on the cross. He knew these things all lay ahead of Him, but He looked beyond them to the certainty of the plan of God.

Jesus knew He must die. But He also knew the Father would raise Him up again.

We can approach any trial we face with the same assurance—God keeps His promises. We can meet each test in the knowledge that God's plan is sure.

And we can trust absolutely in Father, Son and Holy Spirit, looking to eternity with them because the same Lord who kept His promise and raised Christ from the dead has promised to grant us eternal life.

Direction for today: Believe that God keeps His promises.

Prayer for today: "Lord, help me to walk in confidence, knowing that You can be trusted."

February 19: Read Matthew 27,28

Key verse: "He is not here; He has risen, just as He said. Come and see the place where He lay" (Matthew 28:6 NIV).

Journalists constantly compete one with the other to get "scoops"— special, exclusive news stories. But no matter how good their modern-day efforts may be, they will always be striving for second best. The greatest "scoop" ever was given to Mary Magdalene and her friends: "He is not here; He has risen"!

This was, and is, the greatest news in history! Death, the continual enemy of mortal man, has been defeated by the Son of God. Through His resurrection, Jesus proved that He would do what He said. Not only His promise to rise again, but all of His promises to His followers gained eternal credibility.

God has met all of the enemies of man in mortal combat, and God has won. Satan, death, sin and hell are all doomed. Believers in Christ are all set free! What a story!

Direction for today: Rejoice—for you serve a risen Saviour!

Prayer for today: "Praise You, Father, that You raised Your Son Jesus from the dead."

Exodus

The second book written by Moses, the book of the "Exodus," is one of the most dramatic stories in the Bible. "Exodus" is from a Greek word meaning "going out", and this book concerns itself with the deliverance of the children of Israel from the bondage of Egypt by the miracles worked by the hand of the Lord.

The Exodus was *the* most important event in the history of the children of Israel. The event is celebrated throughout the Bible especially in the Psalms, as the historical circumstance to which the Israelites could look as the best example of the victory and salvation wrought by their Lord.

The end of Genesis leaves us with the sons of Jacob and their families living a pleasant life in Egypt, where their brother, Joseph, was Prime Minister. But, early in Exodus, trouble looms: "there arose up a new king over Egypt, which knew not Joseph" (Exodus 1:8). The Israelites quickly became slaves to the powerful Egyptians, and their life became one of terrible hardship.

This book outlines the Lord's action to free His people from these trials. It takes us through the confrontations between Moses and Pharaoh, ruler of Egypt; in every case, God proved Himself to be the supreme, living God. Exodus 12, one of the most gripping stories in the Bible, tells us of the Passover, with the salvation of Israel but the terrible judgement on the first-born of Egypt. The sacrifice of the Passover lamb is one of the best and most detailed pictures in the Old Testament of the sacrifice of the Lamb of God, Jesus Christ, who was later offered up for our sins at the time of the Passover.

The miracles continued as God guided the people by the pillars of fire and of cloud. He parted the Red Sea for the Israelites but used it to engulf the pursuing Egyptians. The people of Israel were free!

But they were not obedient, and the remainder of the book concerns the wanderings of the Israelites in the wilderness for forty years. (In fact, the next three books of the Old Testament, all written by Moses are also concerning this period.

February 20: Read Exodus 1,2

Key verse: "The midwives, however, feared God and did not do what the King of Egypt had told them to do; they let the boys live . . . so God was kind to the midwives" (Exodus 1:17, 20a NIV).

The book of Exodus is a deeply instructive and interesting portion of the Word of God.

Redemption by blood occupies a prominent place. In fact, it characterizes the book. God's many mercies to His redeemed, the patience of His love and the riches of His grace all flow from it. The great question of Israel's relationship to God is settled by the blood of the lamb. Within the blood-sprinkled doorposts, Israel was God's blood-bought people.

It is before this backdrop of the mercy of God that Moses enters the scene. The first five verses of chapter one recall to mind the closing scenes of the preceding book that set the stage for the "new king, who did not know Joseph" and a monarch's fear of the growing strength of Israel. However, it was another fear—the fear of God—that brought His favour and blessing to the Hebrew midwives. The moment God is acknowledged, all of the reasonings of a heart that had never learned to take Him into its calculations fall to the ground.

Direction for today: Take courage in the knowledge that God's counsel shall stand, and He will do all His pleasure.

Prayer for today: "Lord, give us an ear for Your counsel only."

February 21: Read Exodus 3,4

Key verse: "But Moses answered, 'No, Lord. Please send someone else.' At this the Lord became angry" (Exodus 4:13,14 TEV).

We should immediately know that something is wrong with our spiritual life and our relationship with the Lord if we echo the words of Moses: "No, Lord."

When Moses spoke this disobedient contradiction, God became angry. When Peter spoke similar words (Matthew 16:22), Jesus responded most strongly: "Get behind Me, Satan! You are an offense to Me, for you are not mindful of the things of God, but the things of men" (Matthew 16:23 NKJV)

How often do our mouths or our actions speak the same contradiction to our Saviour? How often do we attempt to claim a relationship with our Lord while refusing to do His will?

This kind of attitude angers the Lord. If He is Lord, then He is Lord of everything in our lives. If He is not Lord, we had better immediately re-examine our spiritual condition!

Direction for today: The only consistent response is, "Yes, Lord."

Prayer for today: "Father, You are my Lord. Guide and strengthen me, that my every action and word will reflect that truth."

Memory Verse

"Pride goes before destruction, and a haughty spirit before a fall"
(Proverbs 16:18 NKJV).

February 22: Read Exodus 5,6

Key verse: "And God spoke to Moses and said to him: 'I am the Lord'" (Exodus 6:2 NKJV).

Yesterday, we shared concerning the necessity of making God truly and totally Lord of our lives. We concluded that, if we are truly followers of Christ, our response will consistently be, "Yes, Lord."

Today, we can set this truth into the larger context: God is the Lord of all! Pharaoh was doomed as soon as he hardened his heart against God. He could no more defeat God than you can move a mountain by running headfirst against it.

Moses kept jumping between earthly fears and spiritual sight. When he saw things on an earthly level, he was in deep trouble because there was no way a band of slaves could defeat Pharaoh and his mighty armies. But, when Moses saw the situation from God's viewpoint, he must have felt pity for the Egyptian king, for a mere mortal ruler is as dust against the Lord of all creation.

In our own lives, we can live knowing that Jesus is Lord or we can make ourselves petty lords; if we do that, however, we'll be like Pharaoh—defeated in the end.

Direction for today: Always acknowledge that Jesus is Lord!

Prayer for today: "Lord God, I acknowledge that You are indeed Lord—Lord of creation and Lord of my life."

February 23: Read Exodus 7

Key verse: *"The Egyptians will then know that I am the Lord, when I raise My hand against them and bring the Israelites out of their country" (Exodus 7:5 TEV).*

The whole land of Egypt was made to tremble beneath the successive strokes of the rod of God. All, from the monarch on his throne to those at the mill, were made to feel the terrible weight of that rod. In eleven verses (26 to 36) of Psalm 105, the inspired psalmist capsulizes those appalling afflictions which the hardness of Pharaoh's heart brought upon his people and land. This haughty sovereign had set himself to resist the sovereign will of the Most High God; as a just consequence, he was given over to judicial blindness and hardness of heart.

In contemplating Pharaoh and his actions, the mind is carried forward to the stirring scenes of the book of Revelation, in which we find the last oppressor of the people of God bringing down upon his kingdom and himself the seven vials of the wrath of the Almighty. It is God's purpose that Israel be preeminent in the earth; therefore, whoever presumes to stand in the way of that preeminence must be set aside. He has said to His people, "No weapon that is formed against thee shall prosper". His infallible faithfulness will assuredly make good that which His infinite grace has promised.

Direction for today: Recognize God's great purposes in everything He allows you to go through.

Prayer for today: "Father, we bless You in the hardships, for You desire to bless us even through them."

February 24: Read Exodus 8

Key verse: *"So the Lord did according to the word of Moses" (Exodus 8:13a NKJV).*

This is an important lesson about the kind of spiritual authority the Lord God gives to those who faithfully serve Him. If we are in tune with the Lord, faithful to His Word and His Spirit, then we will be in situations where the word of the Lord will be spoken through our mouths, and God will act accordingly.

The apostles knew this reality. Peter and John raised a lame man as God honoured their declaration of his healing. Paul preached the inspired Word of the Lord, and it was written down and passed on for our instruction.

This does not imply that we can direct God or use Him like a tool. Instead, it is a call for close fellowship with the Lord, so intimate that His thoughts are our thoughts; His words, our words. When we reach that point in our relationship with the Lord—and it need not be far away if we are obedient and faithful—then we will see God do remarkable things through our words and in our lives.

Direction for today: The Lord invests great spiritual authority in those faithful to Him.

Prayer for today: "First, Lord, may I do according to Your Word."

February 25: Read Exodus 9

Key verse: "When Pharaoh saw that the rain and hail and thunder had stopped, he sinned again: he and his officials hardened their hearts" (Exodus 9:34 NIV).

In this chapter, we have an account of three more of the plagues of Egypt. The first of this series of plagues is directed upon the cattle of the land. When Pharaoh was not moved by the death of his cattle, God sent a greater plague (boils) which affected the people themselves. Here God shows the Egyptians their own sin in their punishment; they had oppressed Israel in the furnaces, and now the soot or ashes of those very furnaces are used to be as much a terror to them as the taskmasters had been to the Israelites.

Finally, God inflicted a plague of hail, which caused death to both man and animal alike. When Pharaoh became terrified at the desolation of his land and people, he summoned Moses and repented, only to break his word instantly upon the removal of the plague.

Direction for today: Don't use God as fire insurance and make promises that you have no intention of keeping.

Prayer for today: "Teach me to continue to admonish and pray even for those for whom I have little hope."

February 26: Read Exodus 10,11

Key verse: "Every firstborn son in Egypt will die, from the firstborn son of Pharaoh, who sits on the throne, to the firstborn son of the slave girl, who is at her hand mill, and all the firstborn of the cattle as well" (Exodus 11:5 NIV).

In this chapter, Moses warns Pharaoh of the last and most devastating plague to be inflicted on Egypt. This was the death of all the firstborn and was so vast in its execution that no one, from the highest to the lowest in the land, was to be excluded.

When Moses had delivered his message, it is said that he left Pharaoh "hot with anger" (verse 8). Although Moses was a very meek man, we can understand his righteous indignation against Pharaoh, whose proud heart would not yield—not even to save all the firstborn of his kingdom.

Our Saviour was provoked to holy indignation in His ministry and we can also expect our spirits to be vexed when see people deaf to all the fair warnings given to them. However, we must be careful to be angry at nothing but the sin itself, rather than the sinner.

Direction for today: Maintain a forgiving attitude at all times.

Prayer for today: "Help me, Lord, to break down the barrier of pride in people's hearts."

February 27: Read Exodus 12

Key verse: "This is a day you are able to commemorate; for the generations to come you shall celebrate it as a festival to the Lord—a lasting ordinance" (Exodus 12:14 NIV).

Today, Christ is our passover (1 Corinthians 5:7), and it is interesting to note how the slaying of the lambs in this passage describes perfectly the sacrifice of our Lord Jesus at Calvary:
1) the sacrifice was to be a lamb (verse 3), and Christ is the "Lamb of God" (John 1:29); 2) it was to be a year-old male (verse 5)—that is, in its prime—Christ offered Himself in the prime of His life; 3) it was to be without defect (verse 5), denoting the purity of the Lord Jesus (1 Peter 1:19); 4) it was to be set apart four days (verses 3 and 6), and Jesus entered Jerusalem four days before He was crucified; 5) it was to be roasted over a fire (verses 6 to 9), representing the sufferings of the Lord Jesus till He died; 6) not a bone was to be broken (verse 46). This was fulfilled in Christ's crucifixion (John 19:33, 36).

Direction for today: Remember each day the wonder of God's grace in the sacrifice of His Son, our passover Lamb.

Prayer for today: "Thank you, Lord, for the forgiveness of our sins."

February 28: Read Exodus 13

Key verse: "In days to come, when your son asks you, 'What does this mean?' say to him, 'With a mighty hand the Lord brought us out of Egypt, out of the land of slavery'" (Exodus 13:14 NIV).

Children should be directed and encouraged to ask their parents questions concerning the things of God. We should all be able to explain the reasons why we observe baptism and the Lord's table.

Our service to God is reasonable and acceptable when we perform it intelligently, knowing what we do and why we do it.

Direction for today: Remember that, in the day of Christ's resurrection, we were raised up with Him out of death's house of bondage.

Prayer for today: "Father, we thank You for Your Son, Jesus Christ, the light and guide of our walk."

Thank You, Lord, For Your Love

Lord, how thankful I am that You truly love me;
How marvellously You display that love each day.
When I have failed You so miserably
And taken things into my own hands,
Defiantly going against Your will,
You have waited patiently, 'til I returned to You.

In tears, my heart broken, frustrated
and at wits' end,
I poured out my woes before you
And, in humility, asked Your help.
I knew that, somehow, You were able to fix what I
had ruined,
Mend what I had broken.

You have always been there
To pick up the pieces, draw me to Your side
And assure me of Your love and care.
You've never condemned me for my failures,
Nor reminded me of my errors,
But gently, carefully and lovingly,
You've shown me Your perfect way.

Thank You, Lord, for giving me the assurance
That, wherever I go and whatever I do,
Your presence will always be with me.
Oh Lord, how I thank You for Your love.

— *Nicola Keene*

41

"If we confess our sins, He is faithful and just to forgive us our sins and to cleanse us from all unrighteousness" (I John 1:9 NKJV).

March 1: Read Exodus 14

Key verse: *"The Lord will fight for you; you need only to be still" (Exodus 14:14 NIV).*

Hemmed in between the sea and mountains, with water before them and Pharaoh's forces behind them, the Israelites meet their first big test of faith—and they panic.

As God drives back the waters so they can cross in safety, and as He sends the wall of water rushing down upon Pharaoh's forces, Israel learns the truth of Moses' words: "The Lord will fight for you; you need only to be still."

As long as we have means of resistance put in our power, with a reasonable prospect of success, it is our duty to use them—to exert ourselves to the utmost and make all possible effort. But there are occasions when we can do nothing and all must be left to God. Under these circumstances, our duty is to wait patiently, quietly and courageously. Moses probably did not know how God would deliver Israel, but he was confident that, in one way or another, it would happen.

Direction for today: When you cannot get out of your troubles, give them to the Lord in expectation of deliverance.

Prayer for today: "Help me, Lord, to rise above my fears and to wait on You."

March 2: Read Exodus 15

Key verse: *"Thy right hand, O Lord, glorious in power, Thy right hand, O Lord, shatters the enemy" (Exodus 15:6 RSV).*

The odds had been completely against them. The children of Israel were fleeing on foot, encumbered by families, livestock and all their possessions that they could carry. They were pursued by a trained, efficient army, many of them in chariots. The capture of the people of God was inevitable.

Our situations may often seem like that. But whatever trouble or trauma we face, we must remember that, with the Lord on our side, no one can stand against us! The Lord's victory is sure, for His right hand is glorious in power!

No wonder Moses burst into anointed praise! God had acted to deliver His people; victory had been snatched from what seemed to be sure defeat and God's people had been redeemed!

How can we cease to praise the Lord for the redemption He has brought to us? How can we cease to praise Him for victories won in our lives? How can we cease to praise Him, for His word is powerful and His promises are sure!

Direction for today: Praise the Lord, for truly He is worthy to be praised!

Prayer for today: "Praise the Lord!"

March 3: Read Exodus 16

Key verse: "Your murmurings are not against us but against the Lord" (Exodus 16:8 RSV).

The people murmured against Moses and Aaron. The word "murmur" is found eight times in this chapter. Yet in the face of the unfaithfulness of the people, God proved His faithfulness. The people received "manna", which means, "what is it?"

In John 6, Jesus declared that He is the true Bread from heaven. The people said of Jesus, "Who is this man? Where does He come from?" Yes, He is the living Bread! The Hebrews in the wilderness were to gather the manna fresh each morning. So too, our relationship with Jesus is to be fresh each day.

The manna tasted like wafers and wild honey, but if they kept it overnight, it became wormy. Our stale Christianity becomes "wormy" also. Let "New Direction" and 100 Huntley Street help daily!

Direction for today: Be sure that your experience with Jesus is renewed continually.

Prayer for today: "Lord Jesus, may my relationship with You, and my testimony, be always fresh from day to day."

March 4: Read Exodus 17

Key verse: "Behold, I will stand before you there on the rock at Horeb; and you shall strike the rock, and water shall come out of it, that the people may drink" (Exodus 17:6 RSV).

Jesus is not only the source of living Bread, but also the source of the Holy Spirit. He is the One who baptises believers with the Holy Spirit. This is so beautifully illustrated in today's Scripture. Israel had passed through the Red Sea (saved from Egypt—a type for sin), and had begun to eat manna each day (feast on the living Bread—a type for Jesus). To satisfy their thirst, God gave them water in abundant supply. Are you feasting on Jesus each day? Are you drinking from the fountain of God's supply?

Now they were ready for their first battle with the enemy, Amalek. As a result of prayer, God gave them a mighty victory. Are you walking in the victory God has given you?

Direction for today: God has supplied everything you need to live a victorious Christian life. Make use of it daily.

Prayer for today: "Lord, I need the water from the Rock; I need the fullness of your Holy Spirit. Please fill me now."

March 5: Read Exodus 18,19

Key verse: "You have seen what I did to the Egyptians, and how I bore you on eagles' wings and brought you to Myself" (Exodus 19:4 RSV).

Organization is a vital factor for success. Jethro, Moses' faither-in-law, suggests a type of organization that was very successful and one which Israel thereafter used for many years. God honoured and blessed such a structure, making it fruitful for His glory. Now God is ready to reveal Himself to Moses and all the people in a unique manner. Moses is called to come up Mount Sinai, to meet God and to receive His Word for His people. Moses delivered the first message and the people responded, "All that the Lord has spoken we will do."

God has delivered them from Egypt, led them in victory through the Red Sea, fed them with manna, supplied water in abundance and defeated the Amalekites. Now, for the first time, all the people will hear His voice! He is a personal God. He is ever in the midst of His people.

Direction for today: Walk in the Spirit. Put to death the deeds of the flesh. Rejoice in God's presence with you.

Prayer for today: "Lord, enable me to organize myself and all I do, so that others will see You in me."

March 6: Read Exodus 20,21

Key verse: "I am the Lord your God, who brought you out of the land of Egypt, out of the house of bondage" (Exodus 20:16 RSV).

"I am the Lord your God". What glorious words of love, grace, comfort and acceptance! "Because I am the Lord your God, this is how I want you to act." These are truthful words of encouragement and exhortation.

God begins to reveal His holy character to His people. He is starting to reveal His beautiful plan for their lives. His law is good and perfect and righteous altogether. Here, on the mountain, God begins to reveal some of His great principles of life. If we keep His principles, we are blessed. If we break them we reap punishment.

Sin is a transgression of the law. The wages of sin is death. Whatever we sow, we reap. If we sin we die. We bring the death principle into our life in so many different ways. But because of Jesus' death and resurrection, if we sow to the Spirit and walk in His fullness, we enjoy life; yes, life more abundantly.

Direction for today: Hear the Word of the Lord; search the Scriptures; talk to God and then walk in His principles.

Prayer for today: "Father, give the Spirit of discernment, that I may see Jesus and know Your ways and choose to walk in them."

March 7: Read Exodus 22

Key verse: "You are to be My holy people" (Exodus 22:31a NIV).

In this chapter, as in the previous one, we have the judgments and statutes of God. These were practical rules given through Moses for the purpose of maintaining a well-run, harmonious society.

Only when society has precise and godly laws that are strictly upheld, can we have a peaceful world in which to live. To break those laws not only brings to bear the power of the court, with its resulting discipline, but it also incurs the wrath of God.

In studying judicial history, it is interesting to note the worldwide acceptance of God's civil laws, as outlined in the Bible. Many—if not most—of the laws of our land are based upon these God-given laws, for no man-made plan could be more fair or just then those of God. God knew exactly what He was doing in decreeing each law.

The ultimate purpose of obeying God's law is that we might be a holy people. This truth is further exemplified in I Peter 2:9,10: "But you are a chosen people, a royal priesthood, a holy nation, a people belonging to God, that you may declare the praises of Him who called you out of darkness into His wonderful light. Once you were not a people, but now you are the people of God; once you had not received mercy, but now you have received mercy."

Direction for today: Remember that, though it may seem hard to obey God's strict rules, it is even harder to live with the results of disobedience.

Prayer for today: "Lord, may my life and actions show me to be a holy person, bringing honour to Your name."

Memory Verse

"Rejoice in the Lord always. Again I will say, rejoice!" (Philippians 4:4 NKJV).

March 8: Read Exodus 23,24

Key verse: "See, I am sending an angel ahead of you to guard you along the way and to bring you to the place I have prepared" (Exodus 23:20 NIV).

There are benefits in obeying the commands of God. There is a wholesome purpose in the giving and the living of God's plan for us. After God tells us how to live, He makes it possible to enjoy life to the fullest. Upon the completion of giving the laws, God gave a promise. The promise was that an angel would prepare the way for them.

God is a caring, loving God. He does not leave us to our own devices, but always watches over us. He not only sends us into today's pathway: He prepares the way for us, then watches over us while we walk.

In this Scripture, we also see the results of worshipping God. His blessing will be on what we eat and drink. He will heal our sick bodies, give us children, and grant us a full lifespan. What more could we ask for? All we could ever need is available from God.

Direction for today: Zealously seek a time and a place to be alone with God to develop an intimacy with Him.

Prayer for today: "Lord, lead me to the higher ground where I may experience Your presence."

March 9: Read Exodus 25

Key verse: "Then have them make a sanctuary for me, and I will dwell among them" (Exodus 25:8 NIV).

God desired that the materials for the construction of the tabernacle be donated by His people. This offering was to be given willingly, for God loves a cheerful giver (II Corinthians 9:7). God could easily have supplied a sacrifice or the necessary materials. However, this was to be a special project where He would meet with His people and atonement for sins would be made. For such a special place, God desired a special offering.

Today, God still desires a special gift from the heart of His people, for, when we give, we do not give to a church or an organization, but to God.

In the innermost part of the tabernacle was the ark. It was the focal point for the worshipper. It was in the ark that the words of God to His people were kept. It has been suggested that the wooden box overlaid with gold represents the deity and humanity of Christ.

The lid of the ark was known as the mercy seat, the place of atonement. Our place of atonement, or meeting place with God, is in Jesus Christ. In love and mercy He provided Himself as the one sacrifice man could not provide: redemption for our individual sin.

Direction for today: Whether you are giving of your time or finances, give out of a cheerful heart as a willing sacrifice to God.

Prayer for today: "Father, direct me to that place of meeting with You so that I may receive Your special words for me."

March 10: Read Exodus 26

Key verse: "Set up the tabernacle according to the plan shown you on the mountain" (Exodus 26:30 NIV).

In today's reading, we see the instructions God gave for the building of the tabernacle. Note that God gave an exact design, with precise measurements, using specific materials. These materials needed to be carefully crafted into the shapes and images planned by God. Similarly, God desires to take our lives and make us into vessels that will glorify His name.

It is important for us to follow God's plans and designs very carefully. Just as He had precise instructions for the tabernacle, so God has an exact plan for our lives. We are His modern-day tabernacle.

God's Word is steadfast and sure. Psalm 119:89 says the Word of God is: ". . . eternal; it stands firm in the heavens." God's Word is unchangeable and can be completely trusted as being the best possible plan for each life. Man's philosophies change constantly, but God's Word never changes.

As you read today's text, thank God for ordering your life. You are His tabernacle, better by far than the precious things in the original tabernacle. You are special!

Direction for today: Search God's Word for the precise instructions He has for His children; remember, that includes you!

Prayer for today: "God, help me to carefully and diligently follow Your plan for my life."

March 11: Read Exodus 27

Key verse: "Command the Israelites to bring you clear oil of pressed olives for the light so that the lamps may be kept burning" (Exodus 27:20 NIV).

Today, we continue reading plans for building the tabernacle, the house of God.

An unusual, but predominant, aspect of the altar was the horns. They seem to be symbolic of God's power, protection and help for His children. It is encouraging to know that God desires to care for us simply because we are His children.

The altar was placed just inside the gate of the tabernacle so that no one could come to God without first approaching it. Before we can worship God, we must first have the assurance that our sins are forgiven. Only after salvation is received at the foot of the cross, can we truly worship God from our heart.

The courtyard was a protection for the tabernacle from the outside world. It had only one entrance, as there is only one way to God.

Then we have the oil for the lamps. This oil was to brought daily to the house of God. Our service to God needs to be an ongoing commitment to keep our Christian light burning bright. Oil is often used in Scripture to symbolize the Holy Spirit. As lights in a dark world, we need the daily infusion of the Holy Spirit to keep us burning bright for the Lord.

Direction for today: God's plans have a purpose. Seek always to follow that purpose.

Prayer for today: "Lord, help me to be diligent in my service to You."

March 12: Read Exodus 28

Key verse: "You shall anoint them, consecrate them and sanctify them, that they may minister to Me as priests" (Exodus 28:41 NKJV).

In the days of Moses, only a select few were set aside as priests. The first so chosen were Aaron and his sons. The instructions concerning their clothing, lifestyle and behaviour were very specific.

In our day, according to the words of Peter, all believers in Jesus are members of a "royal priesthood" (I Peter 2:7-9). Nonetheless, the instructions to holiness which applied to Aaron still apply today.

God's people, named by Him to be priests, ministering both to the Lord and to the world around us, are to be anointed, consecreted and sanctified.

The anointing speaks to us of the fullness of the Holy Spirit. We cannot worship properly nor minister effectively if we are not filled by the Holy Spirit of God. Paul tells us to be continually filled with the Spirit (Ephesians 5:18).

Consecration shows that we are set apart, ordained to the particular task of being priests. We need to be sure at all times that our lives are free from sin and our lifestyle honouring to the Lord.

Sanctification speaks of the need for holiness in the lives of priests. We need to be holy—both by asking the Lord to make us clean, and also by living clean lives.

Direction for today: Be filled with the Spirit, consecrated and holy before the Lord.

Prayer for today: "Father, cleanse me and fill me, that I may be a holy and worshipful priest before You."

March 13: Read Exodus 29

Key verse: "You shall also take one ram, and Aaron and his sons shall put their hands on the head of the ram; and you shall kill the ram, and you shall take its blood and sprinkle it all around on the altar" (Exodus 29:15,16 NKJV).

At first glance, this seems like a strange, ugly scene in the midst of the high ceremony and pageantry of the ordination of the high priest and his fellow priests. Suddenly, there is blood and death in the tabernacle.

This death is very immediate and very graphic—Aaron and his sons are compelled to stand in their new, beautiful robes and participate in the death of a ram. As they place their hands on the beast, it is slaughtered, and its blood drained and sprinkled around.

This may seem ugly, but it was very necessary. God ordered this ceremony to remind the people of the ugliness and seriousness of sin, for our sin spawns death.

The ram's death is a picture of God's mercy—an animal was dying in place of Aaron and his sons. This was plainly shown as they laid their hands upon the animal.

Of course, no animal is worth the value of a human being. Ultimately, only a human could die for another human—and Jesus, fully human and fully divine, accomplished that through His death on Calvary.

Remember, as you read this chapter, that it is as though we stood with our hands on Jesus, as He died. Remember, too, that His horrible death was on our behalf.

Direction for today: Consider the horror of your sin and the enormity of Christ's personal sacrifice for you.

Prayer for today: "Thank You, Jesus, for dying for me."

March 14: Read Exodus 30

Key verse: "And thou shalt put it before the vail that is by the ark of the testimony, before the mercy seat that is over the testimony, where I will meet with thee" (Exodus 30:6 KJV).

Moses had gone into the presence of the Lord on Mount Sinai, where he had been instructed to build the tabernacle and provide its furnishings. Here God is telling him how to construct the Ark of the Covenant, and He tells Moses the tremendous importance the ark will play in the everyday life of each of the children of Israel.

The last six words of this verse provide the key to their success and blessing in their walk with the Lord: ". . . where I will meet with you."

God desires to meet with us every day. We will realize the sweetness of His presence and be successful in our Christian walk when we maintain our private altar of devotion.

The verse that God gave for the start of the 100 Huntley Street ministry is, "Day unto day utters speech, and night unto night reveals knowledge" (Psalm 9:2 NKJV).

If, on the other hand, we neglect our daily worship and we do not meet with Him, we find ourselves striving in the power of the flesh and not in the Spirit. This leads to frustration and, sometimes, exhaustion.

Direction for today: Practise the peace of God so that others who desire peace may find it in Christ.

Prayer for today: "Lord, help me to maintain my altar of worship, that I might meet with You each day."

Memory Verse

"And it shall come to pass that whoever calls on the name of the Lord shall be saved" (Joel 2:32a NKJV).

March 15: Read Exodus 31

Key verse: "And I have filled him with the Spirit of God, in wisdom, and in understanding, and in knowledge, and in all manner of workmanship" (Exodus 31:3 KJV).

When God gave Moses the plans to build the tabernacle, with all of its intricate design and details, He didn't for one moment intend that Moses would do it all by himself.

God gave Moses special people to help him. One of them was Bezaleel, whom He filled with His Spirit and to whom He gave wisdom, understanding and knowledge in all manner of workmanship.

As Moses was called to lead the children of Israel, God has called our pastors to lead many of our local congregrations. Like Moses, they often feel that God is leading them to do special projects for Him.

God never expects them to do all the work by themselves, but has given to us His Holy Spirit to enable us to be labourers together in His vineyard.

Direction for today: Offer help to your local congregation and seek opportunities to serve the Lord and His people.

Prayer for today: "Thank You, Father, for Your Holy Spirit. Please help me to glorify Your name with the special abilities You have given to me."

March 16: Read Exodus 32

Key verse: "Yet now, if Thou wilt forgive their sin—and if not, blot me, I pray Thee, out of Thy book which Thou hast written" (Exodus 32:32 KJV).

Although God had done so many wonderful things for the children of Israel, they—like many of us—soon forgot.

One of the reasons so many backslide or turn away from the Lord is that they forget His many blessings and become lazy in their daily devotional life. They look for things which satisfy the desires of the flesh and allow their spirits to go unnourished.

God will, however, always use those who are faithful to Him to intercede for His children who have gone astray and to bring revival to the land.

Moses stood before the Lord and stayed His hand from bringing judgment on Israel. He even requested that his name be blotted out of the Book of Life for their sakes.

God will never blot our names out of His book for such a request, but He will be moved by compassion and love. He will hear and answer positively, even as He did for Moses.

Direction for today: See the plight of the world in the light of eternity.

Prayer for today: "Lord, grant that I might be an intercessor for those who are outside Your salvation."

March 17: Read Exodus 33,34

Key verse: "And he said unto Him, if Thy presence go not with me, carry us not up hence" (Exodus 33:15 KJV).

Moses was a great intercessor. Time after time, we see him standing before the Lord, pleading with Him to spare Israel when they had sinned

so grievously against the Lord.

Here, once more, Moses is standing before the Lord on Israel's behalf. His greatest concern is that God would not withdraw His presence from them.

The presence of God is very important to each of us. In verse eleven of chapter thirty-three, we read that Joshua "did not depart out of the tabernacle"; he desired to stay in the presence of the Lord. Because of his dedication, he became the next leader of the children of Israel.

Moses was so concerned about God's presence being with them, he prayed earnestly that God would go with them, lest they be alone and without protection.

Direction for today: Draw closer to God in prayer, and refuse every obstacle and temptation which comes before you.

Prayer for today: "Father, draw me nearer, that I may experience Your abiding presence."

March 18: Read Exodus 35

Key verse: "Take ye from among you an offering unto the Lord: whosoever is of a willing heart, let him bring it, an offering of the Lord; gold, and silver, and brass" (Exodus 35:5 KJV).

Three times during this chapter we read the words, "a willing heart", in regards to the offering to build the tabernacle of the Lord.

God will build His kingdom and His church and, as with any worthwhile project designed to win the lost to Jesus, there is ever the burden of finances.

There may have been those in Israel during the time of Moses who complained about even the mention of money (gold, silver, brass).

However, God, in His wisdom, had given instructions through Moses that only those who were of "a willing heart" were to give to His work.

The tabernacle of God was not grudgingly built. It was built with love and joy from the willing hearts of those who gave. Therefore, it was with joy and blessing that God came to dwell among the children of Israel.

Direction for today: If you feel you have nothing to give, offer yourself, that God's kingdom may grow.

Prayer for today: "Lord, grant me a willing heart, that I may help to build Your kingdom with love and joy."

March 19: Read Exodus 36

Key verse: ". . . And the people were restrained from bringing, for the material they had was sufficient for all the work to be done—indeed too much" (Exodus 36:6,7 NKJV).

What a problem to have! Every pastor of every church I've ever known dreams of a day when he has to say to his congregation of believers, "enough already"! Every leader of every ministry such as Crossroads Christian Communications Inc., might be considered to have lost his mind if he said to his partners, "You've given too much! Stop! Please don't give any more!" What a problem indeed!

How does one get to this place, the place at which one must say, "Enough"? What might cause such abundance?

To answer that question, we need only look at the story of the Israelites. As we saw yesterday, those who brought an offering did so because they had a **willing** heart (Exodus 35:2,5,21,29). They were grateful for what the Lord had done on their behalf, and showed their gratitude by giving.

We, too, need not wring our hands in desperation that we do not have enough. What the Lord wants from His people is willing hearts. What a difference a willing heart can make!

Direction for today: Condition your heart to willingness and generosity.

Prayer for today: "Lord, give me a willing heart to share what You have given me."

March 20: Read Exodus 37,38

Key verse: "Bezaleel the son of Uri, the son of Hur, of the tribe of Judah, made all that the Lord commanded Moses" (Exodus 38:22 NKJV).

It must have been an absolutely beautiful sight to see the completed dwelling place of the Most High. How glorious to gaze on all that gold, fashioned by Bezaleel into objects of astounding beauty! And what a sense of accomplishment he must have felt as the foreman and chief artisan of such a work of God.

We don't hear much else about Bezaleel in the Scriptures. He's not named with the great men of God in any list of biblical heroes of faith. He would probably not be high on many lists as one after whom we would want to model our lives. Probably not many sermons will ever be preached about him.

But he was chosen by God to do a particular task in a specific way at a certain time. And he was faithful to his calling. So, when he stood back to gaze at his work, his heart was filled with satisfaction because his work had been ordained of God and directed by Him.

We may not feel like we're very important in the kingdom of God. We may not make it to the list of the top spiritual giants of this century.

But let us dare to be a Bezaleel, faithful to the task appointed to him by God, and we will be blessed.

Direction for today: I will be faithful where I have been placed, doing the task assigned to me.

Prayer for today: "Lord, make me faithful like Bezaleel."

March 21: Read Exodus 39

Key verse: "Then they made the plate of the holy crown of pure gold, and wrote on it an inscription like the engraving of a signet: HOLINESS TO THE LORD" (Exodus 39:3 NKJV).

Here we read of the beautiful priestly garments which Aaron and his sons were to wear as they carried out their functions in the tabernacle. Not only were these garments beautiful, but they were also rich with meaning. For example, the breastplate with the 12 stones, one for each of the 12 tribes, was a reminder that God had chosen these people for Himself. Every time the priests stood before God on behalf of the people, it was as if all the people stood there too, for they were represented on his breastplate.

But the key phrase of the entire chapter is the one quoted above: "HOLINESS TO THE LORD." It was affixed to the turban the priests wore. May we suggest that, even with the beauty of all their other vestments, without those words on the head, the priests were somehow incomplete before God?

Unless our hearts are set on holiness, nothing else really matters. Our hearts and minds must be set on the holiness of the Lord in order to be beautiful for Him. He, by the sacrifice of His Son Jesus, made us something beautiful. It's our desire to please Him by offering ourselves to Him and covenanting with Him to live holy lives.

Direction for today: I will be "HOLINESS TO THE LORD" in my words, thoughts and actions.

Prayer for today: "Lord, help me to take time to be holy."

Memory Verse

"And the Word became flesh and dwelt among us, and we beheld His glory, the glory as of the only begotten of the Father, full of grace and truth" (John 1:14 NKJV).

March 22: Read Exodus 40

Key verse: "For the cloud of the Lord was above the tabernacle by day and fire was over it by night, in the sight of all the house of Israel, throughout all their journeys" (Exodus 40:38 NKJV).

In the previous two verses, we read that, when the cloud moved, the Israelites moved and, when the cloud stayed still, the Israelites did not move, either. What a way to follow the leading of the Lord. What a certain signal that God was on the move! There would not have been much of a chance for a mistake.

There are times when I wish I had a cloud by day and a fire by night to lead me. I'd like to be able to see God clearly as He moves or stays; however, God hasn't chosen to show His guiding in that way today. He uses His Word and His indwelling Holy Spirit to lead us. Those ways are as sure and certain as the cloud and the fire.

I suppose it would be good to see God resting because then I could rest, as I like to think the Israelites did. But, knowing what I know about them and their character, I'm not certain they rested even when they could see the cloud resting. People, being what they are, are restless until they have the perfect peace of God.

In our day-by-day situations and circumstances, we need to come to the place of rest which, the Word tells us, is found in God. He is our perfect peace. Rest we must, while God rests, and be ready to move when He moves.

Direction for today: Desire to rest in God and to move when He leads; not until and not later than He leads.

Prayer for today: "Be my Guide, dear Lord Jesus, in all I do."

54

Mark

Mark is the shortest of the four gospels. Some scholars believe this to have been the first gospel written, and that the other writers used it as a foundational work.

Because of its shortness, Mark is a crisp, active narrative account of Jesus' ministry. There is less teaching recorded here than in the other gospels; rather, we see Jesus in action, ministering, healing, and performing miracles.

This book was probably written by John Mark, one of the younger members of the new-born church. Mark was not a disciple but was clearly a follower of Christ; and later, after a shaky beginning, he was a devoted helper of the Apostle Paul.

March 23: Read Mark 1

Key verse: "'Come, follow Me,' Jesus said, 'and I will make you fishers of men'" (Mark 1:17 NIV).

We all know this verse. You probably learned it as a child in Sunday School. And, as often happens, familiarity can rob such an important truth of its real impact.

From the moment they met Jesus, the priorities of the disciples had to change. Suddenly, their occupations could no longer have first place. No more could they be "fishermen" first—Jesus had another plan for them. Now, the first priority in their lives was obedience to the Lord and the building of the kingdom of God.

Notice carefully that Jesus did not first send them to be fishers of men; instead, He told them to follow Him. We will never win others by running after them; we win others by walking with Jesus. At the right time, He will lead us to those who are ready to be saved.

Notice, too, that Jesus claimed the responsibility for producing fishers of men. "I will make . . . ," He said.

Christians generally have one of two problems. Either we are not willing to leave our material pursuits and make God's kingdom our number-one priority, or we run off under our own steam, trying to build the kingdom without help from the King.

Both problems have the same solution: "Follow Me, and I will make you fishers of men".

Direction for today: Follow Jesus and everything else will follow.

Prayer for today: "Lord, make me a fisher of people for You."

March 24: Read Mark 2

Key verse: "While Jesus was having dinner at Levi's house, many tax collectors and 'sinners' were eating with Him and His disciples, for there were many who followed Him" (Mark 2:15 NIV).

Does this dinner party sound like a church supper at your local assembly? If not, perhaps it should. Jesus spent almost all of His time of ministry with the sinners and outcasts of society. Later in Mark 2, He said, "It is not the healthy who need a doctor, but the sick. I have not come to call the righteous, but sinners" (Mark 2:17).

The church is commissioned by Christ to carry on His work. This means that we are called to win the spiritually sick to health and wholeness in Jesus Christ.

There are now many churches where the pews are filled with former alcoholics, one-time drug users, ex-prostitutes, victims of broken homes and all of the other kinds of people to whom Jesus seemed especially to reach out. But there are also some comfortable churches which would discourage such as these at the door.

We were never called to be the comfortable church—we are called to be the conquering church, gaining spiritual victories for all who will receive the good news of Jesus Christ!

Direction for today: We should be unconscious of class, uncaring of economic success and blind to colour. Jesus is an equal-opportunity Saviour and we need to be like Him.

Prayer for today: "Lord, remove all prejudice and fear from my heart, that I may carry the full and true gospel to a needy world."

March 25: Read Mark 3

Key verse: "Whoever does God's will is My brother and sister and mother" (Mark 3:35 NIV).

Jesus used a number of terms regarding His followers. In this chapter, He called them "apostles"; elsewhere, He called them friends. But, in this key verse, Jesus bestows on all who live in obedience to God the ultimate relationship: brother, sister, or mother!

How do we do the will of God? There are basic principles, of course—being filled with the Holy Spirit, obeying the Lord, meditating on the Scriptures, living prayerful lives. But this chapter also points to some specifics that are in God's will.

Mark 3 begins with the healing of the man with the withered hand. Jesus healed hundreds—perhaps thousands—of people during his ministry. Healing—for you and for others—is clearly part of God's plan and in His will.

In verse 9, we see the disciples making plans so Jesus might be seen and heard better. That, too, is God's will for us: that our lives and actions will direct others to Christ; but not our actions alone, for Christ commissioned His followers to speak of Him (Mark 3:14).

All of these things are within the will of God. As we walk in obedience to Him, Jesus declares us to be members of His family.

Direction for today: Live as a child of God, a brother or sister to Jesus.

Prayer for today: "Thank You, Lord Jesus, for Your great love."

March 26: Read Mark 4

Key verse: "Then He arose and rebuked the wind, and said to the sea, 'Peace, be still!' And the wind ceased and there was a great calm" (Mark 4:39 NKJV).

Many people through the ages of history have talked about peace. Some have been completely sincere, seeking to bring peace on an international, national, or personal scale. Others have been liars and madmen, waging war in the name of "peace". Some have been great teachers or political leaders.

Only one of them has even been able to produce the peace which He proclaimed. He is the One of our key verse, the One who stood up in a storm-tossed ship and commanded nature to obey Him. Nature hushed at His voice, for His authority was that of the Creator of all which exists.

The storm in your heart or soul can be changed to peace at the word of Jesus. Whatever storms you are riding through today—whether in your career or your marriage; your family or your health; your friendships or your education—Jesus can speak peace to you and in you.

Direction for today: Hear His voice saying, "Peace, be still".

Prayer for today: "Lord, in the storms of my life, I ask for Your continuing guidance and protection."

March 27: Read Mark 5

Key verse: "When they came to Jesus, they saw the man who had been possessed by the legion of demons, sitting there, dressed and in his right mind; and they were afraid" (Mark 5:15 NIV).

Now, what were your problems again?

Oh, I'm not belittling any of the crises that confront us all from time to time. Perhaps you are facing a very tough situation even today. But our problems do seem to come into perspective when we meet a man like this demon-possessed creature. We would all have to go a long way to match his list of serious problems. He was full of evil spirits, entirely cut off from human contact. He was constantly torturing himself and could not be restrained because of his demonic strength. His home was a cemetery.

In a few words, Jesus solved each of those problems for this tormented man. The people of the town approached fearfully, for they were afraid of the man; they left fearfully because they were even more afraid of the greater power demonstrated by Jesus.

This choice is yours whenever you face a difficulty, regardless of size. Either you can accept the help and deliverance that Jesus so freely offers, or you can run away, afraid of what the Lord might do in your life. The townspeople ran away. The former demoniac remained . . . and was dramatically changed.

Direction for today: Bring your problems and fears to Jesus.

Prayer for today: "Lord, set me free from anything that is binding me spiritually, emotionally, or physically."

March 28: Read Mark 6

Key verse: "Now He could do no mighty work there, except that He laid His hands on a few sick people and healed them. And He marveled because of their unbelief" (Mark 6:5,6a NKJV).

Just imagine: what if Jesus had come one day to a hospital in your community? As He walked through the door, the chief of staff met Him and said, "Welcome to our facility. I'd like to show you around." But Jesus replied, "I've come to heal the people in your wards."

The chief of staff was shocked: "Oh, no I don't think you can do that. That's what our medical staff are for." Jesus reached out and touched a few people who had crowded up to Him, healing each one. Then He turned and sadly walked back through the door.

That's exactly what happened in Nazareth. Sadly, this also happens in our world, in many of our churches, and in our own lives. Jesus has come to us, promising abundant life. But, instead of believing Him and letting Him work the mighty miracles of God, we continue to doubt and try to work things out ourselves—that never works.

Jesus will not impose His grace. We have to accept it gratefully. When we do, we are astounded at the great things He will do in our lives.

Let's not be like the people of Jesus' hometown, nor like the hospital staff in our story. Let's welcome Him into every area of our lives and of our churches, and allow Him to work.

Direction for today: The only thing that prevents Jesus from working in our lives is our own unbelief. Set your unbelief aside!

Prayer for today: "Lord, I believe!"

Memory Verse

"Behold, I stand at the door and knock. If anyone hears My voice and opens the door, I will come in to him and dine with him, and he with Me" (Revelation 3:20 NKJV).

March 29: Read Mark 7

Key verse: "And He said, 'What comes out of a man, that defiles a man' " (Mark 7:20 NKJV).

The Pharisees, in Jesus' time, often held to a very legalistic style of religion. They had added a multitude of details and interpretations to the laws given to Moses, and believed that strict adherence to the law was the only way to satisfy God.

Jesus came with a new message: true faith is inward, founded in a believing heart. He insisted that outward actions could never earn favour with God—we can come to the Father only through the Son, who is the Way, the Truth and the Life.

Too often, we try to prove our faith through outward actions while harbouring sin in our hearts. Jesus teaches that, no matter how good we look on the outside, internal sin will certainly corrupt us.

Be careful not to be the kind of "Christian" who makes an outward show of Sunday religion, but who is vulgar, abusive, dishonest or unkind throughout the week. Our conduct in business, the family or school should reflect the presence of Christ in our lives. The only way outward actions will be truly holy is if they reflect a purity of heart.

Direction for today: Allow the Holy Spirit to cleanse you from the inside out.

Prayer for today: "Lord, remove any defilement from within me, that I may be clean to serve You."

March 30: Read Mark 8

Key verse: "And He commanded the multitude to sit down on the ground. And He took the seven loaves and gave thanks, broke them and gave them to His disciples to set before them; and they set them before the multitude" (Mark 8:6 NKJV).

We all know this story of the feeding of the four thousand, one of two similar miracles of feeding that Jesus performed. Tucked inside this account is a nugget of truth that can teach us a great deal about faith.

Notice that Jesus gave thanks. He turned His eyes heavenward and thanked His Father even before any miracle had been performed. He knew He could trust His Father, and believed that He would never fail Him.

Whatever the situation in which we find ourselves, we can benefit greatly from the same attitude. Often, we come to God begging, pleading and in desperation. But there is no need for this. The Scriptures teach us to cast our anxiety on the Lord; Jesus invited us to come to Him for comfort and rest.

We need not panic. Instead, in every circumstance, we can look to the Lord and thank Him for being in control of our lives.

Direction for today: Come to God with thanksgiving, no matter what your situation.

Prayer for today: "Thank You, Father, because all things are in Your hands and all things are possible with You."

March 31: Read Mark 9

Key verse: "And a cloud came and overshadowed them, and a voice came out of the cloud, saying, 'This is My beloved Son. Hear Him!'" (Mark 9:7 NKJV).

What a powerful witness to the true nature of Jesus Christ! Surely, Peter, James and John left that mountainside with a firm conviction that Jesus was everything He had claimed to be, and even more! They heard the voice of God the Father declaring the eternal truth concerning His Son.

But this amazing occurrence was much more than a declaration of the divinity of Jesus. It was also a command, one as important to Christians today as it was to these three disciples: "Hear Him!"

That is the key to growth as a Christian. It's good to listen to messages, watch Christian television programs, and read Christian books. All of these things will help us to grow. However, we must be sure that at all times, we are hearing the voice of Jesus.

There are two ways to remain familiar with that voice. We hear Him plainly in His Word, the Bible. Each day, as you read the Scriptures, ask the Lord to help you hear His voice in those chapters. We hear Him plainly, too, through the inner witness of the Spirit of God, who lives in all who believe on the Lord Jesus.

Take time to "hear Him." Listen for the voice of the Lord as you read the Bible and as you pray. Ask Him to give you discernment to hear Him through preachers, teachers and writers.

Direction for today: "Hear Him!"

Prayer for today: "Lord, I'm listening. Please speak to me."

4

Abba, Father

The secret hideaway
Beckons me relentlessly
As, time after time,
I take grudging, faltering steps
Toward Your very
Throne-room of patience,
forgiveness, mercy
and abundant blessing—

My reluctance to be just myself
with You, O God,
Stems from nothing but pride—

How shabby an excuse
in light of Calvary;

Thank You for waiting up for me

— Hilda Schnell

April 1: Read Mark 10

Key verse: *"Jesus said, 'With men it is impossible, but not with God; for with God all things are possible'" (Mark 10:27 NKJV).*

Throughout His ministry, Jesus had much to say about the danger of riches and the responsibility of the rich to care for their poor and hungry neighbours. Of all that He said, this is perhaps most ignored by Christians in today's western society. Yet today's reading makes it very clear that Jesus believed riches to be a terrible snare, capable of luring us away from the kingdom of God.

In His advice to the rich young ruler, one principle is evident: our possessions are never to become more important to us than our obedience to Christ. That obedience may mean we must give away our riches in order to follow Him.

The rich young ruler found it impossible to surrender his material possessions for the sake of Jesus. We, too, may be holding on to material things with both hands while trying to serve the Lord as well. It seldom works.

But, with Jesus, there is always hope. He told his followers that it was impossible for a rich person to enter heaven—but the impossible has never stopped God. All who call on the name of the Lord will be saved and as, in obedience, we yield to Him all that we are and all that we have, He will show us what we must do.

Direction for today: Open your bank account and safety box for the Lord today, and then listen to His direction to you. (A helpful book might be "Rich Christians in an Age of Hunger" by Ronald J. Sider.)

Prayer for today: "Lord, may material possessions never get in the way of my obedience to You. If I have done this, I repent. Please show me how to be more faithful."

April 2: Read Mark 11

Key verse: *"If you do not forgive, neither will your Father in heaven forgive your trespasses" (Mark 11:26 NKJV).*

There are a number of things that can block the spiritual channels between you and the Lord. Unconfessed sin is one, of course, as are other forms of disobedience to the Lord. But today's reading speaks of one of the most serious of spiritual blocks—lack of forgiveness.

The words of Jesus are clear: if we fail to forgive someone else, God will not forgive us. It blocks the spiritual channels.

How many lives are spiritually "on hold" because they harbour unforgiveness and bitterness? How many churches are cold and dead because members have blocked up the channels in feuds and grievances, one against the other? How many families are torn apart because someone refuses to forgive someone else?

If we do not forgive, we cannot grow, and the Christian ministries in which we are involved will not grow. No wonder Jesus warns us of this with such force!

The answer is so simple: "If you have anything against anyone, forgive him." If that seems impossible, simply recall how much God has forgiven you, ask Him for the grace, and forgive the one against whom you hold a grudge. Tell the Lord about it first and if He sends you the other person, go and make things right.

These spiritual channels will be reopened, you will know the peace of full forgiveness, and your spiritual life will blossom!

Direction for today: Search yourself for unforgiveness and, by the grace of God, root it out in repentance.

Prayer for today: "Forgive me, Lord, as I forgive others."

April 3: Read Mark 12

Key verse: "Jesus answered and said to them, 'Are you not therefore mistaken, because you do not know the Scriptures nor the power of God?'" (Mark 12:24 NKJV).

How do we come to understand the things of God? Jesus gives us excellent guidance in this verse: we learn about God and His works by knowing both the Scriptures and the power of God.

He accuses the Sadducees, who were once again trying to trap Him in heresy, with knowing neither. It is a terrible condemnation of the spiritual leaders of His day.

In our day, too, there may be leaders who ignore the Word of God and do not seek to know His power. But, more frequently, we see Christians who concern themselves with one or the other, but not with both. This produces a lopsided and ineffective believer.

Many Christians are devoted to the Word of God, reading it faithfully every day and hearing it preached in their churches. Yet they are, for some reason, afraid of the power of God; afraid to allow the Holy Spirit to have free reign to work in their lives and in their church services. They know the Scriptures, but their spiritual lives are dry and uneventful because they avoid the power of the Holy Spirit.

Others make the opposite mistake. They have seen God at work and pursue evidences of His power so singlemindedly that they have little time for serious study of the Word. That extreme is also dangerous and can open the door for false teaching, since such people are unaware of the true doctrines of the Bible.

Be sure you fall into neither error. Spend time in the Scriptures.

Direction for today: Expect and welcome the miraculous workings of the Holy Spirit. Allow the Lord to bless you through the gift of His Word and the gifts of His Spirit.

Prayer for today: "Lord, if I have failed to see You in either of these areas, teach me more of Your Word and Your power."

April 4: Read Mark 13

Key verse: "*Watch therefore, for you do not know when the master of the house is coming—in the evening, at midnight, at the crowing of the rooster, or in the morning—lest, coming suddenly, he find you sleeping" (Mark 13:35,36 NKJV).*

This chapter concerns one of the most exciting truths of the Word of God—Jesus Christ is coming again!

The key verses are the words of Jesus, calling us to live in the conscious awareness of His return. We should live with one eye cocked heavenward, so to speak.

Unfortunately, we do not. Most of us spend most of our time completely oblivious to the fact that Jesus is coming again. If we lived in that continual awareness, how different our lives would be! And how much more productive for the kingdom of God!

If we really believe that Jesus is coming again, and if we are obeying His command to "watch", we will live with our spiritual accounts up-to-date. We will be much less likely to fall into sin. We will be more eager to share the good news of Jesus with our families, friends and neighbours—for it is only that good news which will save them from eternity in hell.

Today's chapter is filled with warnings and signs. We are cautioned against false christs and false prophets, and warned that persecution will surely come. But the most serious message of all is that of our key verses: "watch"! Be prepared for the coming of Christ.

Direction for today: Live in the awareness of Christ's promised return.

Prayer for today: "Father, help me to be ready at all times for the glorious second coming of my Lord Jesus."

Memory Verse

"Your word is a lamp to my feet and a light to my path" (Psalm 119:105 NKJV).

April 5: Read Mark 14

Key verse: "But Peter said to Him, 'Even if all are made to stumble, yet I will not be'" (Mark 14:29 NKJV).

Praise God for the honesty of the Scriptures. Peter was a great man of God and an important leader in the early church. But these chapters make no effort to white-wash him or to hide his errors and sins; thus, we can learn much from him. This declaration by Peter is a prime example of trying to do spiritual things in one's own strength. His intention might have been admirable, but he could not follow through. At the end of the chapter, we read of Peter's horrifying denial of Jesus—the lowest point of his walk as a believer.

But let's not criticize Peter; let's realize that we are continually guilty of the same thing. Every day, we try to accomplish spiritual things without relying on the power of the Spirit. Every day, we try, in own strength to do things only the Lord can do. And every day we fail.

There are two lessons to be learned from this. The first is: be sure you are always tapped in to the spiritual strength that is yours when you are filled with the Spirit. This will prevent you from making vain promises that you cannot keep, and will ensure spiritual victory. Secondly, let us be sure to follow Peter's example in the final verse—he repented of his sin and was restored to fellowship with Jesus. This was not true of his fellow disciple, Judas, who also denied Christ, but who never sought forgiveness.

Direction for today: Beware of vain promises made in your own strength.

Prayer for today: "Lord, may my words always reflect Your presence and power in me."

April 6: Read Mark 15

Key verse: "And the curtain of the temple was torn into two from top to bottom" (Mark 15:38 NKJV).

In our readings in the Old Testament during these months, we are studying the books of Exodus and Leviticus. In these books, we discover the origin of the veil in the temple.

It was placed there under God's instructions as a symbol of the separation between a holy, all-powerful God and His weak and sinful people. Once a year, the high priest could go beyond that veil and make atonement for the sins of the people. At all other times, the veil was a barrier between God and humanity.

At the death of Christ, that barrier was destroyed. A full atonement had been made; the ultimate sacrifice was complete. Because of the love of Christ and His death and resurrection, we can "come boldly before the throne of grace" (Hebrews 4:16).

This torn veil was a perfect symbol of all that had been accomplished by the Lord Jesus. It was torn from top to bottom—from God to man—by an act of God.

The holy of holies stood open, an invitation to all to approach the Heavenly Father in the name of Jesus.

Direction for today: Never fear to come directly to the Lord in prayer.

Prayer for today: "Thank You, Father, that, in the name of Jesus, I can come to You as my Lord and my King, with no barriers between us."

April 7: Read Mark 16

Key verse: *"And He said to them, 'Go into all the world and preach the gospel to every creature. He who believes and is baptized will be saved; but he who does not believe will be condemned. And these signs will follow those who believe: in My name they will cast out demons; they will speak with new tongues; they will take up serpents; and if they drink anything deadly, it shall not hurt them; they will lay hands on the sick, and they will recover." (Mark 16:15-18 NKJV).*

These are astounding promises given by our Lord to His followers before He returned to heaven, leaving with them the responsibility to share the gospel throughout the world.

We instantly notice that the followers of Jesus should expect more than a low-key preaching of the gospel—when the gospel is proclaimed, dynamic things will happen!

Almost all of these prophetic promises were realized in the book of Acts: demons were cast out; the believers spoke in tongues; Paul was attacked by a serpent; Peter, John and the other apostles healed the sick.

But it did not stop there. Wherever the Word was declared, miracles happened—in New Testament times, in the church through the first centuries, and even today.

The promises of Jesus are with us still. We should live, meet together and minister in the expectation that miraculous, powerful, anointed things are going to happen wherever Jesus is lifted up!

Direction for today: Expect Jesus to keep His promises!

Prayer for today: "Lord, use me, in whatever way You see fit, to help build Your church."

Leviticus

"Without shedding of blood there is no forgiveness" (Hebrews 9:22).

The third book of the five-volume "works of Moses" is sometimes perceived to be the most tedious in the entire Bible. Certainly it is full of detail—details of sacrifices, of priestly duties, of rituals and elaborate symbols.

But when we see its place in the divine plan as revealed in the Word of God, Leviticus can become a tremendously exciting book. The Hebrews, though God's chosen people, were not free from the curse of sin which every man and woman has inherited from Adam and Eve.

Here, for the first time, we see a detailed account of God's prescription for sin: a sacrificial system using blood to cover sin.

Thus, we can see Leviticus as a clear message to the people as to how they should deal with sin and continue to walk in obedience to God. But this book is much, much more. As Moses wrote down the Levitical law, he may not have know it but he was painting detailed pictures of the life, work and person of Jesus Christ. As we read of the duties of the priests, we will see the prefiguring of our Great High Priest, Jesus Christ (Hebrews 8:1). As we read of the sacrifices for sin, we can meditate on the ultimate and final sacrifice for sin, Jesus Christ. He was offered on the altar of the cross (Hebrews 10:10) so that we need no longer bring sacrifices, but rather "present our bodies a living and holy sacrifice, acceptable to God, which is our spiritual service of worship" (Romans 12:1).

April 8: Read Leviticus 1,2

Key verse: "If his offering be a burnt sacrifice of the herd, let him offer a male without blemish: he shall offer it of his own voluntary will at the door of the tabernacle of the congregation before the Lord" (Leviticus 1:3 KJV).

The use of the word "voluntary" here emphasizes with great clarity the undergirding idea in the burnt offerings. It leads us to consider the cross as the place where the great question of sin was settled between the eternal Justice and the spotless Victim—as a place where our sin found atonement.

The cross was this, but it was more: it was the place where Christ's love to the Father was told in a language only the Father could hear and understand. Being willing to be "made sin", to endure the wrath of God and the hiding of His countenance, indicates that the burnt offering does not only foreshadow Christ on the cross bearing sin, it was a prefigurement of Christ on the cross accomplishing the will of God.

Christ, in His own words, shrank from His work as a sin-bearer. The thought of contact with sin and losing the light of the Father's countenance was horrifying to Him.

He is pictured as presenting to the heart of the Father an odour of incomparable fragrance. The deep devotion of the Son's heart, presented to and appreciated by the heart of the Father, is the elevated aspect of the cross which is so strikingly foreshadowed in the burnt offering.

Direction for today: Prepare yourself willingly to serve God, even when the tendency is to shrink from the task.

Prayer for today: "Lord, I thank You for the assurance in Your word that, when the tendency is to shrink from the task.

April 9: Read Leviticus 3,4

Key verse: "Anyone who sinned and broke any of the Lord's commands without intending to would have to observe the following rules. . . and he will be forgiven" (Leviticus 4:27, 35b TEV).

The first three chapters of this book explain the intricacies of the "sweet savour" offerings. Six times we read, "the odour of this food offering is pleasing to the Lord". In chapter four, the "sacrifices for sin" are introduced. Within these sacrifices is provision for "sins of ignorance".

The holiness of God and the basis of His association with His people would never be regulated by the standard of man's conscience, no matter how high that standard might be. There are many things man's conscience would pass over, but which God could not tolerate and these would interfere with man's relationship with Him.

If the atonement of Christ merely made provision for such sins as those which come within the compass of man's comprehension, we could find ourselves very far short of the true ground of peace. We need to understand that sin has been atoned for, according to God's measurement. Therefore, that sin, as seen in the light of His inflexible holiness, has been divinely judged.

This is what gives settled peace to each soul. A full atonement has been made for the believer's sins of ignorance, as well as for his known sins.

Direction for today: You can be confident that, even when you offend God unintentionally, this sin, too, is covered by the blood of Christ.

Prayer for today: "Father, I appreciate Your complete plan of salvation. May I be sensitive today to all the areas of my life which do not honour You. Thank You for Your grace."

April 10: Read Leviticus 5,6

Key verse: "This is a very holy offering" (Leviticus 6:25b, TEV).

In none of the offerings is Christ's personal holiness more strikingly presented than in the sin offering. "It is most holy . . . shall be holy . . . most holy" (6:25-29).

The aspect of holiness is emphasized, lest we lose sight of that holiness while contemplating the place our Saviour took in the sin offering. Again and again, we are reminded, "It is most holy."

Never was the Lord Jesus more fully seen to be "the Holy One of God" than when He was "made sin" on the tree. Though a sin-bearer, He was sinless; though enduring the wrath of God, He was the Father's delight; though deprived of the light of God's countenance, He dwelt in the Father's bosom.

How wonderful to see this great mystery so accurately shadowed in "the law of the sin offering"!

Direction for today: Value everything that speaks of the Lord Jesus, that sets Him forth; everything that gives a fresh insight into His excellency and matchless beauty.

Prayer for today: "Holy, Holy, Holy, Lord God Almighty! All Thy works shall praise Thy name, in earth, and sky, and sea" (Reginald Heber).

April 11: Read Leviticus 7

Key verse: "If he offers it for a thanksgiving, then he shall offer, with the sacrifice of thanksgiving, unleavened cakes mixed with oil" (Leviticus 7:12 NKJV).

We often have the impression that the complicated sacrificial system in the Old Testament was a duty and a burden upon the people. But here we read of a voluntary, thanksgiving "peace offering" that God's people were free to bring to the tabernacle.

The sacrificial system was complex—it was designed to teach a number of important things about the holiness of God, the sinfulness of people, and the need for a sacrificial death.

However, it also made provision for joyful worship in acts such as this thanksgiving offering.

The sacrifice involved feasting on the meat offered to the Lord, a picture of the spiritual meals about which we now know: communion and the ultimate marriage supper of the Lamb.

We should follow the example of these Israelites and bring offerings of thanksgiving to the Lord. We can come to Him with our praises, our worship, our service, and with our financial offerings.

As we do so, let us remember the important symbolism of the oil in this offering—each offering had to include oil, the symbol of the Holy Spirit. We must allow the Spirit to move us to such joyful declarations of thanksgiving and service.

Direction for today: Bring a thanksgiving offering to the Lord.

Prayer for today: "Father, thank You for every blessing You have brought into my life!"

Memory Verse

"If we live in the Spirit, let us also walk in the Spirit" (Galatians 5:25 NKJV).

April 12: Read Leviticus 8

Key verse: "What I am now about to do is what the Lord has commanded" (Leviticus 8:5 TEV).

The first seven chapters of Leviticus speak of sacrifice. In chapter eight, we are introduced to the subject of priesthood. These two themes are intimately connected. The sinner needs a sacrifice; the believer needs a priest. We have both in Christ, who, having offered Himself as a sacrifice without spot, entered His priestly ministry in the heavenly sanctuary.

Looking into this chapter, we see three prominent points: the authority of the Word; the value of the blood; and the power of the Spirit.

In verse five, and again in verse thirty-four, we are brought immediately under the authority of the Word of God. Carefully ponder these words. Moses did not say, "This is what is expedient, or agreeable or suitable." Nor did he say, "Traditionally, this is proper." He knew only of the authority of the Word of God, and it was his privilege to bring every member of the assembly into direct contact with that blessed source.

What was to be the result of strick adherence to the Word of God? "The glory of the Lord shall appear to you" (9:6).

Direction for today: Give diligent heed to the Word of God.

Prayer for today: "Father, help me to recognize today if I am departing from or neglecting Your Word."

April 13: Read Leviticus 9,10

Key verse: "...that you may teach the children of Israel all the statutes which the Lord has spoken to them by the hand of Moses" (Leviticus 10:11 NKJV).

A well-known Bible teacher, in speaking of his maturing as a man of God, tells how the Lord spoke to him about going to a movie theatre. He relates that it was as though God said, "Others may; you cannot." He says that settled the matter for him.

In today's reading, we learn about the conduct expected of the priests. They were not to drink intoxicating beverages, for they needed to be able to distinguish between the holy and the unholy, the clean and the unclean, so they could teach Israel all the commands of God.

The thought is this—how often do God's people lose their abilities to discern the difference between holy and unholy and to teach the counsels of God because they taint their testimony with their behaviour? It is incumbent on us all—not just on pastors, elders anbd deacons—to keep our behaviour pure before God so that we will not lose our opportunity to witness. The world watches the Christian, so let us give no opportunity to criticize the Lord because of our behaviour.

Direction for today: Ask the Lord to give you the desire to be willing to pay the cost to be His disciple.

Prayer for today: "Lord, help me always to live a life honouring to Your name."

April 14: Read Leviticus 11,12

Key verse: "I am the Lord your God; consecrate yourselves and be holy, because I am holy" (Leviticus 11:44a NIV).

In these chapters, God gives Israel the first two regulations in a series dealing with ceremonial uncleanness.

Worshiping a holy God demands a holy people. For this reason, the ceremonial laws were given to the Israelites to teach them to sanctify themselves and to be holy. Specifically mentioned here are those dealing with diet, describing edible and non-edible animals, fish, birds, creeping things and insects; and purification after childbirth.

While we are not under the law today, God expects us to live a holy life (1 Peter 1:14). How can we accomplish this? Paul puts it this way; "So then, just as you received Christ Jesus as Lord [by faith, trusting in Him], continue to live in Him" (Colossians 2:6).

In Christ's strength we can live a holy and pure life.

Direction for today: Give thanks that you are not under the yoke of the law. Work on developing the habit of holiness in your life.

Prayer for today: "Teach me to trust in the supernatural provision of our Saviour, Jesus Christ, to achieve holiness."

April 15: Read Leviticus 13

Key verse: "He is a leprous man. He is unclean. The priest shall surely pronounce him unclean" (Leviticus 13:44 NKJV).

This chapter deals, in somewhat graphic detail, with the detection and treatment of a number of skin diseases, including "leprosy". While it is not certain that this disease is the same as that identified as leprosy today, or in New Testament times, the principle is very clear.

The commandments were given for two purposes: to protect the health of the people and to demonstrate the danger of spiritual corruption and infection among the people of God. While the Lord was certainly concerned with physical health, He was even more concerned with the spiritual well-being of His people.

The key here is "separation". Just as those who had a skin disease were to be separated from the camp, so believers are to be separated from sin. Unfortunately, "separation" is a doctrine that seems to have fallen out of favour, as so many followers of Christ partake in almost every worldly pleasure. It is a principle to which we need to return immediately; unless we do so, the infection will continue to spread. Truly, we need to remember that, while we are to be in the world, we are not to be of the world.

Direction for today: Be sure that you are clean, separated from sin.

Prayer for today: "Lord, please give me a longing to be clean always. Give me a heart which yearns always to honour You in all that I do and say and think."

April 16: Read Leviticus 14

Key verse: "The person to be cleansed must wash his clothes, shave off all his hair and bathe with water; then he will be ceremonially clean. After this he may come into the camp, but he must stay outside his tent for seven days" (Leviticus 14:8 NIV).

In yesterday's reading, the priests were given instruction in the detection of leprosy. Chapter 14 deals with the ritual for the cleansing and restoration of the leper. The ritual is quite elaborate. It covers a period of eight days, with special rites on the first and eighth. The ritual of the first day restores the leper to the camp, but not to the intimacy of his home.

If we apply these rituals to the spiritual leprosy of sin, it suggests that, when we withdraw from those who are guilty of improper conduct so that they may be disciplined, we must not consider them as enemies, but rebuke them as brethren (II Thessalonians 3:15).

Also, when God, by His grace, has brought to repentance those who have been shut out of the fellowship of the church, they ought to be received again with tenderness and joy and sincere affection (II Corinthians 2:7,8).

Direction for today: When your brothers sins, rebuke him; if he repents, forgive him (Luke 17:3).

Prayer for today: "Help me, Lord, to forgive others as You have forgiven me."

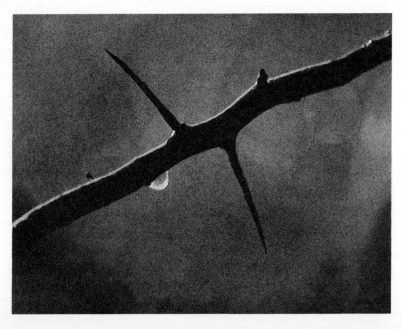

April 17: Read Leviticus 15

Key verse: *"You must keep the Israelites separate from things that make them unclean, so they will not die in their uncleanness for defiling My dwelling place, which is among them" (Leviticus 15:31 NIV).*

We have just read the laws concerning ceremonial uncleanness dealing with matters of sex. In all these laws there seems to be a special regard for the honour of God's dwelling place or tabernacle. The Israelites were taught to preserve the honour of their purity and to keep themselves from all sinful contamination.

While we are not under the yoke of these ordinances today it is a reminder to us of the contagious nature of sin and the danger of being affected by association with bad company as pointed out by Paul in Corinthians 15:33; "Do not be misled: bad company corrupts good character."

Direction for today: In the freedom we have in Christ, remember that, while "everything is permissible not everything is beneficial." (I Corinthians 6:12 NIV).

Prayer for today: "Lord, in this corrupt world, help me not to compromise Your Word."

April 18: Read Leviticus 16

Key verse: *"This is to be a lasting ordinance for you: atonement is to be made once a year for all the sins of the Israelites" (Leviticus 16:34 NIV).*

This chapter describes the institution of the annual Day of Atonement. Only on this occasion was Aaron allowed into the inner-most part of the tabernacle, the Holy of Holies, where the Ark of the Covenant was housed. He must first obtain forgiveness for his own sin; only then might he cleanse the tabernacle and offer sacrifices on behalf of the people's sin.

In this ordinance are typified the two great privileges of direct access to God and the remission or forgiveness of sin, both of which we owe to the mediation of our Lord Jesus Christ.

Firstly, all believers now have the confidence or boldness to enter the "Most Holy Place" through the veil every day (Hebrews 10:19,20). Also, we can come boldly (not as Aaron had to, with fear and trembling) to His throne of grace (Hebrews 4:16).

Secondly, while the atonement made by the high priest pertained only to the congregation of Israel, Christ is the atonement for the sins of the whole world. God laid upon our Lord Jesus "the iniquity of us all" (Isaiah 53:6), and He bore our sins and the punishment of them as He died on the cross (I Peter 2:24).

What a blessed change is made by the gospel of Christ.

Direction for today: Continue, in faith, to rely on Christ, our Saviour, for His blood alone was able to atone for our sins and give us a pardon.

Prayer for today: "Thank you, Father, for Your Son, Jesus Christ, our High Priest, who, by His sacrifice, reconciled us to You."

Memory Verse

"He is not here; for He is risen, as He said" (Matthew 28:6a NKJV).

April 19: Read Leviticus 17,18

Key verse: "You shall therefore keep My statutes and My judgments, which if a man does, he shall live by them. I am Lord" (Leviticus 18:5 NKJV).

There is nothing new about sexual immorality or perversion. The very things that corrupt our cities and towns today are described here in a book penned by Moses. The Bible is very frank about these things and they are mentioned throughout the Scriptures, including the very direct words of the apostle Paul.

And, just as sexual perversion is not new, so, too, God's judgment upon these kinds of sin is not new. Mankind has always been sinful, and God has always been just. Mankind has always sought his own self-gratification, and God has always stated that the wages of sin is death.

In our key verse, written just before a long list of immorality, God promises, once again, that, just as sin leads to death, obedience to Him (which we can accomplish only through Christ) leads to life.

And, even though it is clear in chapter 18 that God hates sexual sin, we have already seen in chapter 17 that He has made provision for even this kind of sin. The sacrifices of the Old Testament are a picture of the ultimate sin sacrifice, that of Jesus, which made a new convenant between us and God.

As always, man is sinning. As always, God hates sin. But, as always God loves sinners and has made provision for them. Praise the Lord!

Direction for today: Like the Lord, we must learn to hate sin and have compassion and mercy toward the sinner.

Prayer for today: "Lead me not into temptation."

April 20: Read Leviticus 19

Key verse: "You shall be holy; for I the Lord God am holy" (Leviticus 19:2 RSV).

This may seem to be an impossible command, but the New Testament says the same thing this way: "For whom He foreknew, He also predestined to be comformed to the image of His Son" (Romans 8:29 NKJV).

It was an impossible command for the Israelites, who were seeking to obey God by keeping the law. Paul tells us—centuries after the law was given—that it was intended to show us our sin and our weaknesses: no one could be "holy" by his or her own effort.

But we are now living in the era in which the Holy Spirit has been poured out upon all believers. Unlike the Old Testament people of God, we have God dwelling right in us, quickening our spirits. Christ is in us, the hope of glory!

The Holy Spirit in us is conforming us into the image of Christ. It is God's plan that we become more and more like our Lord and Saviour.

Because we still battle with sin, we will never be perfectly holy. But, as we allow the Holy Spirit to work in our lives, we are becoming increasingly holy, fitting representatives of Christ.

Direction for today: Holiness is the goal of every Spirit-filled Christian.

Prayer for today: "Lord, by Your Spirit, may I be conformed to the image of Jesus."

April 21: Read Leviticus 20,21

Key verse: "Keep My statutes, and do them; I am the Lord who sanctifies you" (Leviticus 20:8 RSV).

God is holy! God is love. He calls us to Himself in loving fellowship. God wants the best for us, and His desire for us is that His glory be seen in us daily.

In these two chapters, God not only warns us to keep away from those forces that compete for our attention through the various lusts of our fallen nature, but He shows us that we, being sanctified and set apart by Him, must not endeavour to serve Him with weakness (Leviticus 22:18-20). Such weakness might include being spiritually blind; not walking in the Spirit; being dishonest; and being unable to reproduce fruit for Jesus Christ.

The Old Testament, under the law, expressed the negative side. The New Testament, under grace, expresses the positive dynamic of faith and the power of the Holy Spirit. Therefore, let us lay aside every weight and run the race in victory (Hebrews 21:1). Let us praise the Lord for His victory in us! Hallelujah!

Direction for today: Be honest with yourself and with God. Be sure all sin is confessed and under the blood.

Prayer for today: "Fill my life, Lord, with Your holiness and love."

April 22: Read Leviticus 22

Key verse: "Speak to Aaron and his sons, that they separate themselves from the holy things of the children of Israel, and that they do not profane My holy name in those things which they sanctify to Me: I am the Lord" (Leviticus 22:2 NKJV).

All of the utensils used in the tabernacle were made from gifts brought by the people of Israel. The gifts were offered to the Lord, and dedicated to His service.

Although Aaron and his sons were to minister using these gifts, they were warned to keep separate from them. In other words, the gifts of the people were holy in the sight of the Lord, and the priests were forbidden to misuse them or to use them for their own purposes.

That's an important lesson today, as well. God's servants are not to covet or misuse the gifts and offerings that God's people bring to Him. Organizations that depend on the gifts of God's people must be scrupulously careful to use these financial resources only for God and for His glory.

A ministry supported by sincere givers which handles gifts in a way that pleases the Lord will be safeguarded in integrity. However, if such ministries ever move out from the will of God they will been abomination unto Him.

Direction for today: Give from a pure heart and with the joy of the Lord.

Prayer for today: "Lord, keep Your ministries pure and of high integrity for Your glory."

April 23: Read Leviticus 23

Key verse: "On the fourteenth day of the first month at twilight is the Lord's Passover" (Leviticus 23:5 NKJV).

This is a very significant chapter, as it describes all of the key feasts celebrated by the Israelites, ceremonies which consistently point to the coming of Jesus Christ and to the life that God had ordained for His church.

For example, the sabbath was given to the Israelites as a sign that they were sanctified, set apart and made holy by God for Him. So, too, is each Christian sanctified.

The Passover, one of the key feasts of the year, celebrated the deliverance of Israel from Egypt, but was also a graphic picture of Christ's sacrifice on the cross. Jesus was called "the Lamb of God who takes away the sin of the world." The waving of the sheaf, celebrating the first fruits, pointed to the resurrection of Jesus, the "first fruits", from the dead.

The feast of Pentecost, or "weeks", was celebrated 50 days after Passover. Christians know Pentecost as the occasion on which the Holy Spirit was poured out in a dynamic new way upon the people of God.

The feast of booths points to the eventual return of the Lord. It was held for seven days, beginning on the fifteenth day of the seventh month, after harvest had been completed. Jesus will return when the harvest of souls for the kingdom is completed.

Direction for today: Be sure to walk in God's great plan, as revealed to us in Jesus Christ.

Prayer for today: "Help me to watch and wait according to Your will."

April 24: Read Leviticus 24

Key verse: "Command the Israelites to bring you clear oil of pressed olives for the light so that the lamps may be kept burning continually" (Leviticus 24:2 NIV).

Moses was commanded to keep the lamps burning continually. To do this, the Israelites were ordered to bring a daily supply of fresh, pure oil.

To keep God's light shining brightly in our lives, we, too, daily need a fresh supply of oil from Him. This can be achieved only by a intimate relationship with Him through prayer and study of the Word. Only then can we effectively live a dedicated life of service.

This text also shows us the importance of listening before acting. When the blasphemer was brought to Moses, he was held in jail until Moses could hear from God. Only after hearing from God did Moses act.

The story of the blasphemer illustrates the seriousness of violating the character of God. Sin must be punished; it cannot be ignored.

Direction for today: To be effective for God, ensure that you receive a daily supply of fresh oil.

Prayer for today: "Lord, fill me with the oil of Your Holy Spirit, that others might see You in me."

April 25: Read Leviticus 25

Key verse: "Do not take advantage of each other, but fear your God. I am the Lord your God" (Leviticus 25:17 NIV).

This chapter is a real challenge to present-day economists. Here, we have a plan to deal with the poor of the land on a long-term basis.

The Israelites were to consider the land a promised gift from God (hence, really belonging to Him); man was only a temporary caretaker. If one fell on hard times, he might have had to sell his possessions, but such a sale was only temporary. First, his land would be returned to him or, in the event of his death, to his children in the Year of Jubilee. Second, the man or one of his relatives could, at any time, buy back the lost possessions for the price of redemption. This is a beautiful picture of Christ, for His death was the price of redemption for lost humanity. My elder brother, Jesus, paid the redemption price for my possession of a home in heaven.

This Scripture also teaches us to help a brother or fellow countryman who is suffering. We are not to take advantage of another's misfortune, and must treat those who work for us as employees, not as slaves.

All that we have really belongs to God. He gave our possessions as a gift, and they are to be treated as such.

Direction for today: Treat your possessions as though you are a caretaker, not a master.

Prayer for today: "Lord, help me always to seek to bless others through that which You have given to me."

"For I am the Lord, I do not change; therefore you are not consumed, O sons of Jacob" (Malachi 3:6 NKJV).

April 26: Read Leviticus 26

Key verse: "I will look on you with favour and make you fruitful and increase your numbers, and I will keep My covenant with you" (Leviticus 26:9 NIV).

Today's Scripture is exhilarating for the obedient believer, but it should strike fear into the heart of the disobedient.

It pays to serve God. Proverbs tells us over and over, "the fear of the Lord is the beginning of wisdom". Here we have a beautiful outline of the abundance of blessings that God showers upon His favoured children.

God promises victory over our enemies, a fruitful heritage, and the keeping of all His covenants. But the greatest promise of all is: 'I will dwell among you, walk among you, and be your God' (II Corinthians 6:16).

God wants to bless His people. He longs to pour out His blessings upon us. When God gives gifts, He gives in a big way. How do we receive these gifts? Verses three and four tell us that we must be careful to obey God's commands in order to receive His blessings.

An obedience brings God's blessings, so disobedience brings His wrath. It is a fearful thing to fall into the hands of an angry God; but, even in punishment, God shows His love. He punishes just enough to bring about a change. Continued disobedience brings greater punishment but God's purpose is to return us to Himself. His love endures forever.

Direction for today: Remember that obedience brings God's blessing, but disobedience brings His wrath.

Prayer for today: "Lord, help me zealously to follow Your laws so that You may look on me with favour."

April 27: Read Leviticus 27

Key verse: "A tithe of everything from the land, whether grain from the soil or fruit from the trees, belongs to the Lord; it is holy to the Lord" (Leviticus 27:30 NIV).

God's greatest gift to mankind was His Son, who gave His life as a ransom for us. The greatest gift we can give to God is ourselves.

In church, we often hear of the importance of giving all to God. In moments of religious fervour, we can make great promises of dedication to God. These vows are important and very meaningful; it is most important, however, that they also be kept.

Today's reading tells us that which we vow God is forever His. There was no prompting for the making of the vow but, once made, it could not be revoked. A promise made is a promise to be kept. If the original owner desired to regain his possession, it could only be done by an appropriate payment so that the vow might truly be kept.

All that we have and are is from the Lord, and rightfully belongs to Him. No gift of devotion is too great for our God! He is most worthy of all I could ever give.

Direction for today: Be sure you keep any promise which you make to God.

Prayer for today: "Lord, help me to fulfill all my commitments, those I make to You as well as those I make to others."

Luke

If there was a journalist among the New Testament writers, his name was Luke, the writer both of this gospel and of the companion work, the book of Acts.

Luke claimed that he had compiled an account of the life of Christ after careful investigation and interviewing eye witnesses. His inquisitive bent has produced an extremely well documented history. Luke gives us historical links with the events of the time (see 2:1,2) which archaeologists and historians have found always to be completely accurate.

Luke claims that his book is written to show "the exact truth" (1:4). Only a manuscript supervised b y the Holy Spirit could live up to such a claim, and this gospel, penned by one of the stalwarts of the early church, Paul's physician and friend, is certainly honest, accurate, and divinely blessed.

April 28: Read Luke 1

Key verse: "Then to the angel, 'How can this be, since I do not know a man?' And the angel answered and said to her, 'The Holy Spirit will come upon you, and the power of the Highest will overshadow you; therefore, also, that Holy One who is to be born will be called the Son of God'" (Luke 1:34,35 NKJV).

There are many who mock the idea of a "virgin birth", or who discount it as a myth believed only by ignorant people. Such a conception is impossible, they say, and enlightened folk should not accept such a thing. Such people nonetheless often consider Jesus to be a good teacher and a great example.

If Mary was not a virgin, and Jesus was conceived through her union with a man, then He would be no more than a good teacher—perhaps even much less than that. But this Scripture makes it very plain that Mary had never known a man sexually; that Jesus was conceived as the direct result of the miraculous intervention of the Holy Spirit; that He had no earthly father and, therefore, was truly and uniquely "the Son of God."

Doubtless Mary was ridiculed for bearing a son out of wedlock. No doubt Joseph was a laughingstock and Jesus was challenged as an illegitimate child. And today, those who believe the Lord was born of a virgin are still mocked.

But the mockers are wrong, both then and now. Jesus is truly the Son of the Living God!

Direction for today: If the Bible says it, believe it!

Prayer for today: "Thank you, Father, for the miraculous conception of Your Son, Jesus."

April 29: Read Luke 2,3

Key verse: "Now when they had seen Him, they made widely known the saying which was told them concerning this Child" (Luke 2:17 NKJV).

At the end of His life on earth, Jesus told His followers that they were to be "witnesses to Me" (Acts 1:8). Here, at the very beginning of His life, we find one of the best examples of "witnessing" contained in the Scriptures.

These shepherds did exactly what a witness is to do. They told others what they had seen and heard.

Too often, Christians mistakenly think they are not ready to be witnesses because they don't understand theology well enough; they haven't memorized enough Bible verses; or because they can't answer all the tough questions that might come their way.

The shepherds worried about none of those things. Instead, they got excited about what they had experienced and ran out to tell others about it.

There is no need to understand the fine points of doctrine, or to be sure of every difficult point a skeptic might raise. Instead, simply be like the shepherds: since you have experienced something exciting and life-changing, go out and tell others about it. Like the shepherds, you have seen the Christ! Don't keep Him to yourself!

Direction for today: You are called to be a witness to what you have experienced. Be one!

Prayer for today: "Lord, give me the courage to obey Christ's command to be a witness to Him."

April 30: Read Luke 4

Key verse: *"But Jesus answered him, saying, 'It is written, "Man shall not live by bread alone, but by every word of God"'" (Luke 4:4 KNJV).*

We need to understand that Satan will attack us. If you are a believer, you are a declared enemy of the devil, and he knows it! But you need not fear. You can emerge from any attack of the enemy as victoriously as Jesus did following His temptation in the wilderness.

God has promised that, with every temptation, He will provide a way of escape. But that way of escape may require some work on your part.

One of the key tasks of the Christian is to strengthen oneself against the lures of the devil. In order to do this, we must know the Word of God. Each time Jesus was tempted, He responded to Satan with a direct quote from the Bible. The psalmist wrote, "Your word have I hidden in my heart, that I might not sin against You", and Jesus claimed that truth when He was under attack.

Our defence, of course, must be built before the attack comes. Take Bible study seriously; meditate on the Word and memorize the Scriptures that are given to you each week in this guide. The Bible is a prime source of spiritual strength.

Direction for today: Commit portions of the Scriptures to heart through memorization.

Prayer for today: "Lord, I thank You that the Word is a sure defense against the attacks of the enemy."

5

To Him I Am Precious

Cheat! Liar! Fraud! Failure!
The accusations came over and over again.
To many I'd never really measured up,
Never been able to do the right things
at the right time,
Never made the grade.
Nor had I really been what I felt I needed to be,
For I knew what I was like, deep down inside,
And had never learned the difference
between failing
And being a failure.

Now, all the mean things I had said and done
Hurled themselves at me.
They shook their fingers in my face
And clutched their hands around my throat.
I tried to scream but nothing came.
My throat was dry, my lips were parched.
My lungs felt as though they'd burst,
And my body, how it ached.

And then, praise God. I read His Word,
And saw that, though He knows all about me,
Yet still He loves me, and calls me PRECIOUS,
PRECIOUS . . . me?
Yes, not only precious, but beautiful.
I saw, that as the father of a retarded son
Looks upon him with pure love,
Where others view him with pity,
Even so does my Father love me.

Yes, To Him I am precious!
Oh, the healing there is in that knowledge;
Oh, the promise for each new day!
I saw myself forgiven,
I saw my record clean,
Nowhere the condemnation of what I had been.
For I'm cleansed, forgiven, whole . .
And PRECIOUS, PRAISE HIS NAME!

— Doug Burke

May 1: Read Luke 5

Key verse: *"So when they had brought their boats to land, they forsook all and followed Him" (Luke 5:11 NKJV).*

There is an enormous cost to being a disciple of Jesus Christ. Oh, of course, the benefits far outweight the cost; the rewards are eternal. But let us never forget that the cost may also be great.

To be a disciple, we must do what these brave men did—forsake all and follow Christ. We must willingly give up anything that is ours; we must lose our lives to gain them.

Jesus repeated this call over and over again. Peter and Andrew left their business behind; Matthew gave up his job as a civil servant; the apostle Paul left behind a promising career as a leading intellectual and Jewish religious leader. But a rich young ruler failed the test because he would not leave his riches.

The same call comes to us: Jesus wants fully committed disciples.

What is there in your life that you have not left behind? To what do you cling, even though Jesus has shown you that it is preventing your spiritual growth?

Can anything be more valuable than the life that Jesus brings? If God is speaking to you, surrender <u>everything</u>; forsake all that is yours, that you may be fully His.

Direction for today: Never let anything come between you and Christ.

Prayer for today: "Lord, show me if anything is getting in the way of my growth as Your disciple, and I will surrender it to You."

May 2: Read Luke 6

Key verse: *"Then Jesus said to them, 'I will ask you one thing: Is it lawful on the Sabbath to do good or to do evil, to save life or to destroy it?'" (Luke 6:9 NKJV)*

We are surprised and shocked by the attitudes of the religious leaders, as we continually encounter them through the gospel stories. Is it possible they would rather have left this crippled man in his crippled state? Yes, that appears to be true.

But, before we condemn these guardians of the rules and regulations, let's be sure we cannot find ourselves in their midst. How often have churches and individual Christians prevented the moving of the Holy Spirit because the thing that God was doing did not fit into their existing structures?

Too many churches seem to have the motto, "We won't do it because we've never done it that way before."

God is the Creator, and He did not cease to be creative on the seventh day. His creativity is now expressed miraculously in His church by the power of the Holy Spirit. The Lord loves to perform miracles, to meet impossible needs. But, too often, our rigid structures stand as barriers to the work the Lord wants to do.

Paul said it best: "Do not quench the Spirit" (I Thessalonians 5:19). May we trade in our old motto for this new one, and allow the Lord to do whatever He wants to do on the sabbath or any other day!

Direction for today: Be sure that your own private rules and expectations do not quench the Holy Spirit.

Prayer for today: "Work, Lord, as You will."

Memory Verse

"For we do not have a High Priest who cannot sympathize with our weaknesses, but who was in all points tempted as we are, yet without sin" (Hebrews 4:15 NKJV).

May 3: Read Luke 7

Key verse: *"The Son of Man has come eating and drinking, and you say, 'Look, a glutton and a winebibber, a friend of tax collectors and sinners!'" (Luke 7:34 NKJV).*

Christians are commanded to be holy, sanctified and separated from sin. But we are never told to be separated from sinners! Instead, we are to "go into all the world and preach the gospel to every creature."

"Every creature" includes business people, politicians and police officers, but also includes alcoholics and other chemical dependents, as well as prostitutes and criminals. Jesus spent a great deal of His time with people of "ill repute", and He was criticized for it. His critics were wrong.

Too often, Christians side with the critics, and not with the Christ! How comfortable would we be if someone brought a drug addict, an alcoholic or a prostitute to our church? How comfortable would we be if such a person sat next to us in the pew?

Sadly, the people of God are not usually known as friends of sinners. But Christ was, and we are called to follow His example.

Direction for today: Ask the Lord to show you the difference between being separated from sin and separated from sinners.

Prayer for today: "Lord, give me Your love and compassion for every person You have created. Help me to love the unlovely and never to turn away from those in need of Your love."

May 4: Read Luke 8

Key verse: *"No one, when he has lit a lamp, covers it with a vessel or puts it under a bed, but sets it on a lampstand, that those who enter may see the light" (Luke 8:16 NKJV).*

Jesus said, "You are the light of the world" (Matthew 5:14). He also told us: "Let your light so shine before men, that they may see your good works and glorify your Father who is in heaven" (Matthew 5:16).

Yet how many Christians live their lives as "secret believers", afraid to confess their faith and their love for Christ openly?

I am always surprised to be in a church service where no one is willing to speak a word of testimony or praise to the Lord. If we cannot confess our faith before our brothers and sisters in Christ, there is little chance we will ever be obedient to our Lord's command to uncover our light and let it shine before unbelievers.

If you refuse to speak your faith, to let your light shine, you are robbing several different persons. You are depriving those you meet of the opportunity to hear and respond to the gospel. You are stealing joy and peace from yourself because you are living in shrivelled disobedience. And you are robbing God of the glory and honour due Him in your confession of faith and praise.

Let your light shine!

Direction for today: Ask the Lord for strength and the opportunity to shine for Him today.

Prayer for today: "Father, I confess I have failed to let my light shine for You. As You bring opportunity, I will obey."

May 5: Read Luke 9

Key verse: "He said to them, 'But who do you say that I am?' Peter answered and said, 'The Christ of God'" (Luke 9:20 NKJV).

There are some who argue that the Christian church has misunderstood the claims of Jesus and the witness of the Bible about Him. He is a good example, they argue, and a great teacher, but He never claimed to be God!

But, in this chapter, we see several confessions of Christ, all of which He received as truth.

In verse 1, Jesus claims to have incredible power, and even to be able to pass it on to His followers. This is either the raving of a madman or evidence of the presence of God Himself.

In verse 20, we read Peter's confession of Jesus as the anointed one sent by God. In Matthew 16:16, the complete text is included: "You are the Christ, the Son of the living God." To this, Jesus replied that His Father in heaven had revealed this to Peter. If Peter was wrong, Christ should have rebuked him for blasphemy; instead, He commended him.

In verse 22, Jesus predicted that He would rise from the dead. In verse 26, He speaks of his own glory—something due only to God—and of His coming kingdom.

In verse 35, the voice of God the Father testifies to the nature of Christ—the Son of God!

There can be no doubt that Jesus clearly claimed to be God. He is worthy of our praise and glory and honour.

Direction for today: Do not merely follow Jesus' example; worship Him!

Prayer for today: "Thank you, Lord, that the Bible is so clear about the reality that Jesus is Lord and God!"

May 6: Read Luke 10

Key verse: "And He said to them, 'I saw Satan fall like lightning from heaven. Behold, I give you the authority to trample on serpents and scorpions, and over all the power of the enemy, and nothing shall by any means hurt you'" (Luke 10:18,19 NKJV).

Throughout His life, Jesus faced almost every sorrow that a person can know. When we think of Him as God—which He truly was and is—we must also remember that He was wholly man, fully able to know pain, sorrow, and disappointment. He was tempted in every way you are, yet He did not sin.

His sorrows included those of the most devastating kind—the rejection of family and friends. How alone He must have felt when his family declared that He must be crazy (Mark 3:21); when one of His own followers betrayed Him; when Peter, one of His closest friends, denied knowing Him; or when all the disciples ran away at His arrest.

But none of these things plunged Jesus into despair. Why? Perhaps it was because He knew that, whatever happened in the short term, God had won the ultimate victory. Jesus Himself had seen Satan fall in defeat, and would see the final victory over the enemy. He knew this beyond question.

When we are tempted to be depressed or discouraged, we should remember this same truth. Whatever happens today, ultimately God and the people of God will know complete and glorious victory. We can rest with confidence in this promise.

Direction for today: Like Jesus, take hope and joy in the fact that the Lord is the Victor.

Prayer for today: "For Yours is the kingdom and the power and the glory forever!"

May 7: Read Luke 11

Key verse: "If you then, being evil, know how to give good gifts to your children, how much more will your heavenly Father give the Holy Spirit to those who ask Him" (Luke 11:13 NKJV).

What is the best gift that God can give to us? This verse indicates that the ultimate gift is the Holy Spirit.

This is true for several reasons. It is the Holy Spirit who brings us new life in Christ. When we accept Jesus as Saviour and Lord, the Holy Spirit comes dwell within us, bringing our dead spirits to life—eternal life.

The Holy Spirit in us is also our source of comfort (John 15:26), of assurance (Romans 8:16), and of love, joy, peace and the other elements of the fruit of the Spirit (Galatians 5:22,23).

As well, the Holy Spirit living and working within us is the source of the power of God that manifests itself in the gifts of the Spirit and the miraculous workings of the Lord through us (I Corinthians 12:14).

Without the Holy Spirit, we are dead, empty shells, living only to die. But when we are indwelt by the Holy Spirit, we are alive eternally, are empowered to work the works of God, and are filled with the joy and peace of the Lord!

Praise God for His wonderful gift of the Holy Spirit!

Direction for today: "How much more will your heavenly Father give the Holy Spirit to those who ask Him?" So, ask!

Prayer for today: "Lord, may I continually be filled with Your Spirit."

May 8: Read Luke 12

Key verse: "Also I say to you, whoever confesses Me before men, him the Son of Man also will confess before the angels of God" (Luke 12:8 NKJV).

There is nothing you can do to earn eternal life. The Bible makes this very clear: ". . . the gift of God is eternal life in Christ Jesus our Lord" (Romans 6:23).

However, there are certain things that we will normally do if we are, indeed, children of God. One of these is to confess our Lord and Saviour openly. Also in Romans, Paul wrote: "if you confess with your mouth the Lord Jesus and believe in your heart that God has raised Him from the dead, you will be saved. For with the heart one believes to righteousness, and with the mouth confession is made to salvation" (Romans 10:9,10).

That same direction is spoken by Jesus on a number of occasions, as recorded in the gospels. In our key verse, He says that He will confess His allegiance to those who confess their loyalty to Him.

Spoken testimony of your faith in Christ is a natural outcome of having Jesus living within you. If He is there, you will normally want to speak about Him.

Too many Christians have been intimidated into silence. Too often, we are secret Christians, perhaps living good lives, but never telling anyone where that "goodness" is coming from. That is not what Jesus told us to do—He continually called His people to speak boldly of their love for Him.

Direction for today: Confess the Lord with your mouth.

Prayer for today: "Lord, forgive me for my 'guilty silence'".

May 9: Read Luke 13,14

Key verse: *"For whoever exalts himself will be abased, and he who humbles himself will be exalted" (Luke 14:11 NKJV).*

Each one of us has a role to play in the kingdom of God. The Lord has given His gifts to each of us by His Spirit. He has appointed the perfect place for **you** to be working for Him.

Too often, though, we get in the way of His plans. The worst enemy of the effective operation of the church may not be Satan—it just might be pride in the Christians!

How often have people refused to carry out their God-ordained tasks in the church because they coveted a more prestigious role? How often has the advancement of the kingdom and the proclamation of the gospel been hindered because someone's pride was hurt that they were "only" asked to usher or babysit, and not teach or lead?

If we allow our pride to stand in the way of what the Lord is doing, we will suffer, and so will the work of the Lord. Instead of seeking the most visible roles in the church, we should be seeking to know what the Lord would have us do.

It may be that He will put you in leadership; it may be that He wants you to work in the background, with no one noticing; no one, that is, except the Lord. And who else matters?

Direction for today: Allow the Lord to use you wherever He chooses.

Prayer for today: "Lord, cleanse me of any pride that is hindering the work of Your kingdom."

Memory Verse

"Ask, and it will be given to you; seek, and you will find; knock, and it will be opened to you" (Matthew 7:7 NKJV).

May 10: Read Luke 15,16

Key verse: *"What man of you, having a hundred sheep, if he loses one of them, does not leave the ninety-nine in the wilderness, and go after the one which is lost until he finds it? And when he has found it, he lays in on his shoulders, rejoicing" (Like 15:4,5 NKJV).*

I am praying today that the Lord will bring this devotional to the attention of a number of people who are just like that "lost sheep" or like the prodigal son of chapter 5 verses 11-32.

God is using His word and today's commentary to speak to *you* right now. You have wandered far way from the Shepherd, Jesus Christ. Once you were part of His flock, but you have been alone in the wilderness for far too long.

You have been convinced that it is too late—you can never return to

Jesus. Surely, He must have forgotten you, or He must be angry that you abandoned Him all those months or years ago.

Those are lies! The shepherd never stops looking for His lost sheep. He has been waiting to carry you back home, waiting for you to call for help.

This is your opportunity right now. Reach out to the Good Shepherd; allow Him to take you in His arms, to carry you tenderly back to the safety and peace of His fold. He is longing to heal your wounds, to make you whole, and to envelop you in His love.

The Good Shepherd never abandons His sheep!

Direction for today: If you have wandered away from Christ, allow Him to carry you back.

Prayer for today: "Jesus, I have wandered far from You, but I want to come back. Please take me into Your fold."

May 11: Read Luke 17,18

Key verse: "And the tax collector, standing afar off, would not so much as raise his eyes to heaven, but beat his breast, saying, 'God be merciful to me a sinner!'" (Luke 18:13 NKJV).

This is the starting place for each one of us. If we are children of God, we must have come to a point where we stood before the Lord, ashamed and aware of our sin and cried, "God, be merciful to me a sinner."

You may have come a long way in the Lord since that day. It may be years or decades in the past. But it is still a good idea to stand and remember that you are a child of God only because of His great mercy. None of us could earn our way into the kingdom—we are all dirty sinners!

Praise the Lord that He hears that prayer. Praise the Lord for His mercy, which endures forever. Praise the Lord that He reaches down to sinners, lifting us out of our sin and into everlasting life through Jesus Christ!

But never take pride in your status as a child of God. You did not deserve it; you could not earn it; if all things were just, you would not be a son or daughter of the King.

Remember at all times: God has been very merciful to you, a sinner. That in itself is cause for continual joy and thanksgiving.

Direction for today: Always remember God's mercy to you.

Prayer for today: "Thank You, Lord, for Your mercy to me, a sinner."

May 12: Read Luke 19

Key verse: "For the Son of Man has come to seek and to save that which was lost" (Luke 19:10 NKJV).

Why did Jesus come to earth? To teach? To heal? to set a fine example for other human beings? To tell us about God?

Yes, to all of these things. But none of them were His top priority. First, He came to seek and to save all who were, and are, lost.

He saved us through His death on the cross: that God-sized death that was big enough to cover all of us, and that sinless life that was pure enough to cleanse each one of us.

And He seeks us out, even today, by His Spirit and through His people. The task of saving the lost was completed at Calvary, as Jesus died and rose again to proclaim life to all who would hear. But the task of seeking will not be completed until Jesus comes again and history is brought to a halt.

Jesus sought the first believers Himself—He found some mending nets by the sea, another minding tax tables, still more going about their business in Galilee. He no longer walks physically among us, but He has sent His Holy Spirit to convict the lost, and has sent His church to find them and to tell them about the Way to eternal life.

When Jesus ascended to heaven, He left behind His followers to carry on His work. We cannot save anyone, but we are called to seek everyone for the Lord. He will save them.

Direction for today: Seek those who are lost and bring them to the Master.

Prayer for today: "Lord, please guide me as I seek the lost for You."

May 13: Read Luke 20,21

Key verse: "So He said, 'Truly I say to you that this poor widow has put in more than all" (Luke 21:3 NKJV).

It is very easy for the church and for individual Christians to become caught up in the pursuit of riches and in admiration for those who are rich. We have all heard speakers who, when they tell of people finding the Lord, usually talk about someone rich or famous.

And there are many teachings around today which suggest that, if you truly serve the Lord, He will reward you with financial gain.

The Bible is, however, not nearly so generous toward rich people. The Old Testament prophets railed against the injustice of the rich, and their words were echoed by Jesus (Like 6:24,25) and by James and other New Testament writers.

Paul warned us that the love of money is the root of all kinds of evil (I Timothy 6:10).

Instead of trying to get rich or to attract rich people into our congregations, we would be wise to concentrate on what we do with the possessions the Lord has already given us. Remember that Jesus praised the poor widow who gave everything she had to the Lord.

He had no such commendation for rich people who gave significant amounts to the work of the Lord because their gifts had really cost them little.

The key message here is, the Lord is worthy to receive all that we have; if we hold anything back, we may be financially wealthy, but spiritually impoverished.

Direction for today: Be sure that everything you own, whether much or little, belongs to the Lord.

Prayer for today: "Lord, all I have is Yours."

May 14: Read Luke 22

Key verse: "But I have prayed for you, that your faith should not fail; and when you have returned to Me, strengthen your brethren" (Luke 22:32 NKJV).

What a marvellous testimony to the love and forgiveness of Jesus! Peter has assured the Lord that he will not fail Him, but Jesus knows better. The Lord is fully aware that Peter is about to deny Him, to curse and swear and insist that he has never known Him. He knows that Peter will abandon his Master in His hour of greatest need!

So, how does Jesus respond to Peter—in anger or bitterness? Not at all. The Lord looked beyond Peter's sin to the time of his repentance. He looked even beyond that to see Peter's usefulness and faith restored. Despite Peter's rejection, Jesus gave him a job to do after he came back!

Perhaps you feel as Peter did after his sin. Perhaps you have, in some way, denied the Lord. It may be that you have failed in your testimony or refused to obey Him or that you are harbouring sin in your life. You may feel that you have become useless to Jesus and that you are stuck in this rut forever.

Jesus is already looking beyond your sin to your restoration and to the work He has for you to do. His forgiveness and restoration are complete; you can once again be a useful member of the body of Christ.

Unlike Judas, Peter repented and was restored. Which example will you follow?

Direction for today: Even if you are trapped in unconfessed sin, Jesus is eager to restore you and use you in His service.

Prayer for today: "Lord, forgive me, cleanse me, and use me. Thank You."

May 15: Read Luke 23

Key verse: "Then he said to Jesus, 'Lord, remember me when You come into Your kingdom' " (Luke 23:42 NKJV).

This repentant thief was granted an extraordinary insight as he hung on a cross, breathing his last. Others were mocking, accusing Christ of being a fraud: "He saved others, but He cannot save Himself." Pilate had hung a sarcastic sign over His head, proclaiming Him "King of the Jews" even while some of the Jewish leaders, along with Roman soldiers and King Herod, were putting Him to death.

None of them saw what this dying thief was able to see—that even death would not prevent Jesus from coming into His kingdom.

In fact, for Jesus, and now for the thief, death was the entrance to the kingdom. Jesus was already King, but only through His voluntary death could His kingdom grow by the addition of all who would be saved.

Jesus and the thief both died. But they were together that same day in Jesus' kingdom; fulfilling His promise, "Today you will be with Me in Paradise" (verse 43).

It's just the same for each of us. Only through death will we come into the kingdom of God. First, we must accept Jesus' death on our behalf and allow Him to save us from sin, death and hell. And then we must be willing to die to ourselves in order to live for Christ and with Him.

Direction for today: Only through death do we find eternal life in Christ.

Prayer for today: "Thank You, Jesus, for dying for me."

May 16: Read Luke 24

Key verse: "And they worshiped Him, and returned to Jerusalem with great joy" (Luke 24:52 NKJV).

Today we complete the reading of the third gospel, written by Luke. For the third time this year, we have read the glorious account of the triumphant resurrection of our Lord Jesus Christ.

As you reflect on the risen life of Christ and all that this means to you, simply join with the disciples and worship the Lord with great joy.

Praise Jesus for His death, by which He paid the penalty for your sin.

Praise Jesus for His resurrection, by which He proclaimed victory over sin, death and hell.

Praise Jesus for His love, which He showed to His disciples as He appeared to them: this love which He lavishes on you today.

Praise Jesus for His Word, through which we know the wonderful story of the gospel.

Praise Jesus that all of the promises of God are fulfilled in Him.

Praise the Lord! Worship Him in great joy!

Direction for today: Worship God the Father, Son and Holy Spirit in reverence and great joy.

Prayer for today: "Jesus, I praise You and bless Your holy Name."

Memory Verse

"You alone are the Lord; You have made heaven, the heaven of heavens, with all their host, the earth and all things on it, the seas and all that is in them, and You preserve them all. The host of heaven worships You" (Nehemiah 9:6 NKJV).

Numbers

"All of us like sheep have gone astray, each of us has turned to his own way; But the Lord has caused the iniquity of us all to fall on Him" (Isaiah 53:6).

This verse condemns the entire human race for unfaithfulness to God. If each man and woman had to bear his or her own sin, we would all be damned for eternity. But God took our sin and placed it with its penalty upon Jesus as He died on the cross.

The waywardness and unfaithfulness of man is clearly portrayed in the book of Numbers. God's people had seen miracle after miracle since the Lord led them out of Egypt. And yet, even as God provided for them daily, giving them divine leadership, supplying food and water and reminding His people of His great promises, this book tells of their discontent and rebellion.

The first chapter recounts the census or "numbering" (thus the title of the book) of the people, in preparation for the taking of the Promised Land, Canaan. But almost as soon as Mount Sinai, the mountain of the covenant, is out of sight the people begin to complain (Chapter 11). Even Moses' brother and sister speak against his leadership (Chapter 13).

Finally, we see the ultimate faithlessness—the people refuse to attempt to conquer the land that God has given to them, believing the report of faithless spies instead of the promises of God! The rest of the book is largely the account of wilderness wanderings, rebellion and death, surely a sad segment of the history of the people of God.

Toward the end of the book (Chapter 26), we see a dramatic parallel— the fighting men are again numbered, ready to take the land promised by God. But in this census appear only two names which had been on the list 40 years before—Joshua and Caleb, the only two men of Israel who had urged obedience to God on that first opportunity to take the land. The forty years of wandering in the wilderness had seen the death of every other adult who had refused to go in and possess the Promised Land.

May 17: Read Numbers 1

Key verse: "But thou shall appoint the Levites over the tabernacle of testimony, and over all the vessels thereof, and over all things that belong to it: they shall bear the the tabernacle, and all the vessels thereof; and they shall minister unto it, and shall encamp round about the tabernacle" (Numbers 1:50 KJV).

In Matthew 22:21, Jesus said, ". . . render therefore unto Caesar the things which are Caesar's; and unto God the things that are God's."

Here, in our text, we see that God has given instruction to Moses to call the heads of each of the twelve tribes to muster their young men to the great Israelite army.

On the other hand, He has instructed Moses to set apart all the Levites to take care of the tabernacle and to minister to the Lord, and to pray for the nation.

God, in His infinite wisdom, shows the secret of Israel's great power— she was blessed with two powerful armies: one, to stand before God in intercession; the other, of God-fearing men able to fight the enemy. Together, these armies ensure the safety of Israel's borders, both temporal and spiritual.

Direction for today: Endeavour to do only those things which please the Lord, according to His Word.

Prayer for today: "Father, grant me the wisdom and the determination to do Your will."

May 18: Read Numbers 2

Key verse: "Then the tabernacle of the congregation shall set forward with the camp of the Levites in the midst of the camp: as they encamp, so shall they set forward, every man in his place by their standards" (Numbers 2:17 KJV).

In this chapter, we see the order in which the children of Israel were to encamp or travel. God, in His infinite wisdom, had set the Ark and the Tabernacle with the priestly Levites in the midst of all the armies of Israel.

In this way, the fighting men were constantly reminded of their great responsibility for the protection of the Ark and the priests. But, more importantly, they were reminded that the presence of God was in their midst.

God was to occupy the central place in the army and the nation of Israel. Israel came to know that, when God occupied the highest place of importance in their lives, they were safe from their enemies. Then all their needs were met, and they prospered in every way.

The Levites were the ministers of God to Israel, and it was from their central position that they were able to minister to the needs of the people.

Direction for today: Allow God to be the centre of your life and, thus, to minister to all those around you.

Prayer for today: "Father, may I be constantly aware of Your holy presence."

May 19: Read Numbers 3

Key verse: "And I, behold, I have taken the Levites from among the children of Israel instead of all the firstborn that openeth the matrix among the children of Israel: therefore the Levites shall be mine" (Numbers 3:12 KJV).

Here we see the perfect order of the Lord. In the preceding chapter, God has organized Israel by their armies and encampments, with the Levities and the tabernacle in the midst. Here He is organizing the Levites around the tabernacle with Moses and Aaron at the head.

At this point, God commands Moses to separate the Levites from all the children of Israel so they can be consecrated to Him for the service of the tabernacle and to wait upon Him.

God always has those whom He has called to be special vessels for the ministry of His Word and to show His everlasting love to the world. In our key verse, God hints at His great plan of redemption. In this case, it is one Levite for each firstborn male of Israel; eventually, it was to be God's own firstborn Son for all mankind.

Direction for today: Allow God to use you as His vessel.

Prayer for today: "Lord, may Your redemptive love be seen in me so that others may be redeemed."

May 20: Read Numbers 4

Key verse: "According to the commandment of the Lord they were numbered by the hand of Moses, every one according to his service, and according to his burden: thus were they numbered of him, as the Lord commanded Moses" (Numbers 4:49 KJV).

God never intended for one man to do all the work. Everyone in the body of Christ has a part to play in the kingdom work of the Lord.

In the everyday work situation, we readily understand that each part or department of an industry must function in its own way in order to get the job done.

God, in His wisdom, has provided that each individual in His kingdom must be prepared to function as part of a team so that the burden of the ministry is not borne by just one or two. The tabernacle is the forerunner to the church and, as we can see, God placed certain persons under His authority to give direction to the others. In the church setting, God has appointed pastors or elders to give direction to the rest of the body.

God desires that each one of us submit to His leadership and to the leadership of those whom He has given in the church, that together we might complete the great commission to preach the gospel to every creature.

Direction for today: Whatever your task in the local church, fulfill it with all your heart.

Prayer for today: "Lord, show me how I may best help in the work of Your kingdom."

May 21: Read Numbers 5,6

Key verse: *"But if the man hath no kinsman to recompense the trespass unto, let the trespass be recompensed unto the Lord, even to the priest; beside the ram of the atonement, whereby an atonement shall be made for him" (Numbers 5:8 KJV).*

In these two chapters, we see how God makes provision for the forgiveness of sin and the setting apart of the Nazarite or special vessel for Himself.

God is characterized by love and mercy and, although He cannot and will not tolerate sin, He shows His love and mercy to Israel through His provision for forgiveness, or atonement.

Israel is commanded to put out of the camp all of their lepers and sick folk who could contaminate the rest of the nation. Today, we put such people in colonies or hospitals. Later, we shall see how, God makes provision for the healing and reinstatement of these individuals.

God offers forgiveness in the matter of adultery, but forgiveness is obtained only upon an honest confession and repentance from that sin. Once again, we see God's longing for special fellowship because He has provided that, if one would consecrate himself wholly to Him—as in the case of the Nazarite—he would be a special vessel for His use.

Direction for today: Forsake sin and seek fellowship with God.

Prayer for today: "Thank you, Father, for Your love and mercy which You gave through Jesus Christ our Lord."

May 22: Read Numbers 7

Key verse: "And it came to pass on the day that Moses had fully set up the tabernacle that the princes of Israel, heads of the house of their fathers, who were the princes of the tribes, and were over them that were numbered, offered: And they brought their offering before the Lord... (Numbers 7:1-3 KJV).

This is one of those chapters in God's Word which sometime makes me wonder why it's there, for it seems to be so repetitive. Why would God lead the writer of Numbers to list, twelve times over, the gifts which the princes of Israel gave at the dedication of the tabernacle?

I believe there may be several reasons. First, perhaps God had these scenes recorded to show the generosity of the Israelite nation.

I believe that the second reason is summed up in the key verses above. It has to do with the heads of the houses having the responsibility to offer generous gifts to the Lord and, in that way, to teach their children. Each tribe was represented; each offered gifts. But it was the heads of the houses who presented the offerings.

Here is a message for fathers—and mothers, too, for that matter. God, in His Word, asks parents to be responsible to teach their children. Deuteronomy 6:7 is a classic verse. Our key verse should be an encouragement to parents not only to teach the fundamental truths of God's Word to their children, but also to demonstrate to them what it means to walk with God.

Direction for today: Parents, lead your children well, as unto the Lord.

Prayer for today: "Help me, O Lord, to be in my home what You want me to be, so that I and all my family will glorify Your name."

May 23: Read Numbers 8,9

Key verse: "And I have taken the Levites for all the firstborn of the children of Israel" (Numbers 8:18 KJV).

One of the most convincing evidences that the Bible is the Word of God is the way the Old and New Testaments fit together. Things prophesied in the Old Testament have their fulfilment in the New. Events written about by many different authors all point to the same goal.

Another interesting thing about the Bible is typology. This means that there are types of people, events, or things in the Old Testament which are found in the New. For example, in the key verse, the Levites are a type of Christ. That is to say, the way the Bible writer wrote this verse makes us think of Jesus: the Levites are "like" Christ.

Moses wrote: "I have taken the Levites for all the firstborn . . . " In a similiar way, God took His firstborn, Jesus, in our place. It was Jesus who ". . . bore our griefs and carried our sorrows." It was He who stood against sin, death and the devil, and conquered them for us. Jesus is the One who is the firstborn among many brothers. He was the one whom God exalted, that we might be exalted as we believe in Him.

Direction for today: Look to Jesus as the One who endured for You.

Prayer for today: "Father, thank You for Your Word and all it teaches us."

"Assuredly, I say to you, whoever does not receive the kingdom of God as a little child will by no means enter it" (Mark 10:15 NKJV).

May 24: Read Numbers 10,11

Key verse: "I am not able to bear all this people alone, because it is too heavy for me" (Numbers 11:14 KJV).

This chapter records a lot of complaining. First, we are told how the Israelites complained and then we catch a glimpse of Moses crying out to God. In both cases, the complaint was against God. Does this sound familiar? God had rescued Israel because she complained that her burden in Egypt was too heavy. But now they wanted to go back.

But there's more here, especially in Moses' complaint: he was fed up with the whining and complaining of the people. As a result, he went to the only One he knew would be able to help him, and complained to Him. Moses tells God he's not able to bear the people any longer. It seems to me that was just what God needed to hear. The Bible doesn't say so, but it is possible that Moses was trying to do it all on his own. Perhaps, though God had appointed Aaron to assist him, Moses still felt the whole weight resting on his shoulders. Was it time for him to lay down his leadership so that God could swing into action?

I believe so. You see, often it's only when we say, "Okay, Lord, we'll do it your way", that we allow God to work on our behalf. God won't do that for which we're responsible, but He will do that for which He's responsible if we let him.

Direction for today: Yield yourself totally to the Lord. Let go and let Him have control.

Prayer for today: "Lord, please teach me to give all I am and have to You."

May 25: Read Numbers 12,13

Key verse: "And Caleb stilled the people before Moses, and said, Let us go up at once, and possess it; for we are well able to overcome it" (Numbers 13:30 KJV).

One of the really admirable characteristics of great men is courage. The dictionary defines courage as fearlessness. It goes on to say that courage applies to the moral strength that makes a person face any danger, trouble or pain without fear.

Caleb was a man of courage. Not only did he tell the truth about the new land, but he also was not afraid of the opinions of others. Obviously, he was more concerned with telling the truth about what he saw then he was with what other spies might think of him. We could say that his desire to be obedient to God influenced who he was and what he did. Because he desired to be obedient over everything else, he was fearless and willing to face any danger.

Are we people of courage? Are we more eager to be obedient to God than to listen to the voice of the crowd? Are we able to dare to be courageous in the face of difficult odds? Can I entrust my life into the hands of the One who will make me more than a conqueror as I face whatever danger in Him? The answer is "yes". Yes, God is eager to be on the side of those who trust in Him.

Direction for today: Be courageous in Christ.

Prayer for today: "Lord, please give me the courage to be courageous for You."

May 26: Read Numbers 14

Key verse: "Pardon, I beseech Thee, the inquity of this people acording unto the greatness of Thy mercy, and as Thou hast forgiven this people, from Egypt even until now" (Numbers 14:19 KJV).

In Numbers 12:3, we read that Moses was, above all men, very meek. Meekness, or strength under control, was one of the qualities of which Moses needed a superabundance. We see that meekness again in the chapter we read today.

When the people of Israel heard the report of the spies, they began to grumble against Moses and wished they could have been back in Egypt. Probably, they longed for a return to what had become familiar customs and traditions. And all this in spite of the fact that Joshua and Caleb had told them the truth about the new land!

Into this situation Moses is thrust. He was the leader of this people and could very well have agreed with God to destroy the whole lot (verses 11 and 12). Instead, Moses draws on the meekness with which God gifted him and asks God to pardon them.

I believe you and I need to assume, much more often than we do, a prayerful, rather than judgmental, attitude toward those who do wrong around us. We need to ask the Lord, because of His great mercy, to pardon the sins of our nation and its people.

Direction for today: Ask the Lord to pardon those who have wronged you and to forgive the sins of those in your family.

Prayer for today: "Pardon our sins, O Lord because of Your great mercy."

May 27: Read Numbers 15

Key verse: "The Lord gave Moses the following regulations for the people of Israel to observe in the land that He was going to give them" (Numbers 15:1,2, TEV).

The punishment of the Sabbath-breaker is recorded here as an illustration of the severe penalty attached by the law of Moses to wilful and presumptuous sin.

The offender could not possibly claim ignorance of the statute to which already the death penalty had been added (Exodus 31:15). His sin was in open defiance of God. His execution was delayed, not because of any uncertainty as to his guilt or its necessary punishment, but because Moses waited to learn the manner of the penalty to be imposed. The verdict was: "All the congregation shall stone him."

Let us not hastily condemn this cruel punishment of an apparently trifling fault; we need to remember the recent and solemn warnings of the sacred law. Nor are we lightly to dismiss the obligation of the Sabbath observance as an antiquated fragment of a Jewish ritual. Our Saviour, who claimed to be "Lord of the Sabbeth," taught by precept and example that the day, made the more sacred as a memorial of His resurrection, is to be observed as a season of worship and rest, broken only by deeds of necessity and mercy (Mark 2:23 to 3:5).

Direction for today: Show the "good works," generous deeds and holy conduct which are the evidences of a living faith.

Prayer for today: "Thank You, Father, for so eloquently expressing Your pardoning mercy to us today."

May 28: Read Numbers 16

Key verse: "He has let you and all the other Levites have this honour—and now you are trying to get the priesthood too!" (Numbers 16:10 TEV).

This is the essence of jealousy. It is rebellion against the providence of God. He has given to each one of us definite tasks to perform and differing talents to be employed. Why should we seek to fill the places assigned to others?

It is for us to accept gratefully the positions devinely apportioned and to believe that it is honour enough to accomplish faithfully our own allotted work. Further, we should be assured that, for the accomplishment of the work which He assigns, God will give us the abilities, grace and strength needed.

Direction for today: "Godliness with contentment is great gain."

Prayer for today: "Father, may we know the tasks that You wish us to do and, further, know that You have equipped and empowered us to do them."

May 29: Read Numbers 17,18

Key verse: "The Lord said to Moses, 'Put Aaron's stick back in front of the covenant box. It is to be kept as a warning to the rebel Israelites that they will die unless their complaining stops'" (Numbers 17:10 TEV).

The rod which had budded became a continual memorial and seal to the divinely appointed priesthood of Aaron.

Such marvelous attestations and sanctions gave a holy dignity and honour to the office of Aaron, which assumed a new glory when it became a symbol and type of the redeeming work of Christ. The inspiring theme of the Epistle to the Hebrews is the High Priesthood of Christ. It can be understood only by the continual reference to the history of Aaron. His sacrifices, intercession and mediation were all shadows of the realities which were embodied in Christ; the first point of the inspired comparison was that which was pictured by the budding of Aaron's rod. This miracle was a token of his divine appointment, so it was a symbol of the divine commission of our Lord.

Thus, in referring to the priesthood of Christ, the Apostle declares: "No man taketh this honour unto himself, but he that is called of God as was Aaron. So also Christ glorified not Himself to be made an high priest but He that said unto Him, Thou art My son, today have I begotten Thee" (Hebrews 5:4,5).

Direction for today: Accept the Godgiven leaders among you, realizing that complaints against them are really complaints against the Lord (16:11).

Prayer for today: "Lord, lead us to the place where your own wishes and desires are subject to You, that Your will shall be done."

May 30: Read Numbers 19,20

Key verse: "But the Lord reprimanded Moses and Aaron. He said, 'Because you did not have enough faith to acknowledge My holy power before the people of Israel, you will not lead them into the land that I promised to give them'" (Numbers 20:12 TEV).

The charge against Moses was cruel and unjust (verses 3 to 5). The patient, but deeply offended, leader made no reply. As often before, he turned in silence to the place of prayer and fell prostrate before the Lord (verse 6).

Moses was given a new vision of God and, at the same time, he received a specific command and divine promise (verses 7,8).

It was an hour of unlimited possibilities. Moses could have brought to the people a new and impressive message of the goodness and grace of God but, remembering the treachery and disloyalty of the Israelites, he was overwhelmed by a storm of anger, and seemed to forget the message of the Lord. As he and Aaron met the congregation, he cried out with a bitter rebuke to "the rebels" and struck the rock (verses 10,11). Moses had good reason for anger. Again and again, he had interceded for the faithless people. He had been their deliverer, their saviour, their unselfish guide. Now, again, they had turned from him in faithless revolt.

Moses called the people "rebels". This they were. Yet, at that very time, he himself was in rebellion against God. Forgetting his high calling as a representative of the Lord, he assumed an honour which belongs to God alone and does not portray, in any way, the goodness or power of God.

Yet, in spite of Moses' anger and presumption, God was true to His promise. He showed Himself gracious and preserved the nation to which He had assured an entrance into Canaan.

Direction for today: Guard against old weakness which can unexpectedly reappear and overcome the truest servant of God. Watch and pray!

Prayer for today: "Father, it is our desire always to acknowledge Your goodness and power to those around us. To this end, grant us faith."

Memory Verse

"For the love of money is a root of all kinds of evil, for which some have strayed from the faith in their greediness, and pierced themselves through with many sorrows" (I Timothy 6:10 NKJV).

May 31: Read Numbers 21,22

Key verse: "So Moses made a bronze snake and put it on a pole. Anyone who had been bitten would look at the bronze snake and be healed" (Numbers 21:9 TEV).

This story of the serpent of brass holds its immortal place in the literature of the world because of the use made of it by our Lord in His memorable dialogue with Nicodemus. The learned Jewish rabbi was surprised to hear that his own book of the Law contained in such brief form the message of salvation which our Lord was eager to impart.

In interpreting the use which our Lord was making of this historic incident, we should observe:
1) Christ declared that, in the brazen serpent, one could find a type of symbol of the Saviour Himself.
2) The serpent was "lifted up," as was the Son of Man.
3) The condition of being cured was a "look" of faith. Christ's parallel words were these: "Whosoever believeth . . . shall have everlasting life."
4) As the result of a look was "life", so trust in Christ is "life eternal".

Direction for today: In spite of life's discomforts and disappointments, we will not become disheartened if we keep our eyes on Jesus.

Prayer for today: "I look to you, Father, for forgiveness, hope and life."

6

Teach us, O Lord

"One of His disciples said unto Him, 'Lord, teach us to pray'" (Luke 11:1).

Lord, give us the rightful words to say.
Stand by us ever near, and teach us to pray.
Guard Thou our lips henceforth from day to day,
As we walk, trusting Thee, teach us to pray.
Help us to speak true, kindly words — the best;
Teach us to pray with words that stand the test.
Grant to us ever Thy perfect peace and rest.
Teach us to pray.
Teach us to guide our minds into channels fair.
Help us to feel Thy loving and abiding care;
Teach us to pray.
Be with us, day by day, O Lord. And guide —
May we walk quietly, patiently by Thy side,
Dear Lord, whom for our sake was crucified.
Teach us to pray.
May we be like unto Thee in deed and thought,
For by Thy blood, redemption Thou hast bought.
Teach us, O Lord, to be so swift to hear,
So slow to speak, then for Thy wisdom
To quietly wait and seek.
Help us, O Lord, as we walk day by day;
O, Blessed Master, teach us to pray.

— Doris Roberts Moore

June 1: Read Numbers 23,24

Key verse: *"God is not a man, that He should lie, nor a son of man, that He should change His mind. Does He speak and then not act? Does He promise and not fulfill?" (Numbers 23:19 NIV).*

In these chapters, God demonstrates His great love for His people by thwarting an attempt by Balak to curse the nation of Israel. Instead, Balaam blesses Israel and predicts that the nation will prosper.

Our key verse informs us of one of the blessed assurances of our faith: the unchangeable nature of God. While we may renege on our commitment to Him, He never withdraws His promises to us. God loves us so much and His word cannot lie. "He will never leave us nor forsake us" (Hebrews 13:5) and "He is the same yesterday, and today and forever" (Hebrews 13:8).

Praise the Lord!

Direction for today: With the Lord's help, strive to be consistent in your Christian life.

Prayer for today: "Lord, may I continue to live in Christ, rooted and built up in Him, strengthened in the faith and overflowing with thankfulness" (Colossians 2:6,7).

June 2: Read Numbers 25,26

Key verse: *"So Israel joined in worshipping the Baal of Peor. And the Lord's anger burned against Israel" (Numbers 25:3 NIV).*

Balaam knew that the only thing that could separate Israel from God was sin. His idea was simple: if you can't curse a people, corrupt them so that God will have to punish them!

It was on Balaam's advice that the Midianite women enticed Israel to sexual sin and then to further dishonour of God by joining them in pagan worship. God punished the Israelites for their sin by sending a plague. He dealt severely with the Midianites and, subsequently with Balaam himself through death by the sword (Numbers 31:8).

We can note the far-reaching influence of Balaam in Revelation 2:14 and how the effects of his teaching were still being felt 1,500 years later! It is a warning for us today of the insidious nature of immorality and the devastating effect it can have on our lives.

Direction for today: Don't be influenced by the ungodly world.

Prayer for today: "Help me, Lord, to honour You in all I say and do."

June 3: Read Numbers 27,28

Key verse: *"Moses did as the Lord commanded him. He took Joshua and had him stand before Eleazar the priest and the whole assembly" (Numbers 27:22 NIV).*

In Chapter 27, the striking depth of character of Israel's great leader, Moses, is revealed when God tells him that he will soon die and a new leader will be installed to replace him.

Instead of complaining, Moses expresses concern for the welfare of the people and prays for his successor.

Forty years of wilderness travel, during which time his ability and reputation as a leader were frequently under fire, served not to shatter his character but, rather, to shape it.

So, it is not through our successes that God develops and builds our character but rather, through trials and tribulations and difficult circumstances. It is in this way that we can learn to accept God's direction cheerfully, even to denying ourselves and submitting to His will.

Direction for today: "Consider it pure joy, my brothers, whenever you face trials of many kinds, because you know that the testing of your faith develops perseverance" (James 1:2,3).

Prayer for today: "God, build my character as I face the challenges of this day."

June 4: Read Numbers 29

Key verse: "In addition to what you vow and your freewill offerings, prepare these for the Lord at your appointed feasts: your burnt offerings, grain offerings, drink offerings and fellowship offerings" (Numbers 29:39 NIV).

In yesterday's reading, we learned that, while Moses survived God's judgement of his generation, he would not lead the people into the promised land of Canaan. Today, we read that Moses reviewed for the 'new generation' three sacrifices of worship that were to be made. These would ensure the nation of Israel would not overlook any of its holy obligations or divinely assigned remembrances.

As Christians, we are not bound by the law of Moses, but it is a reminder to us not to overlook the need to spend time daily in the Word of God. II Timothy 3:15 tells us that the Scriptures will "make us wise for salvation through faith in Jesus Christ." It is profitable to us for all the purposes of Christian life.

If we consult the Scriptures, which were given by the inspiration of God, and follow their direction, we will "be thoroughly equipped for every good work" (II Timothy 3:17).

Direction for today: Do not only read the Bible, but do what it tells you to do.

Prayer for today: "Help me, Lord, to love Your Word more and keep closer to it than ever."

June 5: Read Numbers 30,31

Key verse: *"So we brought as an offering to the Lord the gold articles each of us acquired—armlets, bracelets, signet rings, earrings and necklaces—to make atonement for ourselves before the Lord" (Numbers 31:50 NIV).*

In this passage, we have a example of the faithfulness and devotion of the commanders of Israel's armies. Instead of coming to Moses to demand a reward for the service they had performed against the Midianites, they brought an offering to the Lord for His goodness to them in saving not only their lives, but the lives of all the men under their command.

It is a lesson for us today to give thanks in all circumstances for God's goodness. Whenever we survive an ordeal or simply return safely from a trip, let us remember to thank God for watching over us.

Direction for today: "Give thanks in all circumstances, for this is God's will for you in Christ Jesus" (I Thessalonians 5:18).

Prayer for today: "Teach us, Lord, to build up our treasures in heaven rather than on earth."

June 6: Read Numbers 32

Key verse: *"For if you turn away from following Him, He will again abandon them in the wilderness; and you will destroy all this people" (Numbers 32:15 RSV).*

Am I my brother's keeper? How often we are challenged to look more deeply into our great salvation. Does it really matter to anyone else how I live and react to Jesus, to His Word and His Spirit?

The gospel comes to each of us individually. But, as soon as one receives Christ, he or she becomes a member of God's family. The word of God clearly teaches family relationships and family responsibilities.

We become stewards of our time, talent and treasure. Whatever we are, whatever we have, belongs to God. The Holy Spirit directs us in using it for God's glory and the good of others.

God is going to conquer and be victorious in the end. But each of us must take our place, as members of His family, and do our part.

Direction for today: Hear the voice of the Holy Spirit and obey.

Prayer for today: "Father, help me to be aware of my responsibility as a member of Your family."

Memory Verse

"You will keep him in perfect peace, whose mind is stayed on You, because he trusts in You" (Isaiah 26:3 NKJV).

June 7: Read Numbers 33,34

Key verse: *"I have given you the land to possess" (Numbers 33:53b NKJV).*

God had promised His people deliverance from Egypt and entrance into the promised land. Because of their unbelief and rebellion, they had wandered in the wilderness forty years.

Now, Moses reviews their progress. It is a good thing to look closely at our past, from time to time, so that we can appreciate our present and look with faith to our future.

The Lord also encouraged the Israelites by pointing out their boundaries in the promised land (chapter 34), a land on which they had not yet set foot. He also named the men who would divide the land among them for their inheritance. All of this planning was certainly a faith-building experience for the people.

Everything we receive from God comes by way of His great and precious promise to us. Have you learned the secret of answered prayer? Can you take hold of these promises and see them fulfilled in your life?

Direction for today: Seek out a promise to meet your need. Pray that promise in faith. Expect the answer.

Prayer for today: "Give us this day our daily bread."

June 8: Read Numbers 35,36

Key verse: *"Therefore do not defile the land which you inhabit, in the midst of which I dwell; for I the Lord dwell among the children of Israel" (Numbers 35:34 NKJV).*

This verse reflects the command of the Lord, but it certainly does not reflect the actions of the people. We do not have to read very far along in the Old Testament before encountering example after example of the defilement of the land.

The entire book of Judges is an account of the way the people ignored God's commands as well as His presence in their midst. By the time we come to the kings of Israel following Solomon, the defilement was so severe that, first, the northern kingdom of Israel, and then the southern nation of Judah were conquered by enemies and physically removed from the land.

Before we judge these people harshly, it would be good for us to look at our own lives. Are we defiling the place where God now dwells? If we are believers, this refers to our lives. Are we indulging in thoughts or actions that similiarly defile the place where the Lord has come to live?

If so, we should take warning from the Word of the Lord and from His judgments which eventually fell upon His people.

Direction for today: The Lord lives in your life; keep it clean.

Prayer for today: "Lord, please make me always willing to obey You in every area of my life."

John

This fourth gospel, so different from the preceding three, is one of the most fascinating books in the New Testament. It is very simple yet eternally profound. John crafts some of the most eloquent and moving passages in the entire Bible, using the simplest vocabulary of any New Testament writer.

He approaches the appearance on earth of Jesus Christ, the God-man, in a matter completely unlike that of the other evangelists. John writes of "the Word" existing at the beginning of all things. The Word was, in fact, the Creator, the Master of the universe. And this Word, who is God, who created all things, "became flesh, and dwelt among us!" (1:14).

This divine, cosmic mystery is John's entire theme. Jesus, the man is Jesus, Son of God. John tells us of His miracles, recounts His teachings, and in passages unparalleled elsewhere, gives us lengthy descriptions of Jesus talking with His disciples and with His Father.

Through his book, the writer carries us along, demonstrating at every turn the truth of his initial claim. Finally, in chapter 20, Thomas, the doubter (perhaps also a picture of John's imagined readers), realizes the truth and exclaims, "My Lord and my God!"

John then turns figuratively, to his readers and says his book "has been written that you may believe that Jesus is the Christ, the Son of God; and that believing you may have life in His name" (20:31).

As we read, let us celebrate this life-giving truth.

June 9: Read John 1

Key verse: "In the beginning was the Word, and the Word was with God, and the Word was God" (John 1:1 NKJV).

This verse is fundamental to our understanding of who Jesus really is. Here, in John 1, we have a clear statement of what the Bible teaches about the man Jesus Christ.

John begins by referring to a being he names "the Word". We quickly begin to discover some pretty amazing things about this "Word". John says the Word has existed from before the beginning since, "in the beginning", the Word was already there. The Word was with God; the Word was God.

The Word is the Creator; all things were made through Him. The Word is the source of life and light.

And, in one of the most powerful phrases to appear in this Spirit-powered book, John tells us that "the Word became flesh and dwelt among us, and we beheld His glory."

Only three verses later, we finally read the given name of this "Word": Jesus Christ.

Don't try to argue that Jesus was anything less than fully God, even as He was fully man. It's all here in these first few verses: John leaves no doubt as to the absolute deity of Jesus.

There are groups today who will reinterpret this chapter to do away with this definite truth. Do not trust their message; John, Jesus' disciple and friend, means exactly what his gospel says.

Direction for today: Worship Jesus as God, Creator, Lord and King!

Prayer for today: "Thank You, Lord, that the Bible leaves no doubt as to Your true nature."

June 10: Read John 2,3

Key verse: "For God so loved the world that He gave His only begotten Son, that whoever believes in Him should not perish but have everlasting life" (John 3:16 NKJV).

There are many wonderful truths in these two chapters of the gospel of John, but no one can deny that this verse is key to the chapters, and perhaps even key to the entire Bible.

Here is the message of Christ in 25 words. Here is the joy, the truth, the life of the gospel. Here is all you need to know to begin a walk with Jesus that will lead to eternal fellowship with God our Creator.

There is so much in these 25 words. We read that God loved us. That, in itself, can give reason for thought, for prayer, for praise, and for exceeding joy. Just think—God loves you!

He loves you so much that He gave the greatest gift that could ever be given—His own Son, Jesus Christ. Jesus willingly "emptied Himself" (Philippians 2:7) and became a real, live human being, a man who lived and died for us.

And, in Jesus' death, is the gift of life. He died carrying your death. He rose to life again, winning your victory over death and your everlasting life!

Read the verse again. And praise the Lord with all your being!

Direction for today: Live in the consciousness of how much God loves you!

Prayer for today: "Thank You, Jesus, for the greatest gift: everlasting life."

June 11: Read John 4

Key verse: "But whoever drinks of the water that I shall give him will never thirst. But the water that I shall give him will become in him a fountain of water springing up into everlasting life" (John 4:14 NKJV).

The Bible is filled with amazing, wonderful stories. Moses is told to speak to a rock, and water will flow forth . . . and it does. Elijah promises a woman, in the name of the Lord, that her small supply of oil and flour will never run out and it doesn't. Jesus blesses five loaves and two fish and then feeds thousands and thousands of people.

God frequently demonstrated His power by producing water or food from a totally impossible source.

This is the same miracle that Jesus longs to perform in our lives. The late gospel singer Keith Green asked, "What can be done with an old heart like mine?" Jesus spoke the answer that Green celebrated: He can make it a fountain of joy, a well-spring of life to you and to others around you.

The same God who can bring water out of a rock can bring spiritual life bubbling up from our cold hearts. As we drink Jesus in, He will produce in us real, vital, overflowing life.

If you have never known that life, receive Jesus today. If you have, but the fountain has dried up to a mere trickle, ask Him to uncap His Holy Spirit in your life once more and drink freely of the life-giving spring.

Direction for today: Allow the Holy Spirit to flow freely in your life.

Prayer for today: "Lord, I confess any blocks to the flow of the Spirit in me. May Your fountain of life spring up in me."

June 12: Read John 5

Key verse: "Most assuredly, I say to you, he who hears My word and believes in Him who sent Me has everlasting life, and shall not come into judgment, but has passed from death into life" (John 5:24 NKJV).

I recently attended the funeral of an 85 year old woman who had served and loved the Lord throughout her life. Her final years were times of struggle against disease and the failings of an aged body, but her faith never wavered and her joy was never quenched.

As we sat in the funeral service, we were keenly aware that all was not as it seemed. The coffin was before us and we were commemorating the passage of this woman from life into death—at least, that is what we seemed to be doing.

In reality, every Christian in the room knew that we were at a celebration of a passage from death to life! Our dear sister had long known the onslaught of death—the failing senses and growing weakness of the body, the memory lapses, and all of the reminders that our mortal bodies die. But, as we sat in *our* mortal bodies in a funeral parlor, our friend had crossed over the final passageway from death into life.

The Christian can celebrate this victory every moment of this life, and especially at the time of the death of a believing loved one. Jesus' promise of life is sure!

Direction for today: Remember that death has lost its sting, and the grave its victory.

Prayer for today: "Thank You, Father, that death is swallowed up in victory!"

June 13: Read John 6

Key verse: "But He said to them, 'It is I; do not be afraid'" (John 6:20 NKJV).

What are you afraid of?

One of the enemy's favourite methods of attack against a Christian is through fear. Sometimes, Christians will admit that their fears have increased since they found the Lord. That happens because the enemy increases his attacks on those who join the King's army, and because the new Christian has not yet learned to live in the presence of Jesus.

The Bible has much to say about fear, and the message can be summed up simply: if you are with the Lord, you have nothing to fear.

What are you afraid of? Whatever it is that causes you to fear, that fear can be defeated. "The Lord is my light and my salvation; whom shall I fear?" (Psalm 27:la). "For God has not given us a spirit of fear, but of power and of love and of a sound mind" (II Timothy 1:7).

Face your fear. Confess it to the Lord. Cover yourself spiritually with the blood of Jesus, and rejoice in the fact that He is with you, so you have nothing to fear.

Each time you fear, turn to the Lord in praise and thanksgiving for the victory over fear that He has won. Each time you do this, remember that Jesus said, "It is I; do not be afraid" (Matthew 14:27).

Direction for today: Give all your fears to Jesus.

Prayer for today: "Yea, though I walk through the valley of the shadow of death, I will fear no evil; for Thou art with me."

Memory Verse

"For as the body without the spirit is dead, so faith without works is dead also" (James 2:26 NKJV).

June 14: Read John 7

Key verse: "For even His brothers did not believe in Him" (John 7:5 NKJV).

We live in a world in which relationships are crumbling. More and more people feel abandoned, alone or betrayed. Families are breaking up; marriages are fractured; friendships are short-lived.

Perhaps you can identify with those feelings. It may be that you, too, feel alone and even betrayed.

Take hope from two things: first, you are not alone. Jesus is with you, and He fully understands how you feel. Today's reading tells us that He knew the feeling of family betrayal, for His brothers refused to believe in Him. He also knew what it was to feel completely alone, for He said, "the world hates Me." He understands, and He is the source of all comfort.

As well, remember that situations change, and that the Lord can bring joy and happiness, friendship and fullfillment to your life. The same brothers of Jesus who did not believe at this point are found among the believers at Pentecost (Acts 1:14). Two of them, James and Jude, wrote books that are part of the New Testament.

Direction for today: Jesus knows your sorrow, your hurt and loneliness.

Prayer for today: "Lord, I thank You for saying You would never leave me nor forsake me. I am grateful for Your presence. with me, now and always.

June 15: Read John 8

Key verse: "And you shall know the truth, and the truth shall make you free" (John 8:32 NKJV).

Everyone longs to be free. The search for freedom lies at the heart of every social and cultural movement in history. Revolutions are started as a fight for freedom. Young people take drugs, hoping to be freed from the tensions and constraints of their lives. Criminals steal money to buy freedom. But none of this brings real freedom.

Politicians promise freedom; so do rock stars, dictators and beer commercials. None of them deliver on their promises.

Freedom is found only at one source. The truth shall make you free, and the truth is Jesus, who named Himself "the Way, the Truth and the Life."

In Jesus we find freedom from the bondages of sin. We are freed from addictions, emptiness and vain pursuits. Only in Jesus can black and white in South Africa—or the southern United States, or anywhere else—be free to love and care for each other. Only in Jesus can a wife and husband be free truly to respect and nurture one another. Only in Jesus can we be free from strife and anger and warmongering.

Only in Jesus are we free from the multitude of temptations we face every day. Without Him, we are all slaves to something or someone. But in Him we are free.

Direction for today: Be sure you have the only real freedom: that found in Jesus Christ.

Prayer for today: "Praise You, Lord, for the truth that has set me free!"

June 16: Read John 9

Key verse: "Jesus answered, 'Neither this man nor his parents sinned, but that the works of God should be revealed in him'" (John 9:3 NKJV).

It is so typical of human nature that Jesus' disciples wanted to lay blame for the blindness that afflicted the man who stood before them.

114

So often, we see a scandal when we should be seeing an opportunity to minister; we seek to judge instead of to help; we fall into gossip instead of falling on our knees in prayer.

Jesus saw each situation as an opportunity to bring glory to His Father. He who is the Judge of all the earth did not judge. He who knows all things rejected the opportunity to speak of past sins of the man or of his parents. Instead, He acted to bring honour to God.

He healed the blind man.

Often, we see the Pharisees as the villains of the Scriptures, and the disciples as heroes. But here, the followers of Christ were acting exactly like their opponents, abandoning compassion for criticism.

Let's be sure that, when we encounter a need, we see it as an opportunity for ministry, compassion and prayer.

Direction for today: Ask God to reveal to you the opportunity for ministry and for spiritual growth that lies in each situation you will encounter.

Prayer for today: "Lord, may I be a minister and not a judge."

June 17: Read John 10

Key verse: "I am the good shepherd. The good shepherd gives His life for the sheep" (John 10:11 NKJV).

What a beautiful image! Jesus is our good Shepherd, our protector, our provider, our comforter.

In the hills around the Sea of Galilee, the shepherds literally became the door for the sheep. The sheep were housed for the night in a cave, and the shepherd lay across the opening as a protective guard.

Jesus promises that, when we are His sheep, no enemy will be able to attack us, for He will bear that attack. He is our deliverer, our Saviour.

Jesus also promises abundant life to all who are His. He knows what is best for His sheep, and He is able to provide it. Our Shepherd is the source of life and of blessing.

Our good Shepherd has already laid down His life for us. We need fear no evil, for He has overcome the evil one and won victory over death and hell.

The good Shepherd promises that He knows His sheep, and that they know His voice. Just now, take a moment in silence and listen for the voice of the Shepherd. He has a message of peace, comfort and hope for you today.

Direction for today: Listen to the voice of the good Shepherd.

Prayer for today: "Praise You, Jesus, that You laid down Your life for me!"

June 18: Read John 11

Key verse: *"Jesus said to her, 'I am the resurrection and the life. He who believes in Me, though he may die, he shall live'" (John 11:25 NKJV).*

People in our age have a compulsive fascination with death. Even as our "youth-oriented" culture tries vainly to delay the aging process, and thus to delay death, classes on death are filled and books about dying are best-sellers.

We fear death because it is the ultimate enemy. Yet we are drawn to look closely at it because it is the inevitable end for each of us.

No one wants to reach that end. No one is happy to think about a time when they will no longer breathe, walk, talk and laugh. No one wants to die.

Yet everyone will reach that end. Everyone will cease to breathe, to walk, to talk and to laugh. Everyone will die.

There are many who despair because they believe that is the final reality. But Jesus has exploded that myth and opened the doors for us to see the triumph, the laughter and celebration that can be ours beyond death. "Though he may die, he shall live!" This is a tremendous proclamation of victory. It is the message that our death-obsessed and dying world needs to hear!

Jesus is the resurrection and the life. The sting of death and the victory of the grave are gone. Praise His wonderful name!

Direction for today: Tell someone who lives in fear of death about life in Christ.

Prayer for today: "Thank you, Lord, for life."

June 19: Read John 12

Key verse: *"But the chief priests took counsel that they might also put Lazarus to death, because on account of him many of the Jews went away and believed in Jesus" (John 12:10,11 NKJV).*

What kind of an impact does your life have for Jesus? Do people look at you, notice the changes God is bringing about in your life, and turn to Him? Do people see your good works and glorify your Father who is in heaven?

Sadly, many believers would have to answer "no" to those last two questions, for the impact of their lives upon those around them is not great.

But it should be! Like Lazarus, we have been raised from the dead! Like Lazarus, we have received an infusion of new life by the Spirit of God! Like Lazarus, we are living proof that Jesus is real, and that He brings new life where there was only death.

Perhaps there is one key difference between most of us and Lazarus—he did not stay in the tomb, while we often do. Either we refuse to leave behind the graveclothes of the world or else we find a cave in which to hide so that no one will know we are "born again."

Let's come triumphantly out of our caves, abandon our graveclothes, and proclaim to the world that we are alive in Jesus!

Direction for today: Every Christian has already experienced the miracle of being raised from death to life!

Prayer for today: "Lord, may my life be a witness to Your life-giving love."

June 20: Read John 13,14

Key verse: *"By this all will know that you are My disciples, if you have love for one another" (John 13:35 NKJV).*

How do you rate on this scale of love?

Several times, especially in the accounts included in this Gospel of John, Jesus stressed the importance of love among the believers. Here, He says we will be recognized as Christians because of our love. Later in the gospel, He went so far as to say that the world would judge whether or not Jesus had come from God by our love for one another.

And yet, sadly, the history of Christianity has more often been a story of dissensions, fights, rebellions and divisions. Too many times, unbelievers have looked to those bearing the name of Christ and have seen no evidence of love.

Can we blame an unbeliever who refuses to trust Christ because he or she sees nothing but strife and hypocrisy in the church? Jesus Himself said we would be the evidence that the world could consider.

The conclusion is obvious: we are to love one another. If you have suffered a breakdown of love between yourself and another Christian, go and make it right. If you are breaking the bonds of love through gossip, greed or pride, confess and heal those bonds. Your relationship with your fellow Christians is evidence for good or ill.

Direction for today: Love one another.

Prayer for today: "Lord, forgive me for failing to love. Grant me a special anointing of Your love."

Memory Verse

"Go therefore and make disciples of all the nations, baptizing them in the name of the Father and of the Son and of the Holy Spirit" (Matthew 28:19 NKJV).

June 21: Read John 15,16

Key verse: "Abide in Me, and I in you. As the branch cannot bear fruit of itself, unless it abides in the vine, neither can you, unless you abide in Me" (John 15:4 NKJV).

"Happy anniversary, darling. These are for you." And, for a number of days, a dozen lovely red roses sit in a vase on a table or mantlepiece.

They are beautiful for a day or two, and nice for a few days more. But, eventually, the petals darken and fall, the stems droop, and what were once beautiful roses are now withered and ugly.

Everyone knows this. No one would bring home a dozen roses and expect them to last forever. They can't for they have been cut off from the source of their life.

That's the same message Jesus was giving to us. But many people who completely understand the principle when it comes to roses reject it when it concerns themselves.

That may be why your own spiritual life feels withered and dry.

Jesus said that we will find our source of life, health and growth only in Him. Only as we "abide" in Him will we flourish. And we should expect that, if we cut ourselves off from fellowship with Him through the Word, prayer, teaching and worship, we will be in danger of spiritual death.

Direction for today: Abide in Jesus.

Prayer for today: "Lord, help me always to remain in You."

June 22: Read John 17,18

Key verse: "Jesus answered, 'My kingdom is not of this world. If My kingdom were of this world, then My servants would fight so that I should not be delivered to the Jews' " (John 18:36a NKJV).

In the Old Testament era, God's people formed a political nation. They occupied a specific land, served under prophets and kings, and went to war to defend their land or to serve their God.

Jesus came to expand the kingdom of God on a global basis. As His followers carried the good news of salvation from Jerusalem through Judea and Samaria and unto the uttermost parts of the earth, the kingdom grew.

No longer was the kingdom of God identified with a specific nation or land—Jesus' holy nation came to include people from every continent, inside every political border.

When He spoke these words, His followers were few, and all came from the small nation known as Israel. But, even before the New Testament was completed, the kingdom had spread to include people from Asia, Africa and Europe. Now, God has His people around the globe.

If you are a believer, you are a part of the kingdom of Christ! You have been commissioned to expand its borders, to take the loving message of the gospel to other potential citizens of the eternal kingdom of God!

Direction for today: Remember that of all nations that have ever existed, only the kingdom of God will last.

Prayer for today: "Praise to the King!"

June 23: Read John 19

Key verse: "So when Jesus had received the sour wine, He said, 'It is finished!' And bowing His head, He gave up His spirit" (John 19:30 NKJV).

Too often, these three words, "It is finished," are interpreted as words of despair or loss. In reality, Jesus was proclaiming eternal triumph and ultimate victory just before He offered up His life in voluntary sacrifice.

It was truly finished. He had completed the work the Father had sent Him to do.

He had been obedient. Faced with all the temptations that other men and women know, Jesus had triumphed over sin. He did not sin, and thus prepared Himself as the perfect sacrifice for sin.

He had been a teacher. All of the truths that His followers needed to know had been taught to them during three years of itinerant ministry in Israel. They didn't yet understand everything, but they would, under the guidance of the Holy Spirit.

Jesus had died as our sacrifice, in place of the world which God so loved; that sacrifice was big enough to cover all the sins of all who ever lived or will live.

And He knew that while the task was finished, the triumph was not. As He had told the disciples, after three days, He would rise again and initiate a victory celebration that continues in the church to this day.

Direction for today: Walk in the knowledge that all God wanted to accomplish for you was finished in Christ.

Prayer for today: "Thank You, Jesus, that the victory is completely won!"

June 24: Read John 20, 21

Key verse: *"Then, the same day at evening, being the first day of the week, when the doors were shut where the disciples were assembled, for fear of the Jews, Jesus came and stood in the midst, and said to them, 'Peace be with you' " (John 20:19 NKJV).*

Many people have used "peace"—as a greeting over the years. In some cultures, it is the standard form of salutation.

While anyone can wish another, "Peace,", only Jesus can speak it as a gift. When He appeared among His frightened and confused followers, Jesus not only wished them "peace" He brought them peace. Many, many believers from that day to this have known that same gift.

Missionaries, trekking through dark jungles, have suddenly sensed the peace of the presence of Jesus. Parents, praying and hoping by the bedside of a sick child, have known that peace. Men and women, in times of war or danger, have realized that Jesus was there and that everything would be all right.

Whatever your problem, Jesus can give perfect peace.

Direction for today: Allow the Lord to speak peace as a gift to you.

Prayer for today: "Lord Jesus, I need to know Your peace."

Acts

The foundation of our faith has already been laid, as is clearly shown in the four gospels. All four writers agreed that "Jesus is the Christ, the Son of the Living God." Now, one of those four, Luke, takes us on into the building of the superstructure of the church and, very carefully, under the inspiration of the Holy Spirit, shows that Jesus Christ is indeed doing what He said He would do: "I will build My church and the gates of Hell shall not prevail against it" (Matthew 16:18).

The promises of the gospels are proven true here. The Holy Spirit comes upon the disciples; God confirms His Word with signs following; there is testing, persecution and great victory. The proof of Christ's resurrection is here. The people seen thousands converted to Jesus Christ. Miracles are on every page; even the dead are raised. A pattern of the action of the Holy Spirit in this present age is offered here.

As we read this book, let us prayerfully and with fervency open our lives to the same acts of the Holy Spirit as these first Christians did, and let us expect God's wonders to happen to us, in us and through us.

This book tells not only of signs and wonders, but also of the practical living of the early church. It teaches us the importance of taking our place faithfully in a local fellowship and shows that, no matter how glorious the spiritual life, there must be organization authority and responsibility.

As we read, let's check up on ourselves. Are we enjoying the normal Christian life?

June 25: Read Acts 1, 2

Key verse: "But you shall receive power when the Holy Spirit has come upon you; and you shall be witnesses to Me in Jerusalem, and in all Judea and Samaria, and to the end of the earth" (Acts 1:8 NKJV).

There can be no question that this is the key verse of these chapters; indeed, it might be called the key verse of the entire book of Acts and, perhaps, even of the rest of the New Testament.

This is Christ's program for His people. Here we have His command to be witnesses to Him; His promise of power, given to us through the Holy Spirit to enable us to carry out His command; and His goal, that the whole world will hear the good news of Jesus Christ.

It is easy for believers to be diverted from this primary command. We may simply become comfortable in our own salvation and cease to be concerned for the salvation of others. We may enjoy meeting with Christians in fellowship so much that we completely neglect this command to be witnesses to those who do not know Christ. Or we may hide behind excuses such as, "I don't know enough" or "I need to understand the Bible better," and thus try to escape our assignment as witnesses. Remember: Jesus said that all we need to enable us to share the gospel is the power of the Holy Spirit!

Let's be sure we are obeying the Lord we claim to love, and that we are following the example of the early believers.

Direction for today: To obey Christ, be a witness for Him.

Prayer for today: "Lord, release in me the boldness and grace to share the good news of Jesus Christ with others."

June 26: Read Acts 3, 4

Key verse: "Nor is there salvation in any other, for there is no other name under heaven given among men by which we must be saved" (Acts 4:12 NKJV).

The power promised by Jesus was quickly evident in the young church: Amazing things began to happen: people spoke in tongues they had never learned; miracles of healing were performed; thousands came to hear the new message being preached.

The power was evident in the miracles—a lame man lept to his feet and walked. The power was evident in the messages—Peter and his friends preached with amazing authority.

But, most importantly, the power of the Holy Spirit was evident in the way lives were being changed. Thousands were declaring that the risen Jesus was Lord of their lives, and their lifestyles immediately bore witness to the changes that had taken place.

That is the greatest miracle of all—the salvation of lost people. As our key verse says, only in Jesus can we find salvation, freedom from the bondage of sin, death and hell, and the ability to live up to the potential God had in mind when He made us.

While we thank the Lord that His salvation has been revealed to us, let us not forget yesterday's study—the command of Jesus to share this wonderful news with a lost world.

Direction for today: Salvation is yours; claim it and share it, rejoicing!

Prayer for today: "Thank you, Father, for the eternal salvation I have found through your Son Jesus."

June 27: Read Acts 5, 6

Key verse: "Then Peter and the other apostles answered and said: 'We ought to obey God rather than men' " (Acts 5:29 NKJV).

The Bible teaches us that, whenever possible, we are to be good citizens, obeying the laws of the country in which we live. As in all matters of morality, freedom in Christ does not mean freedom to be sinful or irresponsible.

But, as Peter and the other apostles realized, there are times when the laws of God will differ from the laws of the land. There are countries in the world today where it is illegal to become a Christian or to preach the gospel. And yet, the believers in those lands courageously continue to tell others about Jesus, and for this they are imprisoned or even killed.

Let us remember to pray for these persecuted brothers and sisters.

But, even in our own western lands, there are laws that stand in contradiction to the laws of God. Terrible examples of this are the laws that allow abortion in Canada and in the United States. Christians who recognize the value of every life created by God must stand against such laws, choosing to obey God rather than men.

Direction for today: Always stand with God, no matter who is opposing you.

Prayer for today: 'Lord, help me to be sensitive and discerning in my obedience to the government and to You."

Memory Verse

"Blessed is the man who walks not in the counsel of the ungodly, nor stands in the path of sinners, not sits in the seat of the scornful; But his delight is the law of the Lord, and in His law he meditates day and night" (Psalm 1:1,2 NKJV).

June 28: Read Acts 7

Key verse: "And he knelt down and cried our with a loud voice, 'Lord, do not charge them with this sin.' And when he had said this, he fell asleep" (Acts 7:60 NKJV).

In Romans 8:29, Paul tells us that we are intended to be "conformed to the image of His Son". God's plan for us is that we might come to resemble Jesus Christ.

This does not mean that we will be perfect and without sin, although that should always be the goal for which we strive. But, as we grow in the Spirit, our lives, our temperaments and actions will come to be like those of Jesus.

Stephen is a great example of this. We have learned that he was full of the Holy Spirit; thus, we see that he was acting, speaking and loving as Jesus did.

His defense at his trial was not an attempt to be released; instead, with a boldness born of the Spirit, Stephen challenged all who had rejected Christ, warning them of their error and their peril. Their violent reaction was predictable but Stephen did not flinch from the true proclamation.

And, when he faced his executioners, Stephen echoed the attitude and words of Jesus: "Father, forgive them." Here was a man who had come to be like Christ.

This is God's will for each of His children.

Direction for today: Allow the Holy Spirit to conform you to the image of Christ.

Prayer for today: "Father, help me to be like Jesus."

June 29: Read Acts 8,9

Key verse: "And he said, 'Who are You, Lord?' And the Lord said, 'I am Jesus, whom you are persecuting. It is hard for you to kick against the goads' " (Acts 9:5 NKJV).

What a surprise for this earnest, devout persecutor of the church! Saul, who knew so much, discovered in an instant that he really knew nothing at all. Much of what he was sure of disappeared in that moment on the road to Damascus. All his efforts were empty; all his righteousness was as filthy rags.

Praise the Lord that all of this occurred, for Paul was a key to the growth of the early church. Without him, the church might not have been carried through Asia Minor to Rome; without him, our New Testament would be cut in half.

The Lord had much for Paul to do, and He set him on that path in a very dramatic way. But the Lord also has much for you to do and, although He may not get your attention as dramatically as He did that of Paul, He is calling you just the same.

Think about how much we would miss if Paul had not listened. Now, think about how much others may miss—and how many may miss the kingdom—if *you* do not listen to God's call!

Direction for today: Listen to the Lord's direction for you and then follow it!

Prayer for today: "Lord, I want to hear and to obey."

June 30: Read Acts 10

Key verse: "While Peter was still speaking these words, the Holy Spirit fell upon all those who heard the word" (Acts 10:44 NKJV).

There is a valuable lesson here for each one of us who is involved in any kind of Christian leadership. Perhaps you are a pastor or a worship leader. Maybe you teach a Sunday school class or lead a Bible study or help out in some other way.

Whatever your role, the message is the same: God does things unexpectedly.

Notice, in the story of the conversion of Cornelius, that the Holy Spirit fell on the people while Peter was still speaking. God interrupted Peter's message with a miraculous outpouring of His Spirit!

It hadn't happened that way before in any of the Acts accounts. But here, while Peter was on the second of his three points (or something like that), people began to speak in tongues and praise God. Peter had to quit preaching!

If this had happened in many of the churches in our day, these rowdy types would have been asked to be silent or been shown politely to the door so that the preacher could properly complete his sermon. Too often, we try to fit God's work into our moulds.

But God doesn't fit into any mould. He will work His will sovereignly, as He chooses. He is creative and always perfectly right.

In whatever service or group we have responsibility, let's be sure we leave room for the Lord to do the unexpected, or we may find He does nothing at all.

Direction for today: Allow the Spirit freedom to work at all times.

Prayer for today: 'Lord, help me to stay in Your will and out of Your way!"

7

Conformed to His Image

The pressure's on Lord,
And I don't much like it,
This conforming to Your image.
You mean to say
I'm supposed to be like You?
Willing to be a servant;
Loving without being loved;
Ministering without reward;
Laying down my life for those
Who don't want it anyway;
Dying, yet going on to live,
Not for myself but others?
Is this what it's all about, Lord?

It's what You did, isn't it?
You turned the other cheek
And didn't answer back.
You kept on sharing truth,
No matter what was said.
And You shared it, in Love,
With those who wished You dead.
You cared, and kept on caring
Even when all Your friends had fled.
You prayed and kept on praying,
Even as You bled to death.
But that was You, Lord,
That was <u>Your</u> calling.

Oh! . . . I see! . . . It's mine, too,
To be conformed to be like You!   — *Bunty Burke*

125

July 1: Read Acts 11,12

Key verse: "And he killed James the brother of John with the sword" (Acts 12:2 NKJV).

There are two deaths recorded in Acts 12—the death of James and the death of Herod. They stand in stark contrast one with the other.

James was put to death by Herod, who was seeking to stamp out the newborn church. Yet nothing that Herod intended to accomplish actually took place. He did not smother the church; instead, "the word of God grew and multiplied". He did not frighten the other church leaders into silence; the church continued to meet and the gospel was preached.

He did not truly harm James, for John's brother became one of the first members of the early church to join his Lord and Saviour in eternity.

Despite its appearance, James' death was entirely victorious.

Not so for Herod. The kingdom he sought to hold soon crumbled. The glory he claimed for himself was lost instantly. The worship he accepted was false, and the result of his blasphemous pride was undoubtedly eternal damnation.

The king was destroyed; the simple fisherman he attempted to destroy now sits with the King.

Direction for today: Be assured of victory. Remember that those who are on the Lord's side always win!

Prayer for today: "Lord, may I not be deceived by appearances, but have the discernment to know what is of true eternal value."

July 2: Read Acts 13

Key verse: "As they ministered to the Lord and fasted, the Holy Spirit said, 'Separate to Me Barnabas and Saul for the work to which I have called them' " (Acts 13:2 NKJV).

Many Christians express frustration because they are seldom sure what God's will is for them. They say, "If only I knew the will of the Lord, I would surely do it." But instead they live aimless, unfulfilled lives, never certain of how they should be serving God.

There are two sure answers to this problem. First, much of God's will for you is directly revealed in the Bible. People who complain they don't know the will of the Lord probably don't know the Word of the Lord either. God's Word is full of instructions for the believer.

The second answer is found in our key verse, and appears many times through Scripture: prayer and fasting. The church at Antioch was ministering to the Lord—praying, worshipping, praising—and fasting. As they sought the Lord's presence and fasted as a symbol of holiness, purity and rejection of sin, they heard the voice of God. "The Holy Spirit said . . . " and they listened.

And, after hearing God's will, *they did it!* Sometimes we know what the Lord has for us, but we don't like the idea very much, and so we don't do it. It's not surprising that we don't hear from Him again for a while!

Direction for today: Listen to God through His Word and in prayer and fasting, and you will hear His voice!

Prayer for today: "Lord, I am listening and I will obey."

July 3: Read Acts 14, 15

Key verse: "Then the contention became so sharp between them that they parted from one another. And so Barnabas took Mark and sailed to Cyprus" (Acts 15:39 NKJV).

This may seem like a strange passage to included as a "key verse" for today's reading. It stands in sorry contrast to the accounts of the victorious spread of the gospel in this section of Acts.

But it carries two important messages for us.

The first has to do with leadership: we are called by God to respect and honour our Christian leaders, but we must never expect them to be perfect.

Too often, Christians place their pastor or their favourite evangelist on a pedestal, expecting him never to fail or make any mistake. That is an unrealistic expectation—even Paul and Barnabas failed in this case, disagreeing so strongly that it shattered their partnership.

The only One upon whom we can utterly depend to be perfect and unfailing is Jesus. Let's be realistic and, when necessary, forgiving, toward our brothers and sisters in positions of spiritual leadership.

The second lesson concerns forgiveness. It is obvious that the Lord forgave Paul and Barnabas for their falling-out, for He continued to bless their ministries. As well, Paul, so offended by Mark at this point, later welcomed him back as a co-worker (II Timothy 4:11).

As God forgives, we must also forgive one another.

Direction for today: Respect your Christian leaders, but do not expect perfection from them.

Prayer for today: "Lord, strengthen, guide and keep my pastor and the Christian leaders in our land."

July 4: Read Acts 16

Key verse: "And they said, 'Believe on the Lord Jesus Christ, and you will be saved, you and your household' " (Acts 16:31 NKJV).

It is unlikely that the Philippian jailer was asking Paul and Silas about the path to eternal life. Instead, his question, "What must I do to be saved?", had to do with the very practical and immediate issue of the possibility of the escape of prisoners from jail!

But the two apostles were not going to miss an opportunity to tell a lost man about their Lord and Saviour, and they used his question for a chance to share the good news of Jesus.

There is a lesson here for us. Too often, our fear keeps us from seizing such opportunities to speak about Jesus. We are not abiding in the Spirit, and thus lack the holy boldness that Paul and Silas had on this occasion.

Every day, the Lord will give us clear *opportunities* to speak about His salvation. But we need to be listening to those around us with ears and spirits tuned to detect those opportunities. Perhaps one will come as a colleague explains that he or she is not feeling well, and you might pray for them. Maybe someone will say something negative about church or about 100 Huntley Street, and you can (gently now!) tell them why you appreciate those ministries.

Perhaps someone will come to you, sounding a lot like the jailer and saying: "My life is in a mess. How can I get out of this?" Like Paul, you can answer, "I know the One who can rescue you."

Direction for today: Be open for opportunities to share Jesus.

Prayer for today: "Lord, give me discernment of ear and of spirit."

Memory Verse

"Now faith is the substance of things hoped for, the evidence of things not seen" (Hebrews 11:1 NKJV).

July 5: Read Acts 17,18

Key verse: "Then the Lord spoke to Paul in the night by a vision, 'Do not be afraid, but speak, and do not keep silent; for I am with you' " (Acts 18:9,10a NKJV).

The young woman had been in Zambia for only a few months, stationed at a hospital in a remote village. So much of her life was new, for Marie had come from a small community on the Niagara Peninsula in southern Ontario.

One night, she was the only staff member working in the primitive hospital when one of the patients died. The family cried and mourned, but none moved to take the relative's body to the morgue, located outside the hospital, a few steps into the jungle.

Marie lifted the body onto her shoulder as the family members wept. She had never had any duty like this before and, with considerable fear, she stepped outside the hospital bearing the heavy corpse.

She had carefully to wend her way through sleeping bodies on the ground, for the families of patients slept outside the building, huddled around smouldering fires. In the midst of that jumble of human forms, smokey fires, and piles of possessions, in the dark of the night, Marie's flashlight failed. She began to panic, but suddenly realized that someone was beside her, taking her hand in His.

And then she knew who it was—Jesus had come to guide her the rest of the way on that terrible journey. She finished her task and returned to the hospital in peace and great joy, knowing Jesus was with her!

Not many weeks later, Marie contracted cerebral malaria, and she herself died in that same hospital. But we know that the Lord's promise, "I am with you", was true; it remains true for Marie, and for each of us who is His child today.

Direction for today: Remember that the Lord is always with you, and will never leave you.

Prayer for today: "Thank You, Lord, that You are with me in every situation."

July 6: Read Acts 19,20

Key verse: "And when Paul had laid hands on them, the Holy Spirit came upon them, and they spoke with tongues and prophesied" (Acts 19:6 NKJV).

The gift of the Holy Spirit is for all who believe in Jesus Christ. The gifts poured out at Pentecost were not exclusively for the people assembled at that time. On several occasions throughout the book of Acts, we again encounter "personal Pentecosts", as individuals or groups of believers are baptized with the Holy Spirit.

Here, at Ephesus, Paul encountered a group of sincere believers who had not known the full experience available to the Christian. He immediately instructed them, laid hands upon them and prayed for them.

The result? "They spoke with tongues and prophesied."

We should never try to tell God what to do—Jesus is Lord, not you! But we should always allow God to tell us what to do, and He tells us, through His Word, to "be filled with the Spirit" (Ephesians 5:18).

Direction for today: Ask God to fill you with the Spirit and to minister through you.

Prayer for today: "Lord, help me never to place roadblocks in the path of Your Holy Spirit."

July 7: Read Acts 21

Key verse: "I am ready not only to be bound, but also to die at Jerusalem for the name of the Lord Jesus" (Acts 21:13b NKJV).

In the early years of the eighteenth century, a group of men and women caught a vision for something almost unknown in the church of that day—world missions! This Christian community, known as the Moravian Brethren, began to pray ;as they did so, the Lord laid a burden on their hearts to spread the gospel of Jesus around the world.

In those days of slow, precarious travel, before there was adequate medical care or innoculation, dozens of the Moravians headed off into the unknown, taking with them their love for Christ and their burden to preach the gospel.

They went to places as diverse as the West Indies, Greenland, India and the Ivory Coast in Africa. They were the first Protestant missionaries to Canada, working with native people in Labrador (where the first Moravian missionary was murdered) and in southern Ontario.,

Scores of them died. They were struck down by disease and hardship, and a few were killed by those they were trying to reach.

As word of a multitude of deaths came back to their community in Germany, the Moravians did the only thing they could do: they sent out scores more to take their places. Such dedication, loving Jesus and the gospel more than life itself, brought eternal results on almost every continent of our world.

Direction for today: Examine your life to discover all of the things you love more than you love Jesus and the kingdom of God.

Prayer for today: "Lord, I promise to keep You as my first love always."

July 8: Read Acts 22,23

Key verse: "And I persecuted this Way to the death, binding and delivering into prisons both men and women" (Acts 22:4 NKJV).

Paul was a bitter enemy of the church of Jesus Christ. Before his encounter with Jesus on the road to Damascus, this zealot was killing and imprisoning Christians. Right afterward, he was afraid to try to associate himself with Christians for fear they would harm him for his persecution of them.

As we know, that did not happen. Through the welcoming ministry of men such as Ananias and Barnabas, Paul, after many years, became a trusted leader of the church.

God delights to turn enmity into friendship, hostility into love. And, in our world of constant strife, it soon becomes apparent that much of the conflict would end if only the combatants gave their lives to the Lord.

Every once in a while, we see just such a thing happen—a former member of the Ku Klux Klan is embraced by a black brother; Protestant and Catholic in Ireland abandon their struggle in the name of Jesus; black and white in South Africa declare they are brothers in the Lord.

Let us pray for peace in our war-torn world, and allow Jesus to continue to unite enemies in His love.

Direction for today: Blessed are the peacemakers. *Be one.*

Prayer for today: "Lord, bring peace where there is strife through the love of Christ."

July 9: Read Acts 24,25

Key verse: "But after two years Porcius Festus succeeded Felix; and Felix, wanting to do the Jews a favour, left Paul bound" (Acts 24:27 NKJV).

Our timing is not always God's timing.

How long would you have left Paul to languish in prison, being brought out every once in a while to speak with a ruler who gave no indication that he was listening to him?

There were continents which still needed to hear the gospel. Paul had many places that he longed to visit, and thousands of people to win or to nurture in the faith.

But here he was, in jail. How impatient would you have become?

It wasn't that God couldn't get him out—the Lord had already broken Paul out of jail in Philippi and done the same for Peter in the early days of the Jerusalem church. God could certainly have freed his faithful servant to continue the missionary work he had so successfuly begun.

But Paul remained in prison.

We may never know—in this life, anyway—why God chose to do it this way. But we do know that Paul used his various sojourns in prison to write his letters, the letters that now comprise such a significant part of the New Testament. Had he been freed from jail to minister to thousands, he would not have reached the millions who have read Romans or Galatians in the centuries since.

Direction for today: Be content with God's timing.

Prayer for today: "Lord, by Your Spirit, please cause patience to grow in me."

July 10: Read Acts 26

Key verse: "Therefore, King Agrippa, I was not disobedient to the heavenly vision" (Acts 26:19 NKJV).

Not many Christians could stand beside Paul and make that statement. Too many of us have received a "heavenly vision," some kind of direction or guidance from the Lord, and yet have chosen to ignore it.

It may be that, as you read this today, the Lord will remind you of a command He gave you, or a promise you made to Him that has never been carried out.

Paul acted immediately upon the Lord's command, but not all of the followers of Jesus did so. A few days ago, we read about Mark, who failed but eventually returned to serve the Lord. We know that all of the disciples abandoned Jesus the night of His arrest, yet they were restored.

If you have been disobedient to the heavenly vision, you can be restored. The Lord will enable you to accomplish that to which He has called you!

Direction for today: Return, in obedience to the Lord, and allow Him to complete the work to which He has called you.

Prayer for today: "Lord, I want to obey the heavenly vision that You have given to me."

July 11: Read Acts 27

Key verse: *"Indeed God has given you all those who sail with you" (Acts 27:24b NKJV).*

Philip Cameron is a great friend of 100 Huntley Street. He came to us with a deep burden for what he called "Household salvation", and has ministered mightily in this area. As people have begun to pray for their families and to claim them for the Lord, miracles have taken place. We have received reports of entire families accepting Christ as Saviour, and others where, every week, a new family member has come into the kingdom of God.

We praise the Lord for these mighty miracles of the Spirit.

Today's key verse reminds us of these truths. Although each person is ultimately responsible for his or her own decision about Jesus, we can have a great influence on those around us.

In a very real sense, God has granted to you all those who "sail" with you. It is your responsibility to live a Christ-like life before them, to speak to them about Jesus, and to pray for them continually.

As you are faithful in these things, the Lord will move through your prayers and your witness, and wonderful things will happen!

Direction for today: Take spiritual responsibility for those who share in your life.

Prayer for today: "Father, I pray for those who work alongside me and who need to know you. I also pray for those members of my family who are yet unsaved (name each one individually)."

Memory Verse

"And the Spirit and the bride say, 'Come!' And let him who hears say, 'Come!' And let him who thirsts come. And whoever desires, let him take the water of life freely" (Revelation 22:17 NKJV).

July 12: Read Acts 28

Key verse: *"And from there, when the brethren heard about us, they came to meet us as far as Appii Forum and Three Inns. When Paul saw them, he thanked God and took courage" (Acts 28:15 NKJV).*

As believers, we have a vital ministry one to another. The Lord has made us members of a family that is intended to build up, encourage and comfort one another.

In today's reading, Paul was making the long trip from southern Italy to Rome. He was tired, and perhaps even a bit fearful, for he was on his way to his trial before Ceasar.

But, when brothers and sisters from Rome went far out of their way to meet him and to minister to him, he took courage and was able to praise the Lord.

We must remember this today, as well. Too often, our churches are cold places, where we meet with relative strangers once or twice a week. That isn't God's plan; He calls us "brothers and sisters", and expects us to reach out in love, compassion and hospitality to each other.

This week, the Lord can use you to encourage another believer. Ask Him to direct you to a brother or sister who needs a word of comfort or encouragement, and then be ready to minister to that one.

Direction for today: Be sensitive to the needs of brothers and sisters in the Lord.

Prayer for today: "Lord, use me as an encourager."

Deuteronomy

Moses, the man who had met God, the man who was called the "friend of God", is near the end of his life. He has led the people of Israel through extremely important years. He has stood between the people and the Lord, interceding on several occasions, for his rebellious charges.

Now, once again, he takes the mediating position, standing before the people as God's representative, to remind the Israelites of all that God has done for them and all that He will continue to do as they are willing to obey Him.

Because this book is essentially a "reminder" of laws and events already stated in Moses' first four volumes (Genesis through Numbers), this final book of Moses is called the Deutero-Nomos, the second law. This not because it is a new law replacing the old, but a restatement of God's laws and works towards His people.

The heart of the book can be found in chapter six: "Hear, O Israel! The Lord is our God, the Lord is one! And you shall love the Lord your God with all your heart and with all your soul and with all your might. And these words, which I am commanding you today, shall be on your heart: and you shall teach them diligently to your sons" (6:4-7).

Moses was not simply giving a lesson in history or divine legalism. Rather, the great man of God was providing his people with a spiritual textbook, a book that would direct them toward a deeper love for God and would enable them to teach these same truths, grounded in love, to their children.

As we read the final book of Moses, let us ask God to work this same growth in our own hearts.

July 13: Read Deuteronomy 1

Key verse: *"The Lord our God said to us Horeb, 'You have stayed long enough at this mountain' " (Deuteronomy 1:6 RSV).*

Isn't it rather amusing, yet painful, that we like to stay and be confronted by our mountains?

"Oh, but you should see my mountain!"

"My mountain is bigger than yours!"

Stop and think! God has delivered us from Egypt. We are new people in Christ Jesus. My sins are gone. I am a Christian. I'm given the Promised Land, a land flowing with milk and honey! Hallelujah! Thank you, Lord!

"But, Lord there is this mountain."

"What mountain?„

"Lord, are You blind? Can't you see this terrible problem I have?"

"No, but I see the Promised Land. It is a land flowing with milk and honey. The ground is fertile. The fruit is plenteous; the pastures are large and green. My blessing is upon it. I give it to you."

"Lord, what land are You talking about? I can't see past this mountain . . ."

So many of us are like that. But the Lord requires that we put our trust in Him, that we accept His Word and His promises—by faith.

Direction for today: Praise God for His promises.

Prayer for today: "Mountain, in the name of Jesus, be removed and cast into the sea."

July 14: Read Deuteronomy 2

Key verse: *"For the Lord your God has blessed you in all the work of your hand. He knows your trudging through this great wilderness. These forty years the Lord your God has been with you; you have lacked nothing" (Deuteronomy 2:7 NKJV).*

Many Christians are living in defeat. It's sad but nonetheless true. One of the major causes of that sense of defeat is the underlying awareness that, sometime in your past, you have failed God. Perhaps He called you to a specific ministry and you refused. Perhaps there was some other clear instruction of the Lord which you ignored. Furthermore, you know that, because the situation is long past, you cannot recover the opportunity to obey.

This is a root of much defeat among believers.

But notice our key verse: it was spoken by Moses to a nation of people who had failed the Lord. God had sent them into the Promised Land; they had refused to go. God had provided for them in the wilderness; they had grumbled.

And yet, God continued to bless them. He was with them through the wilderness wanderings. He had cared for them and guided them. And He was ready to restore them to victory.

This can also be true for you. You can rise above that defeat, for the Lord is always ready to forgive, restore, and bring you into complete victory. You need not carry your failure with you, for Jesus took it to the cross with Him.

Direction for today: Confess your rebellion and defeat and allow Jesus to bring you into total victory right now!

Prayer for today: "Lord, restore me to Your victory in Jesus."

July 15: Read Deuteronomy 3

Key verse: "Do not be afraid of them; the Lord your God Himself will fight for you" (Deuteronomy 3:22 NIV).

Moses recounts how the children of Israel were a few short weeks from entering the Promised Land. Enroute there, they won a number of battles and the conquered land was divided amongst the tribes of Israel.

He tells how, from the Plains of Moab, he made an impassioned plea to God to be allowed to enter the Promised Land. As we have read of Moses' leadership of this rebellious people; as we have seen his frustrations, and yet his love of the people; as we have read of his prayers to God on behalf of the Israelites, even asking that his own life be taken but that they be spared . . . surely we, too, desire to see him enter the land of promise.

But God is adamant. He rejects Moses' petition and tells him never to speak of it again. He sends him to the top of Mount Pisgah to view the Promised Land from there and then tells Moses to commission Joshua as his successor and to encourage him for the task ahead.

Direction for today: Remember—as God required from Moses absolute obedience, so He requires it of you.

Prayer for today: "Father, help me always to be totally obedient to You, and never to question Your authority."

July 16: Read Deuteronomy 4

Key verse: "What other nation is so great as to have their gods near them the way the Lord our God is near us whenever we pray to him?" (Deuteronomy 4:7 NIV).

God delights in the special relationship that exists between Himself and His children. In our key verse, Moses reflects on the false religions of the nations around them. The god of each of these nations was one of terror and immorality. The people were afraid of their false gods, but there was never a sense of affection or closeness.

Not so with Israel—or with the believer today. God loves us so much that He dwells among us and has established His own guidelines to show us how we should live. As we obey Him, we will live a good, suc-

cessful and peaceful life.

But Israel was instructed to go beyond mere enjoyment of the blessings of their relationship with the Lord. They were to be a light to the nations, a testimony to the joy of relationship with the one true God.

They often failed in that calling, as has the church of Christ. We, too, need to remember that we are called beyond enjoyment to evangelism.

Direction for today: Enjoy the good things of God, and be sure to share them.

Prayer for today: "All praise to the one true God, the Lord and Creator."

July 17: Read Deuteronomy 5,6

Key verse: "And if we are careful to obey all this law before the Lord our God, as He has commanded us, that will be our righteousness" (Deuteronomy 6:25 NIV).

Forty years have passed since the exodus from Egypt. In a few days, Moses is to turn over the reins of leadership to Joshua. Before he does this, he preaches his final sermon. He reminds the people where they came from, refreshes their minds regarding God's laws—which were established for their own good—and pleads that they remain faithful to God.

To be successful in the Christian walk, we must listen to God's Word, learn God's Word, and live God's Word. We must be doers and not hearers only. In the Book of Deuteronomy, the word 'hear' occurs 30 times; 'learn', 7 times; 'keep,' 39 times; and 'do', 100 times.

Moses told the children of Israel that God's laws and covenants were not for their forefathers only, but for them also. They were to make them predominate over every aspect of their lives. Whether they were walking or sleeping, the Word of God was always to be a part of them. And since God's Word does not change, they were to teach it to their children and their children's children for generations to come. It still applies today.

The challenge from Moses is: "To learn them (the laws of God), and be sure to follow them" (5:1 NIV). Only then can we fulfil righteousness and enjoy the fruit of God's promises.

Direction for today: Listen to God's Word. Learn God's Word. Live God's Word.

Prayer for today: "Lord, help me to be careful not to forget Your Word."

July 18: Read Deuteronomy 7,8

Key verse: "Know therefore that the Lord your God is God; He is the faithful God; keeping His covenant of love to a thousand generations of those who love Him and keep His commands" (Deuteronomy 7:9 NIV).

In today's reading, Moses emphasizes the special place of honour held by God's chosen people. God's family is "His treasured possession." In I Peter 2:9 (NIV) we read: "But you are a chosen people, a royal priesthood, a holy nation, a people belonging to God, that you may declare the praises of Him who called you out of darkness into His wonderful light." We are special!

When parents raise children they want to provide for them, to protect and guide them and help them make decisions. But the day comes when they must be sent to school. As they grow older, they venture further from the safety of home. Eventually, they "leave the nest" to live their lives without the help of their parents. Parents can identify with Moses as he sends the Israelites into the Promised Land. He longs to go in with them but God has forbidden him.

Moses told them what to expect when they crossed the Jordan and how to defeat their enemies. He pleaded with them to detest evil and to have no part of the evil in the land. He shared with them the importance of yielding to God's discipline and begged them never to forget the Lord their God but to praise Him to a thousand generations for His goodness and faithfulness.

Direction for today: "Remember the Lord Your God" (Deuteronomy 8:18).

Prayer for today: "I praise You, Lord, for Your goodness to me."

"He is the Rock, His work is perfect; for all His ways are justice, a God of truth and without injustice; righteous and upright is He" (Deuteronomy 32:4 NKJV).

July 19: Read Deuteronomy 9,10

Key verse: *"But be assured today that the Lord your God is the One who goes across ahead of you like a devouring fire. He will destroy them; He will subdue them before you. And you will drive them out and annihilate tham quickly, as the Lord has promised you" (Deuteronomy 9:3 NIV).*

As we read the history of the Israelites, we see a very stiff-necked people. When things went wrong, they turned to God and pleaded for mercy. God answered their prayers and got them out of their troubles in spite of themselves. But, in short order, they forgot the promises they had made to God during their hour of crisis, and began to slip back into their old sinful ways. This made God very angry.

Moses said that God was angry enough to destroy them in the wilderness. It took all of God's mercy and compassion to allow His children to enter the land. In fact, he says it was not because of them, but in spite of them. There were three reasons God took them into the Promised Land: first, because of the wickedness of the other nations; second, because of His promise to their forefathers; third, because Moses pleaded on their behalf for forty days and forty nights.

To win the favour of God, we must fear Him, walk in His ways, love Him, and serve Him with all our hearts. How we live our lives is important to God, and He is to be feared and obeyed.

It is by faith that we New Testament believers win God's favour. He, in turn, asks us for lives fully consecrated to Him. Give Him your all so He can give you His all.

Direction for today: God desires obedience rather than sacrifice.

Prayer for today: "All to Jesus I surrender, all to Him I freely give."

July 20: Read Deuteronomy 11,12

Key verse: *"Therefore thou shalt love the Lord thy God, and keep His charge, and His statutes, and His judgments, and His commandments, always" (Deuteronomy 11:1 KJV).*

The Lord God, as a loving Father who knows what is best for His children, is here preparing Israelites for their entry into the Promised Land.

God knew that the Canaanites who inhabited the land were wicked and idolatrous. He also knew that, if the children of Israel were to live among them, they would be influenced by their sinful lifestyle and, in due time, would turn their hearts away from Him.

God commanded the Israelites to be obedient to Him for their own good and safety. He also had great plans for their blessing, joy and prosperity. However, this obedience was to be based on love, rather than fear of judgment and reprisal at the hand of a vengeful God.

In Psalm 103:13, we understand something of the love of God as we read, "As a father pitieth his children, so the Lord pitieth them that fear (hold in awesome reverence) Him." It is only as we truly love Him that we will keep His commandments.

Direction for today: Plan to walk in obedience to God's Word.

Prayer for today: "Lord, enable me to demonstrate my love to You by my obedience."

July 21: Read Deuteronomy 13,14

Key verse: "Thou shalt not hearken unto the words of that prophet, or that dreamer of dreams: for the Lord your God proveth you, to know whether ye love the Lord your God with all your heart and with all your soul" (Deuteronomy 13:3 KJV).

In these two chapters, the Lord is laying the groundwork for spiritual and physical health. In the thirteenth chapter, God gives instructions to deal very strongly with false prophets or anyone who would try to entice others into a religious cult which would turn them from the truth.

This is as important a message today as it was in the time of Moses. There is never any lack of false teachers and fradulent prophets who will try to deceive others. We frequently hear of individuals or groups who have been led astray, to their own harm or even their destruction.

We can be thankful today that the Lord has not left us alone; He indwells us by His Spirit and ministers to us through His Word and His people. As we are faithful to Him, we can be sure we will not be led into error.

Direction for today: Our spiritual safety lies in our intimate, ongoing relationship with Jesus.

Prayer for today: "Deliver us from evil, for Thine is the kingdom."

July 22: Read Deuteronomy 15,16

Key verse: "Thou shalt remember that thou wast a bondman in the land of Egypt, and the Lord thy God redeemed thee" (Deuteronomy 15:15a KJV).

Here the emphasis is on remembrance and kindness. The Lord expects us to remember the poor of the land, to open our hearts and hands to them, and to help them in their plight.

God says that, for all we do for the poor, He will give us a special blessing.

The reason the Lord wants us to remember the poor is that they are in a type of bondage. In our key verse, we are reminded of our own bondage in the old life of sin, which is typified by Egypt. This remembrance will cause us to be thankful to God for His great mercy. Out of deep love and gratitude, we will want to offer a sacrifice of worship and praise to the Lord. This is typified in the feast of the Passover, which is Israel's reminder of her deliverance from Egypt.

Direction for today: Remember to do good deeds of kindness.

Prayer for today: "Remind me, O Lord, from whence You have brought me."

July 23: Read Deuteronomy 17,18

Key verse: "And it shall be with him, and he shall read therein all the days of his life: that he may learn to fear the Lord his God, to keep all the words of this law and these statutes, to do them" (Deuteronomy 17:19 KJV).

Throughout these two chapters, there is a strong emphasis on the Word and the importance of it in the lives of the Lord's children.

God has made provision for His people to be spiritually alive, healthy, protected, prosperous and blessed in this present world, but these things are not automatic just because we believe in Him.

There are evil forces at work, both in mankind and in the spiritual realm. We must be on guard against these, and God has provided us with His Word so that we can combat them.

In Chapter 18, verses 15, 18 and 19, there is a prophetic reference to the Lord Jesus Christ; in verse 19, God says, "Whosoever will not hearken unto My words which he shall speak in My name, I will require it of him".

The importance of the Word of God is given to us by Jesus when He said, "Man shall not live by bread alone, but by every word that proceedeth out of the mouth of God" (Matthew 4:46 KJV).

Direction for today: Make a continual habit of reading God's Word.

Prayer for today: "Thank you, Father, for Your holy Word."

July 24: Read Deuteronomy 19,20

Key verse: "For the Lord your God is He that goeth with you, to fight for you against your enemies to save you" (Deuteronomy 20:4 KJV).

The Lord is on the side of those who are His; He watches over us at all times. The Lord is against all evil, and there will come a day when He will judge all evil-doers who refuse His salvation.

From time to time, we as believers may feel very much alone. It seems that the evil of the world is so overwhelming and we are so insignificant. But our key verse proclaims that the Lord is with us.

Many times, Israel had to face enemies that were much more powerful and greater in number than she, but God fought for her and she was able to overcome her enemies. Similarly, we who believe in Christ as Saviour and Lord are given assurance that the Lord is on our side and will always be with us.

Paul the Apostle recognized this as he made the statement, "We are more than conquerors through Him that loved us" (Romans 8:37 KJV).

Direction for today: Walk in confidence that victory is your right as a believer in Jesus Christ.

Prayer for today: "Thank You, Lord, for Your abiding presence and the assurance of victory."

July 25: Read Deuteronomy 21,22

Key verse: *"If a man has committed a sin worthy of death, and he is put to death, and you hang him on a tree . . . he who is hanged is accursed of God" (Deuteronomy 21:22,23 NKJV).*

I imagine that Moses spoke these words soberly and carefully, for he was dealing with a sombre subject. But can you imagine the heart of God as He gave these laws to Moses? While Moses was thinking of the people of his day, God was undoubtedly looking to the day when His Son would hang, accursed, on a tree.

Jesus was executed in the worst possible way. Not only did He have to bear the tortures inflicted by man and the humiliation of hanging, naked, from a cross; He also carried the stigma of being "accursed", for his countrymen knew well that every man who is hanged on a tree is accursed of God.

And He was accursed, for on Him was placed all of the sin of the world. Your sin and mine made Him accursed. The One who is more beautiful than anything in His creation became the most despised, laden with sin and sweating blood.

Jesus carried my curse and yours, and hung from a tree. Moses may not have been aware of it, but he was pointing to that most terrible, and greatest, of days when he spoke these verses to the people of Israel.

Direction for today: Live in the awareness that Jesus carried your curse.

Prayer for today: "All praise and thanksgiving to the One who bore my curse, that I might be delivered from my sin."

Memory Verse

"For God did not send His Son into the world to condemn the world, but that the world through Him might be saved" (John 3:17 NKJV).

July 26: Read Deuteronomy 23,24

Key verse: "And thou shalt remember that thou wast a bondman in the land of Egypt" (Deuteronomy 23:24a).

"Remember" is a good word.

In the context of the key verse, the Lord was talking to the Israelites and asking them to remember their own bondage in Egypt. He instructed them to be kind and generous to those among them who were poor and needy. As they remembered their own plight, they would become more responsive to the needs of others.

Similarly, we, too, need to be moved by those who don't have as much as we do. We need to remember that, before we became children of God and of the light, we were children of darkness. We need to remember that great love of God that moved us from one kingdom to another. We need to remember that it is the Lord who supplies our every need and that without His mercy we would not be where we are.

This would be a good day to remember what the Lord has done for us.

Direction for today: Remember what the Lord has done for you, and be thankful.

Prayer for today: "Lord, thank You for all You've done for me. Help me now to reach out to others with Your love."

July 27: Read Deuteronomy 25,26

Key verse: "And now, behold, I have brought the firstfruits of the land which You, O Lord, have given me" (Deuteronomy 26:10a NKJV).

Giving to the Lord is such a precious privilege.

Giving allows us to acknowledge that God is the One from whom we receive everything. I am often amazed at the ungratefulness of people. To eat in a restaurant provides a real education in ungratefulness. People receive their food and, from all appearances, begin to "dig in" without a pause to give thanks for what has been set before them. From time to time, this is true even of Christians. How sad!

Giving makes me turn my attention to God, who made my giving possible. If He hadn't given, I would not be able to give.

Giving also allows me to tell God that I trust Him for all I need. I could hoard all I have and be greedy but, when I give, I show God that I trust Him to provide all my needs—even needs which could have been met with what I gave to Him.

Direction for today: I will let God know I am grateful.

Prayer for today: "Father, thank You for all You mean to me, for all You have provided for me. Most of all, thank You for my salvation through Your Son Jesus."

142

July 28: Read Deuteronomy 27

Key verse: "Cursed is the one who does not confirm all the words of this law! And all the people shall say, Amen!" (Deuteronomy 27:26 NKJV).

"Do not think that I have come to destroy the Law or the Prophets. I have not come to destroy but to fulfil. For assuredly, I say to you, till heaven and earth pass away, one jot or one tittle will by no means pass from the law till all is fulfiled. Whoever therefore breaks one of the least of these commandments, and teaches men so, he will be called least in the kingdom of heaven; but whoever does and teaches them will be called great in the kingdom of heaven" (Matthew 5:17-19 NKJV).

Most of the curses recorded in Deuteronomy 27 are ignored today. People in our "enlightened" society see the commands of God as irrelevant and totally unnecessary. Why should there be any restrictions on anyone if he doesn't want restrictions? Today's generation says, "If it feels good, do it!"

You will notice in this list that most have to do with interpersonal relationships. In any society, there must be laws for harmonious living. Without laws to provide safety for all, there is chaos.

Jesus' words in the Sermon on the Mount provide us with all the incentive we need to live by His laws and to avoid His curse. His laws were not made just to give man restrictions but, rather, to steer us clear of pitfalls to a good life. Those who have children know only too well their responses to parental rules: "Why do I have to go to bed so early?"; "Why can't I go to that movie? All the other kids have seen it." Why? What for? Why not? One day, our teenagers will understand our rules, but it may take some time before they understand it was for their good that we had such restrictions.

God has His rules too, and He expects us to obey them. Are you doing all that He requires of you? Are you staying away from those things and those habits which His Word declares to be wrong?

Direction for today: Obey the Lord in all things.

Prayer for today: "Father, help me never to question the wisdom of some of Your laws but, rather, to obey them."

July 29: Read Deuteronomy 28

Key verse: "And all these blessings shall come on thee, and overtake thee, if thou shalt hearken unto the voice of the Lord thy God" (Deuteronomy 28:2 KJV).

It's interesting to read this chapter of blessings and curses and to note that, of the sixty-eight verses, only the first fourteen have to do with blessings. The rest of the verses deal with curses.

The issue is one of obedience to the Lord. The Lord says through Moses that, if the people obey, they will be blessed; if they choose to disobey, then curses will follow.

This is the principle of sowing and reaping. Paul, inspired by the Holy Spirit, writes in Galatians 6:7, "Be not deceived; God is not mocked: for whatsoever a man soweth, that shall he also reap."

Somehow, we like to think that our actions do not have consequences. To think that is to believe a lie of the enemy. We can take something as simple as our weight. If we overeat, there will be consequences. This may mean nothing more than an upset stomach. If done often enough, however, overeating causes gain in weight.

Every action has a consequence.

That's what the Lord wants us to know. He wants us to walk in obedience so that the consequence will be blessing. By giving us restrictions, God desires to free us to live in the blessings. He has provided for those who love Him and, therefore, obey Him.

Direction for today: Walk in obedience so that you may walk in blessing.

Prayer for today: "Teach me, O Lord, to be aware of my actions and to know there are consequences. Give me the ability to be obedient."

July 30: Read Deuteronomy 29,30

Key verse: "Love the Lord your God, obey Him and be faithful to Him, and then you and your descendants will live long in the land that He promised" (Deuteronomy 29:20 TEV).

At Mount Sinai, the children of Israel had learned that communion with God is a gift. Now, in the land of Moab, just before entering the land of Canaan, Moses gave them another promise: they would receive prosperity when they responded to the call of God.

Note that Moses taught that blessing would come from God in response to their faith and obedience. In both of these chapters, these things are clearly spelled out, starting with a history lesson on the exodus. This would encourage them to believe God and trust Him. They apparently did not yet have the capacity to understand this, and so were given more explicit guidelines: "Therefore keep the words of this covenant, and do them, that you may prosper in all that you do" (29:9 NKJV). Four times in these two chapters, Moses emphasizes this to stress the importance of choosing wisely.

Obedient response to the revealed will of God brings blessing. Walking with the Lord brings constant guidance by His Holy Spirit and, as we follow Him, we can expect His continuous blessing.

Direction for today: Be faithful to the Lord with all of your heart and He will bless you.

Prayer for today: "Father, I turn to You with all of my heart in love and obedience. Thank You for Your promise of mercy and blessing."

July 31: Read Deuteronomy 31

Key verse: *"Be strong and of good courage: for you shall bring the children of Israel into the land of which I swore to them: and I will be with you" (Deuteronomy 31:23b NKJV).*

We often hear those words: "Be brave." Parents say it to their children as they walk into the doctor's office. Dentists say it to parents as *they* sit down in the chair!

These words are spoken on battlefields and sports fields; before exams and concert performances; in thunderstorms and in the dark.

The problem is, the person saying "be brave" often cannot give any real reason to support that admonition. The doctor's treatment may hurt; the football team may lose; the soldier may die.

But, when God says "be brave", He backs up His admonition with the greatest promise ever made: "I will be with you."

What more could anyone ask? Is there any circumstance you might face where that promise would not be sufficient?

Of course not; it is the perfect answer to any problem, test, temptation or trial that might come our way.

"I will be with you."

We could desire nothing else.

Direction for today: God is always with His people.

Prayer for today: "Father, may I always, and in every situation, be conscious of Your presence."

8

Coming Soon

They are building up the Kingdom
For the coming of the Lord.
They are telling out the gospel
As recorded in God's Word.
It's the good news of salvation;
In your heart for Him make room,
Listen to the Gospel message,
Christ is coming — coming soon!

They are working in God's vineyard
Every hour of every day.
They are building up the kingdom,
And preparing now the way.
As the Holy Spirit bids you,
In your heart for Him make room.
Hear the simple gospel message,
Christ is coming, coming soon.

They are toiling by the wayside,
They are working in the field,
For the precious grains of wheat
That the harvest soon will yield.
They are giving time and talent
'Ere the reapers will descend,
And the tares in bundles gather,
And the wheat be garnered in.

— Rebecca Hoffner

August 1: Read Deuteronomy 32

Key verse: "Set your hearts unto all the words which I testify among you this day, which ye shall command your children to observe to do, all the words of this law" (Deuteronomy 32:46 KJV).

Moses had been with the children of Israel for forty years, and they had heard him many times. While he had often instructed and guided them, he realized the importance of this: his final message. This is what he told them: taking up the things of the Lord is a matter of life and death—we come to God or we do not; we walk with God or we do not. No decision is more important.

Moses was prepared to leave this world. He had spent a lifetime serving the Lord, and had served well. As his life was coming to a close, he prepared to enter God's presence. To the people, he emphasized, "Set your hearts on what I have said today and stress them to your children". Nothing was more important than their decision to obey God. Things in this world come to an end, but the things of God are eternal.

Direction for today: Live your life in the light of eternity.

Prayer for today: "Father, help me to measure each part of my life and to be aware of its eternal impact."

Memory Verse

"For as the earth brings forth its bud, as the garden causes the things that are sown in it to spring forth, so the Lord God will cause righteousness and praise to spring forth before all the nations" (Isaiah 61:11 NKJV).

August 2: Read Deuteronomy 33

Key verse: "God has always been your defense; His eternal arms are your support" (Deuteronomy 33:27 TEV).

Moses blessed the people of Israel when he came to the end of his days. This was a very natural thing for him to do, as they had constantly been in his prayers for forty years. This chapter begins with praise to God, and then follow one statement after another of blessing upon all of the tribes, except that of Simeon (see Genesis 49).

As He came to the end of his days, Moses blessed the people of Israel whom he had led for forty years. In this chapter, we read of the blessing he gave each of the tribes—but none was given to that of Simeon. In Genesis 49, we read of the blessings Israel gave to his sons and note that he had only rebuke, not blessing, for Simeon and Levi.

In the closing verses, Moses reveals one of the most wonderful promises of assurance in the Bible: "The eternal God is thy refuge, and underneath are the everlasting arms" (verse 27). God is a shelter in the time of storm. Believers do not have to run for safety because His eternal arms are their support.

Verses 28 and 29 picture a people who, having been threatened by enemies, have turned to the Lord and found that they are now a "people saved by the Lord." The "shield of help" is for protection, and the "sword of excellency" is a weapon for attack.

We are beset on every side by persons and events that shake our confidence. But these are enemies over which we have already victory in the Lord Jesus Christ.

Because the eternal God is our refuge, and underneath are His everlasting arms, we can be saved and victorious all the time.

Direction for today: Remember, God will grant the necessary strength this day requires. Trust Him for it!

Prayer for today: "Father, how reassuring it is to know that Your strength is made perfect in our weakness."

August 3: Read Deuteronomy 34

Key verse: "There has never been a prophet in Israel like Moses; the Lord spoke with him face to face" (Deuteronomy 34:10 TEV).

Moses shared his own spirit and his personal blessing with Joshua. Joshua would now lead Israel. Moses was glad to relinquisah unselfishly the leadership so that the people could continue to be blessed by Joshua.

Moses was great because he knew and obeyed God. Because he knew God, he received guidance and encouragement. But notice what the Scripture says: "the Lord knew him." The word "knew" connotes the idea of accepting, respecting and sharing with. We are not told of Moses' human abilities, but we do see him as a faithful "servant of the Lord" (verse 5). He was the leader of the people, but the servant of the Lord. He lived all his life as unto God.

Direction for today: Encourage a leader who has been a particular blessing to you by expressing your appreciation.

Prayer for today: "Lord thank You for the godly leadership you have ordained in our midst. May my life be an encouragement to them."

Romans

The book of Romans holds a primary place in several ways—it is the first of Paul's letters as they are included in the New Testament, and it is also first in the hearts of a great many Christians, from those who have found the Lord by following the "Roman Road" plan of salvation to learned theologians who are always enthralled by the writing and doctrine of Paul.

It is believed that Paul wrote to the Romans while in Corinth, in A.D. 56. during his third missionary journey. It was not the first of his letters to be written but is placed first because of its length and doctrinal importance.

In this book, you will encounter many of Paul's key teachings. The Holy Spirit inspired him to write about themes ranging from the depravity of man to the wonder of God's grace; from the horrow of rebellion to the glory of obedience; from the failure of our own attempts at righteousness to the victory that is ours in the Spirit.

This is a letter to be read with heart and mind; allow the Lord to speak to your intellect but be sure to read with a heart open to conviction and to great opportunities for joy.

August 4: Read Romans 1,2

Key verse: "The wrath of God is being revealed from heaven against all the godlessness and wickedness of men who suppress the truth by their wickedness" (Romans 1:18 NIV).

The first chapter of Romans is a powerful condemnation of wickedness. Paul speaks out very strongly against those who willfully practice evil.

The message seems to be directed especially against those who know the truth about God and their own sin, but who continue in disobedience. Against such, the wrath of the Lord will be outpoured.

In our world, the most wicked nations may not be those who know little or nothing about the gospel of Jesus Christ. Instead, unbounded evil can be found right here in North America, where almost everyone has some knowledge of the Word of God.

Let us pray that God's wrath will be withheld, that others may have the opportunity to find the truth of Jesus. And let us do all we can to stand against wickedness in our land and to bring others into the kingdom of God before the righteous judgment of the Lord falls.

Direction for today: Work, for the time is short.

Prayer for today: "Lord, in Your mercy, may many more of our neighbours be brought into Your kingdom."

August 5: Read Romans 3

Key verse: "For all have sinned and fall short of the glory of God" (Romans 3:23 NIV).

For many years, I have had a friend who is a really wonderful person. He's not a Christian, but he is kind, generous and humble—many things that a lot of Christians could not even claim to be. And because his sins seem to be so small, he sees no reason to be saved!

But the truth is, all have sinned. It doesn't take a great big sin to cut us off from God; sin, *any* sin, is so evil in His sight that we instantly fall under the penalty of death.

This is because all sin is the same: conscious rebellion against God. The *form* of rebellion is not what matters; the spirit of rebellion dooms us to godless eternity.

So, whoever you are, your sins be they little or huge have cut you off from eternal life. I am so grateful that Paul continued: "and are justified freely by His grace through the redemption that came by Christ Jesus" (verse 24).

Direction for today: Remember, it is not the magnitude of sin, but the *fact* of sin, that condemns us.

Prayer for today: "Thank You, Lord, that You have given the gift of forgiveness and eternal life."

August 6: Read Romans 4

Key verse: "He did not waver at the promise of God through unbelief, but was strengthened in faith, giving glory to God, and being fully convinced that what He had promised He was also able to perform" (Romans 4:20,21 NKJV).

Someone has defined faith as "believing that God tells the truth." Abraham had that kind of faith—no matter how impossible God's promises seemed to be, Abraham knew the Lord would do what He said He would do. When God promised a child, though Abraham and Sarah were too old to bear children, Abraham believed. When God told him that his descendants would be as countless as the stars, Abraham believed. When God told him his children would live in a wonderful promised land, Abraham again believed.

Abraham's faith was stronger than the physical evidence of his own age and that of Sarah. Later, his faith was stronger than the confusion and fear he must have felt when God told him to sacrifice Isaac.

That is real faith. And that faith was not based in Abraham; it was founded in God, whom Abraham knew to be faithful.

Celebrate God's faithfulness today. He has promised to save you; He will. He has promised to give you the gift of His Spirit; He will. He has promised eternal life, starting now; it's yours for the believing.

Direction for today: Believe God.

Prayer for today: "Praise You, Lord, that You are always faithful!"

August 7: Read Romans 5,6

Key verse: "For he who has died has been freed from sin" (Romans 6:7 NKJV).

Everyone has sinned. Our key verse two days ago made that very plain, as Paul wrote, "all have sinned" (Romans 3:23).

In addition, everyone has been trapped in sin. Not only do we choose sin, we are also born into an environment and with a nature that make sin inevitable.

But Jesus has set us free! Not only has He freed us from the penalties of sin, He has also released us from the necessity of sin. Those who have been born again are set free from that bondage and given the potential to live as obedient children of God.

That makes sin a very serious thing for the believer because, when we sin, we have probably consciously chosen to do so. All the excuses and rationalization cannot alter the fact that we have knowingly offended God.

Direction for today: The Christian is freed from the necessity to sin. Walk in that freedom. Do not become encumbered with sin.

Prayer for today: "Thank you, Lord, for this wonderful freedom You granted me."

August 8: Read Romans 7

Key verse: "O wretched man that I am! Who will deliver me from this body of death? I thank God—through Jesus Christ our Lord" (Romans 7:24,25a NKJV).

We should thank God that chapter seven is included in the book of Romans. As we read yesterday, Paul has shown us how we are meant to be completely free from sin, delivered from bondage.

Yet, while we rejoice in that potential, we know that sin continues to lure us and, sometimes, to defeat us. We know the sense that our very being—our mind, our will, our emotions and our senses—is at war within itself.

Paul understood that feeling. He knew what it was to intend to do good, but to be drawn toward sin. He knew the inner battle between serving Christ and gratifying oneself.

He had even reached the realization that there was nothing, absolutely nothing, that he could do to win these battles himself. Thus, he cried out, in the words of our key verse: "Who will deliver me?"

Praise God, the answer to the cry that has echoed in each of our hearts is Jesus Christ our Lord. Whenever the battle is too difficult, our Deliverer is right there. Whenever temptation looms, Jesus is at your side. Victory is assured, when we call upon Him with all our hearts.

Direction for today: Remember that Jesus is your Deliverer.

Prayer for today: "Lord, whenever sin beckons, draw me to Your side and protect me."

Memory Verse

"Do not fear, little flock, for it is your Father's good pleasure to give you the kingdom" (Luke 12:32 NKJV).

August 9: Read Romans 8

Key verse: "For I am persuaded that neither death nor life, nor angels nor principalities nor powers, nor things present nor things to come, nor height nor depth, nor any other created thing, shall be able to separate us from the love of God which is in Christ Jesus our Lord" (Romans 8:38,39 NKJV).

What are you worried about? Which fears haunt you? Which anxieties rise up to make your life miserable?

Most of us worry. Most of us are anxious. Most of us have fears. And, when we do, most of us are wrong!

These verses, like many other promises in the Bible, offer the perfect answer to worry, anxiety or fear. They tell us that, no matter what happens, we can depend on the Lord and on His presence. Nothing can separate us from the Lord.

Many people fear death. The Lord assures us that death will not cut us off from Him or His love. Some Christians are afraid of the devil or His legions. These verses promise that these things will never have the power to do us eternal harm.

Many people worry about the future. However, Paul says that nothing which will come can separate us from the Lord. No created thing—and all things are created except the Lord Himself—can cut us off from God.

If we remain faithful, we will abide in the love of God. That leaves no room for fear or worry or anxiety.

Direction for today: Christians have no cause for fear or anxiety.

Prayer for today: "Lord, take my fears and my worries and replace them with Your love."

August 10: Read Romans 9,10

Key verse: "If you confess with your mouth the Lord Jesus and believe in your heart that God has raised Him from the dead, you will be saved" (Romans 10:9 NKJV).

It was a family in which everyone had gone their own way, and all had made the wrong choice. Finally, the single mother found Jesus Christ, and God worked great miracles in her life. She was full of joy and praise to the Lord, and urged her sons to commit their lives to Him as well.

For a while they would not listen. But, one day, one of the sons, who knew he was heading for serious trouble, prayed and asked Jesus to be his Saviour.

To his surprise—especially after having seen the very evident joy in his mother's life—nothing significant seemed to happen. He sensed no new joy; in fact, he sensed nothing new at all.

He continued in this way for several days, until the moment when his mother once again asked him if he would give his life to Jesus.

"Mom, I already did . . . ", he began to say and, even as the words came out of his mouth, he was filled with joy and happiness. He practically exploded with the spiritual excitement that suddenly welled up inside him.

As the apostle Paul wrote, believing is vital to salvation, but God also calls us to open, verbal confession of Jesus as Lord.

Direction for today: Speak about your love for Jesus.

Prayer for today: "Lord, give me boldness and opportunity to confess You openly."

August 11: Read Romans 11

Key verse: "Oh, the depth of the riches both of the wisdom and knowledge of God! How unsearchable are His judgments and His ways past finding out" (Romans 11:33 NKJV).

Theologians talk about three very special attributes of God: His omnipresence, omnipotence and omniscience. In normal language, omnipresence means being everywhere at all times; omnipotence means all-powerful; and omniscience means all-knowing and all-wise.

These attributes of God mean that we are never going to be able to understand Him. He knows all; we know only a little. He is everywhere, seeing everything; we have an extremely limited perspective. He is all-powerful; we are weak in every sense—physically, emotionally and spiritually.

Perhaps you have already encountered in the Book of Romans many things which you do not understand. Paul hit those same kinds of blocks; that is why he pauses here to celebrate the omniscience of God. Paul knew it would be foolhardy to try to grasp the totality of God and His plan—He is simply too big, too wise, too . . . well, God is both infinite and eternal.

That's why it is all right sometimes to lack understanding when we read the Scriptures. That's why we will never know all things. Instead, we rely on our all-powerful, always-present, all-knowing God to teach us the things we need to know.

Direction for today: Seek the special lesson God has for you, and be sure to learn it well.

Prayer for today: "Thank You, all-wise Father, for teaching me by Your Spirit."

August 12: Read Romans 12

Key verse: "Do not be overcome by evil, but overcome evil with good" (Romans 12:21 NKJV).

Phillip Cameron, the teacher and proponent of "Household Salvation" who has frequently appeared on 100 Huntley Street, tells of a vision from the Lord. Cameron saw all of his loved ones in a meadow. They were happily living their lives, and even serving the Lord. But in the corner of the field, hiding and laughing fiendishly, was Satan.

This is a starkly true picture of the life many Christians lead. We are born-again believers, but have not taken our place in the spiritual battle against the evil one.

Unfortunately, even if we do not fight, he does; and, if we do not properly and spiritually resist him, the devil may score many victories against us and our loved ones.

Cameron relates that the Lord showed him Satan could be driven completely from his field. The same message lies at the heart of much of the teaching in the letters of Paul.

Here, we are told there are two options: to be overcome by evil or to overcome evil with good. But make no mistake—there is no third, passive choice. Either the devil is in your field or he has been driven out. Either God is winning, through you, or the enemy is chalking up victories.

A true believer is a true battler, fighting the spiritual war, eagerly seeking to overcome evil with good.

Direction for today: Allow the goodness and power of Christ to flow through you, that you may defeat the enemy.

Prayer for today: "Deliver me from evil, for Thine is the kingdom."

August 13: Read Romans 13

Key verse: "Owe no one anything except to love one another, for he who loves another has fulfilled the law" (Romans 13:8 NKJV).

Have you ever realized that love is a debt you owe? So often, we treat love as an option, a choice we can make. If we are feeling spiritual, we choose to love others; if we are not feeling very well that day, we don't bother.

But, in our key verse, we read that we are debtors; we are required to love.

If we owe money to a bank, the manager will not allow us to pay it back if and when we feel like it. If we borrow a book from the library, it is not ours. We must return it. A debt is something that requires specific repayment.

We owe a debt of love. We owe it to God, of course, but also to our fellow believers and to the non-Christians whom the Lord brings to us.

We honour God when we consistently pay this debt by acting in love toward those around us. We honour God as we share the good news of Jesus, the ultimate love-gift. But we dishonour God when we refuse to pay this very real debt.

Direction for today: "Walk in love, as Christ also has loved us" (Ephesians 5:2a).

Prayer for today: "Lord, remind me of my debt of love; help me to follow the example of Jesus in the power of the Holy Spirit."

August 14: Read Romans 14

Key verse: "For the kingdom of God is not food and drink, but right-eousness and peace and joy in the Holy Spirit" (Romans 14:17 NKJV).

What is the greatest enemy of the joy of the Christian? It might be Satan; it might be spiritual laziness on the part of the believer. But, for a great many Christians, their freedom, peace and joy has been withered away by legalism.

So often, Christians start their spiritual lives in joy and spiritual excitement, but quickly begin to adhere to a set of rules and traditions that rob them of the freedom they knew at the beginning of their walk. Paul deals with the issue in several of his letters, notably Galatians. Here in Romans, he raises the same issue and warns the believers against being bound up in rules about appropriate food and drink.

Too often, such mundane things bog us down and we are trapped in a legalistic swamp. Many Christians need to be set free from such legalism in order to walk in the Spirit. Notice that both the legalist and the one walking in freedom seek to live a righteous life. Freedom is not licence to sin.

But, while the legalist may strive for righteousness, he or she will never achieve it; all our efforts are filthy rags. Instead, holy living is a result of the Holy Spirit's presence within, not from an outward religious observance.

Direction for today: Walk in freedom, in the Spirit.

Prayer for today: "Lord, free me from dead legalism and grant me peace, joy and righteousness."

August 15: Read Romans 15

Key verse: "Now I beg you, brethren, through the Lord Jesus Christ, and through the love of the Spirit, that you strive together with me in your prayers to God for me" (Romans 15:30 NKJV).

Some years ago, a popular Christian song suggested that God doesn't want any "Lone Ranger" Christians. No matter how talented or gifted a Christian may be, it is not the Lord's will that he or she stand alone in ministry.

Instead, every believer from the most public figure to the least noticed brother or sister is part of the body of Christ. We all need one another.

One of the most vital methods of support for those on the front lines of ministry is prayer. In our key verse, Paul pleads with his friends to pray untiringly for him and for the Lord's ministry through him. He urges them to "strive" in prayer.

This principle stands today. Our leaders today need our fervent, continual prayers as much as Paul did. I urge you to pray for your pastor today. Take more than a few seconds; instead, truly bring your leader and his or her needs to God.

As well, pray for the leaders of Christian ministries which you value,

and please include prayers for the leadership and all the team at 100 Huntley Street. Make this a special day of intercession, and continue in this pattern in the days ahead.

Direction for today: Pray for all those Christian leaders who have touched your own life in any way. Ask God to keep them from harm and from error. Ask Him to bless their ministry and their families.

Prayer for today: "Lord, please bless and protect my pastor and other Christian leaders, including, (name each one)."

Memory Verse

"Therefore, whether you eat or drink, or whatever you do, do all to the glory of God" (I Corinthians 10:31 NKJV).

August 16: Read Romans 16

Key verse: "Greet Mary, who laboured much for us" (Romans 16:6 NKJV).

This chapter can be a tremendous encouragement to all of us who work in the church, especially to those who work behind the scenes and receive little attention—particularly women! In Romans 16, Paul commends friends and fellow workers, many of whom were not people in primary positions of leadership. Every job in the work of the Lord is important!

He commends Phoebe, a woman who was a key servant of the church, one of the people entrusted with service to the needy among the congregation. He greets his old friends Priscilla and Aquila, a husband-and-wife team who did much to build the kingdom of God, working alongside Paul.

He greets Mary, identifying her only as someone who worked for himself and his friends, enabling them to minister. Many others are named as vital co-workers who aided Paul in the work of the Lord; several of those particular co-labourers were women: Junia, Tryphena, Tryphosa and Julia.

God has just the right place for each one of us in His church. As we faithfully serve Him, our work will form a key part in the spread of the gospel and the salvation of souls, whether we preach like Paul, serve like Phoebe or, like Mary, "help" in some less-noticed way.

Direction for today: The Lord has specific, important work for you to do. Ask Him to show you what it is.

Prayer for today: "Father, show me my place in Your church; I know You have a special task for me to do, and I thank You for counting me worthy to be used."

Joshua

This sixth book of the Bible is a vitally important completion to the five books of Moses. Without the conquest and settlement of the Promised Land recorded in this book, the history that began back in Genesis would not have been completed as the Lord had promised.

Joshua and the Israelites claimed a promise given to Abraham, as recounted in Genesis 12:7: "Now the Lord appeared to Abram and said, 'To your descendants I will give this land.'"

The book is named for the valiant successor to Moses, Joshua, whose name literally means "The Lord is salvation". God had indeed saved His people, and this book demonstrates the practical outworking of this salvation as He led His people into their new homeland.

It is important to understand that God did not simply displace or kill innocent people to provide a homeland for His people. At the same time that God was fulfilling His promises to Israel, He was judging the inhabitants of Canaan for terrible occult and immoral practices. "Whoever does these things is detestable to the Lord; and because of these detestable things the Lord your God will drive them out before you" (Deuteronomy 18:12).

Joshua is an account of the conquering of the land under the leadership of Joshua, guided the aided by God, and of the settlement of the Promised Land. It is a testament to the faithfulness of the Lord.

August 17: Read Joshua 1,2

Key verse: "This book of the Law shall not depart from your mouth, but you shall meditate in it day and night, that you may observe to do according to all that is written in it. For then you will make your way prosperous, and then you will have good success" (Joshua 1:8 NKJV).

Do you ever wonder why you bother to pick up the Bible and this Bible Reading Guide every day? Has this exercise become more of a habit than anything else? Do you read through quickly to get it over with, and then feel good about having done your duty?

If any of these things are true, you have been attacked by the enemy. If he cannot stop you from reading the Word of God, then he will try to drain the power, the excitement and spiritual victory from the act of reading the Word of God.

But God has much bigger things in mind. He told Joshua that if he read the Word, spoke the Word, meditated on it and obeyed it, he would find success in everything the Lord gave him to do. The same is true today for each of us—that includes you.

Perhaps you haven't seen much success lately. Maybe your marriage or your family is crumbling; perhaps your ministry is becoming feeble; it may be that your own spiritual life is in the dumps.

You hold in your hand the answer. Don't read the Word because you think you should; read it because it is the key to spiritual prosperity, to victory and to triumph in whatever situation you now find yourself.

Direction for today: Read the Word; speak the Word; meditate on the Word; obey the Word.

Prayer for today: "Lord, may I know the peace and the power that come through Your Word."

August 18: Read Joshua 3,4

Key verse: "And those twelve stones which they took out of the Jordan, Joshua set up in Gilgal" (Joshua 4:20 NKJV).

Throughout the Old Testament, we see God's people setting up stones or enacting rituals to remind them of the good things God had done for them. The feasts of Israel were all reminders of God's great provision. And here, Joshua is establishing another reminder. Each time children saw the pile of stones, their parents were to tell them of the Lord's deliverance.

We need reminders as well. Because we forget so easily, we need to be reminded of the great things God has done for us.

How often have you been depressed, having forgotten that God's wonderful hand is on your life? How often have you been sick, forgetting that the Lord has healed in the past and is able to heal *you*? How often have you been short of money, forgetting that the Lord provided in the past and is able to do so again?

We continually need to remind ourselves of the great things the Lord has done for us because this is a good foundation for faith.

Take time today to build a pile of memory stones; reflect on the good things God has done for you: miracles, healings, provision, salvation for you, your family and friends. Perhaps you will want to write down a list of God's work in and through you and tuck it into your Bible as your own personal pile of memory stones.

Direction for today: Never forget the great things God has done in your life.

Prayer for today: "Thank You, Lord, for working in my life and in my circumstances; thanks for being the same today as You ever were."

August 19: Read Joshua 5,6

Key verse: "Then the Lord said to Joshua, 'See, I have delivered Jericho into your hands, along with its king and its fighting men' " (Joshua 6:2 NIV).

The writer to the Hebrews describes faith as "being sure of what we hope for and certain of what we do not see" (Hebrews 11:1 NIV). The fall of Jericho is a story of faith.

The instructions of God to Joshua for the deliverance of Jericho into Israel's hands would, in human terms, seem foolish. Yet, when the Israelites obeyed in faith, without using force, the walls of Jericho fell down. Not even the strongest and highest walls can withstand God's almighty power.

We can have faith in the absolute certainty of Christ's return when our "Lord Himself will come down from heaven, with a loud command, with the voice of the archangel and with the trumpet call of God" (I Thessalonians 4:16), and all opposing powers will be defeated.

Direction for today: Trust in the Lord always.

Prayer for today: "Father, thank You for Your Word which cannot lie."

August 20: Read Joshua 7

Key verse: "Israel has sinned; they have violated my covenant, which I commanded them to keep. They have taken some of the devoted things; they have stolen, they have lied, they have put them with their own possessions" (Joshua 7:11 NIV).

Israel's incredible victory at Jericho, of which we read yesterday, illustrates the importance of following God's instructions down to the smallest detail, no matter how trivial it may seem. This lesson is painfully reinforced at Ai, where the disobedience of one person leads to defeat and death.

The gold and silver pieces taken by Achan (7:21) were worth only a few thousand dollars. In exchange, they cost the lives of 36 soldiers, a humiliating defeat for the nation, and death by stoning for Achan and his entire family.

Although only one person sinned, the children of Israel are said to have violated the covenant because one of their body did so. Achan's sin brought guilt upon the whole nation, of which he was a member. This should be a warning to us to be careful not to sin so that others are not affected. Also, we need to watch over one another in love to keep each other from falling into sin.

Direction for today: "See to it that no one misses the grace of God and that no bitter root grows up to cause trouble and defile many" (Hebrews 12:15).

Prayer for today: "Teach us, Lord, that obedience brings victory and disobedience brings defeat."

August 21: Read Joshua 8

Key verse: "Then the Lord said to Joshua, 'Do not be afraid; do not be discouraged. Take the whole army with you, and go up and attack Ai. For I have delivered into your hands the king of Ai, his people, his city and his land' " (Joshua 8:1 NIV).

It would be understandable if Joshua were a little hesitant about pushing forward against Ai, in case there was another Achan in the camp. But, after disciplining His people, God patiently encourages them and leads them to victory in the rematch against Ai. He tells Joshua not to be afraid or discouraged because the same power that keeps Israel from being ruined by their enemies will keep them from ruining themselves.

When we faithfully put away sin, we can expect to hear from God. He comforts, directs and encourages us to go forward, not in our own strength, but in His.

Direction for today: Like your heavenly Father, offer encouragement to someone.

Prayer for today: "Thank You, Father, for the comfort and encouragement of Your Word."

August 22: Read Joshua 9

Key verse: "The men of Israel sampled their provisions but did not inquire of the Lord" (Joshua 9:14 NIV).

Just as the Lord commended the unjust steward because he had acted wisely for himself (Luke 16:8), we have to commend the prudence of the Gibeonites in arranging a peace treaty with the children of Israel.

On the other hand, the leaders of Israel acted unwisely in making a decision without consulting God. Their decision was based on false appearances and deceiving words. In the years ahead, this foolish pact with Gibeon would be a source of heartache to Israel.

How about you? Are you making decisions without consulting God? Have you decided that you can handle things on your own, and that there's no need to bother God about trivialities?

Talk to Him first. God delights in directing those who acknowledge Him. Avoid the consequences of acting without first receiving His direction.

Direction for today: "Trust in the Lord with all your heart and lean not on your own understanding; in all your ways acknowledge Him and He will make your paths straight" (Proverbs 3:5,6).

Prayer for today: "Help me, Lord, to be completely dependent on You in all things and at all times."

Memory Verse

"And He shall stand and feed His flock in the strength of the Lord, in the majesty of the name of the Lord His God; and they shall abide, for now He shall be great to the ends of the earth; and this One shall be peace" (Micah 5:4,5 NKJV).

August 23: Read Joshua 10

Key verse: "The Gibeonites then sent word to Joshua in the camp at Gilgal: 'Do not abandon your servants. Come up to us quickly and save us! Help us, because all the Amorite kings from the hill country have joined forces against us' " (Joshua 10:6 NIV).

Today, we read that the king of Jerusalem (not conquered by Israel until King David's time) forms an alliance with other kings in southern Canaan and attacks Gibeon, the nation which tricked Israel into a treaty. The Gibeonites send word to Joshua of their distress and he, true to the pact, comes to the defense of Gibeon and destroys the Amorite kings.

When spiritual enemies attack us and threaten to overpower us, let us, by faith and prayer, appeal to Christ, out Joshua, for strength and help. Just as Paul did, we will receive the answer: "My grace is sufficient for you, for My power is made perfect in weakness" (II Corinthians 12:9).

Direction for today: "Do not be anxious about anything, but in everything, by prayer and petition, with thanksgiving, present your requests to God" (Philippians 4:6).

Prayer for today: "Thank you, Lord, for the grace by which we are saved."

August 24: Read Joshua 11,12

Key verse: "As the Lord commanded Moses His servant, so Moses commanded Joshua, and so Joshua did; he left nothing undone of all that the Lord had commanded Moses" (Joshua 11:15 RSV).

God had assured Abraham, Isaac and Jacob that He would give the Land of Promise to their descendants, of whom He would make a mighty nation. God promised this to Moses and he passed it on to Joshua.

Today, we see the fulfillment of God's promises.

The remarkable thing about these "wars" of conquest is that Israel's losses were so small. God promised to fight for them, and He did.

I apply this to my life. God's Word promises me total victory over my sinful nature. Romans 6 points out that I am crucified with Jesus; therefore, if I will consider myself dead, the old sinful nature will have no power over me. Though all my lusts, desires and appetites may crave for self-expression, Jesus promises victory.

Direction for today: Examine your life carefully under the searchlight of God's holy Word.

Prayer for today: "Lord, give me victory throughout my entire being so my life will bring honour to Your name."

August 25: Read Joshua 13,14

Key verse: "You are old and advanced in years, and there remains yet very much land to possess" (Joshua 13:1b RSV).

We are all growing older. Has the blessed Lord yet conquered your sinful nature? Is there much land left to possess? Why not surrender yourself completely to Jesus right now?

Think of all those areas of your life in which the flesh is allowed to rule. Do you still have a violent temper? Is your heart fixed on worldly fame and gain? Are you having problems with lust? Do you cover up by telling lies?

The precious blood of Jesus cleanses from all sin.

Will you confess your sins, small or great? Will you repent and turn away from every known sin? Will you forgive everyone who ever wronged you—especially your parents? Perhaps they are dead now, but you still hold bitterness against them for something which happened, even a long time ago.

Confess this right now to Jesus. Claim the cleansing of His precious blood. You will be made whole and know the joy of being forgiven.

It is never too late to begin to conquer the promised land.

Direction for today: Be totally honest as you examine yourself. Let the Holy Spirit lead you to complete victory.

Prayer for today: "Thank You, Lord, for setting me free! May I praise and extol only You."

August 26: Read Joshua 15

Key verse: "Caleb drove out the three sons of Anak from there" (Joshua 15:14a NKJV).

Caleb was accustomed to victory. Unlike the ten spies who had returned with an account full of fear, Caleb and Joshua had urged the children of Israel to conquer the promised land in the name of the Lord.

Unfortunately, the people did not listen, and thus doomed themselves to wandering in the wilderness and to death for every adult—except Caleb and Joshua—before they would finally enter the land of promise.

When the people finally got there, Caleb was one of the two oldest in the entire nation, but his confidence was as strong as ever. He took part in the battles and drove out mighty warriors to claim the inheritance the Lord had given him.

Here we see the power of faith. Caleb consistently believed God and expected Him to work on his behalf. Because of this, he was one of the few who consistently experienced complete victory.

Perhaps you have been like the Israelites, easily daunted and turned aside by fear. Today is the day to become like Caleb—not strong in your own might, but mighty in the Lord!

Direction for today: Like Caleb, believe God and trust Him for victory. And, like Caleb, you will see great victories in the Lord.

Prayer for today: "Lord, help me to keep my trust in You."

August 27: Read Joshua 16,17

Key verse: "And it happened, when the children of Israel grew strong, that they put the Canaanites to forced labour, but did not utterly drive them out" (Joshua 17:13 NKJV).

This is a very familiar story because it is repeated time and again in our own lives. God had told the Israelites utterly to drive out the inhabitants of Canaan. He did this with very good reason—the Canaanites followed wicked, immoral worship practices, such as sacrificing their children to heathen gods and the Lord knew that such corruption would soon influence His people.

But the Israelites were sure they were strong enough to handle the situation, and they disregarded the command of the Lord. After all, they thought, Canaanite slaves would be very useful!

It wasn't long before the Canaanite influence had corrupted the Israelites. The next seven books of the Bible are full of stories of idol worship and lack of faith on the part of the people of God. The forced labourers had become spiritual saboteurs!

There are often things in our own lives—material possessions, friendships, habitgs—that seem good or useful, so we keep them, even though the Lord has said they must go. Think again, friend; God requires complete obedience!

Don't fall into the same trap as the Israelites did. Many Christians marry non-Christians, hoping their spouses will find the Lord under their good influence, but it usually works the other way. Many business partners become "unequally yoked" in order to have a successful business, but find that their Christian stand becomes compromised. Many

Christians acquire too many material possessions, claiming they will use them to better serve the Lord; instead, they wind up serving Mammon.

Direction for today: When God says, "Clean out the land", clean it out!

Prayer for today: "Lord, show me if there are any corrupting things in my life; if there are, help me to get rid of them."

August 28: Read Joshua 18

Key verse: "So Joshua said to the people of Israel, 'How long will you be slack to go in and take possession of the land, which the Lord, the God of your fathers, has given you?' " (Joshua 18:3RSV).

What a challenge! Sadly, it seems that God's people are almost always reluctant to take Him at His word! How many things are part of our inheritance as the people of God, and yet we refuse to take possession of them?

It is foolish for believers to be satisfied with anything less than the abundant life that the Lord has promised. Yet, so often, we miss the abundance just as the children of Israel were prone to do.

Perhaps this is because, in order to take possession of the good things of God, we have to surrender many of the less than good things to which we now cling. We need to empty our hands of the things of this world in order to receive the things of eternal value.

But the comparison is ridiculous! How can temporal treasures compare with the great blessings of the kingdom of God?

Direction for today: How long will you be slack in taking possession of God's gifts to you? Empty your hands and your heart of earthly treasures. Take possession of the amazing blessings which are yours in Jesus.

Prayer for today: "Lord, I want to know Your blessings in fullness."

August 29: Read Joshua 19,20

Key verse: "When they made an end of dividing the land as an inheritance according to their borders, the children of Israel gave an inheritance among them to Joshua the son of Nun" (Joshua 19:49 NKJV).

It is important to realize that, when Joshua supervised the division of the land among the tribes of Israel, he gave to others before receiving any himself. He did not reserve the best for himself, but received the final portion—a small inheritance in comparison with the others. This is so different from the actions of other kings and rulers, who always took the best for themselves.

But God says, "The first shall be last, and the last first" (Matthew 19:30).

Where do we put ourselves in relation to others? As God's children, we, too, receive an inheritance. But we also receive responsibilities, and one of our assignments is to put others ahead of ourselves. Like Joshua, we are to be servants, not masters. And, as with Joshua, there is an inheritance already prepared for us, an eternal treasure laid up in heaven.

Direction for today: Have the heart of a servant, the heart of Jesus.

Prayer for today: "Lord, help me to put others before myself."

Memory Verse

"And He said to me, 'My grace is sufficient for you, for My strength is made perfect in weakness.' Therefore most gladly I will rather boast in my infirmities, that the power of Christ may rest upon me" *(II Corinthians 12:9 NKJV).*

August 30: Read Joshua 21

Key verse: "Not one of all the Lord's good promises to the house of Israel failed; every one was fulfilled" (Joshua 21:45 NIV).

Our friends will fail us; they are not utterly reliable. Our relatives will disappoint us; we cannot depend on them to be infallible, for they are as human as we are.

But God never fails. His promises are true. What He says, He will do.

Ask yourself: do I really live as though those statements are true? The Israelites often did not. When God promised victory, they ran away, fearing defeat. When God promised prosperity, they broke all of His rules so He could not bless them as He wanted to. When He promised to lead and guide them, they asked for a king to be their leader. When He promised to protect them from their enemies, they made their own unsuccessful battle plans.

They were almost as foolish as we are! God has promised to meet our needs, yet we worry and fret. God has promised to be our healer and our deliverer, yet we are anxious and defeated.

Not one of the Lord's promises will fail. Every one will be fulfilled!

Direction for today: Depend on the Lord's promises!

Prayer for today: "Praise You, Lord, that You are completely dependable."

August 31: Read Joshua 22,23

Key verse: "They were glad to hear the report and praised God" (Joshua 22:33a NIV).

With the land settled and secured, Joshua saw that it was time to allow the armed men from the east side of the Jordan to return to their homes.

The Reubenites, the Gadites and the men from the half-tribe of Manasseh had served well. When they returned, they took with them the blessings of God and the fruit of the land, for the workman is worthy of his hire.

Upon their arrival in their homeland, they built an altar to God as a witness to future generations of their dedication to Him.

Their action was misinterpreted by the other tribes, who feared that they were establishing a false religion for themselves. The western tribes were ready to go to battle to stop such heresy.

Fortunately, peace and understanding were restored. But it is refreshing to encounter this kind of loyalty to the worship of God: later in the story of the nation, we will discover that the northern tribes did establish a false religion, and this led to their complete defeat.

As we appreciate the loyalty to God shown by the people, let's also be aware of the problems that misunderstandings can cause—they almost led to war between brothers! This can also happen in our churches unless we always allow the Holy Spirit to unite us in Jesus.

Direction for today: Be loyal to the Lord and understanding toward your brothers and sisters.

Prayer for today: "Lord, may I see others through Your eyes."

9

I Am Your Temple

I am your temple, Lord; fill me.
Cleanse me so Your kingdom will grow.
Reflect in me Your compassion
Break me and let Your love flow.

Set me apart for Your use, Lord.
Let me seek to be holy like Thee,
Pressing on to take hold of the prize
Which You have prepared for me.

Reveal to my soul Your glory;
Touch and strengthen me this day
That I might move in strength and power
As you make plain to me Your way.

Protect and unite Your people, Lord,
That we may Your body become,
Uplifting and strengthening each other,
Bringing glory to Jesus Your Son.

— Rebecca Bell

Key verse: "But if serving the Lord seems undesirable to you, then choose for yourselves this day whom you will serve, whether the gods your forefathers served beyond the river, or the gods of the Amorites, in whose land you are living. But as for me and my household, we will serve the Lord" (Joshua 24:15 NIV).

Today's scripture is the record of a powerful revival service. Joshua preaches his final sermon, and reminds the people of the mighty victories God has won for them in the previous forty years. He emphasizes the faithfulness of God.

Joshua presents a personal challenge: to fear the Lord and serve Him faithfully. He then asks them to make the ultimate choice: "Choose today whom you will serve." Today, each of us has to make that choice as well. It is your decision: either you serve God or you do not serve Him. It is one or the other.

Joshua tells them to do what they will, "but as for me and my household, we will serve the Lord." It is not difficult to stay on the straight and narrow road when you are in dire need of God's involvement in your life, but when all is going well, you need to live by a firm, unwavering commitment.

The children of Israel are, at long last, securely settled in the Promised Land. Now they must make their decision of commitment. After he warns them of the disastrous cost of forsaking God, the people say to Joshua, "We will serve the Lord."

Direction for today: Find yourself a place of fresh commitment.

Prayer for today: "Lord, I *will* serve You."

Judges

The book of Judges might be as appropriately termed: "The Dark Ages of Israel". The people of Israel had conquered Canaan, and settled the country — but they had failed to obey the commandment of God to utterly drive out or destroy all of the previous inhabitants. The faith of the Israelites was quickly corrupted. They abandoned the Lord God to worship the false gods of the Canaanites and participated in all of the occult, corrupt, and immoral practices associated with those religions.

The theme of the book, stated over and over, is: "In those days there was no king in Israel; every man did what was right in his own eyes" (Judges 17:6). Relative morality is certainly no new thing!

The book runs in cycles. Over and over again the same progression is repeated. The Israelites fall into sin and false worship; God raises up a foreign people to punish the Israelites for their unfaithfulness; the

Israelites repent and cry to the Lord for deliverance; the Lord raises up a deliverer, a "judge", to save His people.

If that happened only once, this might be a beautiful book. But sadly, it is repeated many times — God's people were, over and over again, unfaithful to Him. The end of the book contains some genuine horror stories which graphically demonstrate the depths to which the people have fallen.

This is by no means a pretty book; but it is included in Scripture as a stark warning about what will happen to God's people who abandon Him. Yet there is a promise of deliverance for those who are willing to repent and return to the Lord.

September 2: Read Judges 1,2

Key verse: *"Then the Lord raised up judges, who saved them out of the hands of these raiders" (Judges 2:16 NIV).*

The book of Judges is a tragic story of a downtrodden nation. While it contains a record of conquests and victories, this book also tells of a series of defeats.

It is not a pretty story, but Judges contains a valuable truth. Moses and Joshua had pleaded with the people to hold firm to the Word of God, and never to forsake Him. But, when that generation passed away, "Another generation grew up, who knew neither the Lord nor what He had done for Israel" (2:10). As a result, they "did evil in the eyes of the Lord" (2:11).

God's wrath was strong and sure. After forty years of victories, the children of Israel now suffered defeat after defeat. They did what was right in their own eyes, and this always leads to disaster.

God, in His patience and love, provided a solution. He raised up judges over them, leaders whose role was to bring them back into righteousness. But "they refused to give up their evil practices and stubborn ways" (2:19). How tragic! They would not listen and learn—but we can. God longs to watch over and bless His children, but the decision is ours.

Direction for today: Learn from history; disobedience to God is a tragic mistake.

Prayer for today: "Lord, help me to stay on the way of life, that I might not run headlong into disaster."

September 3: Read Judges 3

Key verse: *"Now these are the nations which the Lord left, to prove Israel by them, even as many of Israel as had not known all the wars of Canaan" (Judges 3:1 KJV).*

The children of Israel, like many modern-day believers, were prone to forget the Lord and all of His goodness to them. Therefore, God, in His great wisdom, allowed them to dwell among the unbelieving nations which were antagonistic towards them. The Israelites were safe from these enemies while they remained obedient to the Lord. But, when they began taking Him for granted, they soon forgot that it was He who protected them. They began to be careless and sinned against Him.

Then God allowed their enemies to prevail against them, taking them into captivity and forcing them to serve as slaves.

We are living among unbelievers, with many worldly—and even sinful—pleasures offered to us. God does not remove us from these things, but allows us to be surrounded by them in order that He might prove our faithfulness to Him.

Direction for today: Determine in your heart to serve the Lord.

Prayer for today: "Lord, strengthen me, that I might stand."

September 4: Read Judges 4

Key verse: "And the children of Israel cried unto the Lord: for he had nine hundred chariots of iron; and twenty years he mightily oppressed the children of Israel" (Judges 4:3 KJV).

When the Israelites turned from the Lord, they automatically opened the door which allowed their enemies to triumph over them. They suffered much oppression and their lives were constantly in danger.

All the while, God waited patiently until they called out to Him before He would act in their defence and deliverance. God does not necessarily bring trouble into the lives of those who turn from Him—it's simply that they abandon His protection and then try, in their own strength, to overcome their problems and difficulties.

But, when we come to our senses and call on God, He has promised to deliver us.

Direction for today: Call upon the Lord for your deliverance.

Prayer for today: "Thank You, Lord, for Your great protection."

September 5: Read Judges 5

Key verse: "Hear, O ye kings; give ear, O ye princes; I, even I, will sing unto the Lord; I will sing praise to the Lord God of Israel" (Judges 5:3 KJV).

Israel has been delivered from twenty years of oppression by her enemies. It was a direct intervention by God, who raised up Deborah and Barak. Suddenly, they were free and God was now their great delight. A wonderful spirit of rejoicing and praise begin to flow from the lips of the children of Israel.

This is like a revival, for a new awareness of the Lord is prevalent in the nation. They begin to remember all the great victories which God has given them in the past.

God delights in making His people rejoice by giving them great victories over evil. He longs for us to be able to experience His blessings and to rejoice in fellowship with Him.

Direction for today: Turn from evil and experience God's great blessing.

Prayer for today: "Lord, I praise You for Your goodness towards me."

Memory Verse

"But you are a chosen generation, a royal priesthood, a holy nation, His own special people, that you may proclaim the praises of Him who called you out of darkness into His marvellous light" (I Peter 2:9 NKJV).

September 6: Read Judges 6

Key verse: "And he said unto Him, Oh my Lord, wherewith shall I save Israel? Behold, my family is poor in Manasseh, and I am the least of my father's house" (Judges 6:15 KJV).

The children of Israel had again done evil in the sight of the Lord.

They were constantly up and down. When things went well for them, they forgot the Lord; when things went badly they cried out to Him for deliverance and He, in His mercy, sent them a deliverer.

When God chooses a deliverer, He always looks for a humble vessel: someone who truly has a servant's heart and is willing to be sensitive and obedient to His Holy Spirit. It has been said that God is not just looking for those who have ability, but for those who offer their availability. He often equips the most unlikely people as vessels for His great purposes.

Direction for today: Walk humbly before the Lord.

Prayer for today: "Lord, use me for the welfare of others."

September 7: Read Judges 7

Key verse: "Then the three companies blew the trumpets and broke the pitchers—they held the torches in their left hands and the trumpets in their right hands for blowing—and they cried, 'The sword of the Lord and of Gideon!' " (Judges 7:20 NKJV).

Gideon was a man filled with the light of God. God had raised him up to be the deliverer of Israel. It is evident in these chapters that he was a humble man, a man of prayer and of worship. In this chapter, we see that God spoke to him and that Gideon worshipped the Lord even in the presence of his enemies.

Just as Gideon was filled with the light of the Lord, God used light to defeat the enemies of His people. As light burst forth with the breaking of the pitchers and as the trumpets and the shouts of triumph were sounded, victory over the Midianites was secured.

We are involved in spiritual warfare if we are followers of Christ, our Deliverer. We too, will know victory if we walk in the light of God's Word, allow our light to shine out to others and proclaim with our lips the good news of Jesus Christ.

However, like the earthen vessels carried by Gideon's men, we often have to be broken before the light inside can shatter the darkness around us.

Direction for today: Be a light in this dark world.

Prayer for today: "Thank You, Lord, for the light of Your Word."

September 8: Read Judges 8

Key verse: "Thus the sons of Israel did not remember the Lord their God, who had delivered them from the hands of all their enemies on every side" (Judges 8:34 NAS).

When Moses spoke to the children of Israel, he several times reminded them to remember God—not to forget Him and all He did for them. In fact, in Deuteronomy 8:19, God, through Moses, warned that Israel would surely perish if she forgot God and served other gods.

Yet we know how short a time it took Israel to forget these words. During the period of the judges, Israel was continually turning from God. It was only as God brought enemies across Israel's path that she remembered to turn to Him. In troubled times, He was their only refuge. The judges, like Gideon, led Israel back to God. Unfortunately, as indicated in the key verse, Israel again soon forgot.

In I Corinthians 1:6, Paul writes, "Now these things happened as examples for us . . ." "These things" would include Israel's experience during the time of the judges. "These things" include forgetting God. How quickly we, too, forget the Lord! Too easily, the daily events of life become merely coincidental and we forget that God is directing all things for our good. Too often we are victims of our circumstances rather than victors over those circumstances.

Too often, we forget who has given us every good thing.

Direction for today: Reflect on God's goodness towards you and thank Him for all His blessings.

Prayer for today: "Father, teach me to see Your hand directing the affairs of my life and to be grateful to You."

September 9: Read Judges 9

Key verse: "Then Jotham escaped and fled, and went to Beer and remained there because of Abimalech his brother" (Judges 9:21 NAS).

At first glance, it would appear that Jotham ran away from something which he should have carried out by himself. His father, Gideon, did not want to rule over the Israelites. Jotham's brother, Abimelech, however, being power-hungry, claimed the rule over the nation.

When he discovered what Abimelech had done, Jotham challenged the Israelites to examine their integrity in choosing Abimelech. It seemed to him that their action was inconsistent with what Gideon would have desired. Jotham told the people a parable about the various trees of the forest being asked to rule. Except for the bramble, all the trees declined. Jotham compared Abimelech to the bramble, then he fled.

One can look at Jotham's action in two ways. Either he was simply a coward who ran away from a possible confrontation with Abimelech, or he showed wisdom in leaving the whole matter up to God. So often, we take matters into our own hands. Jotham could perhaps have tried to kill Abimelech; instead, he left him to God. Sometimes we take things into our own hands and cause confusion. We need to remember always to ask God to direct us.

Direction for today: Strive to perceive things God's way.

Prayer for today: "Father, into Your hands I commend my spirit, soul and body."

September 10: Read Judges 10,11

Key verse: "Now Jephthah the Gileadite was a valiant warrior, but he was the son of a harlot . . ." (Judges 11:1 NAS).

Do you sometimes wonder why the sacred writer recorded certain things and what the exact intention of such a recorded comment might be? In the key verse, we are told that Jephthah was the son of a prostitute. To what end might the writer of Judges record that little bit of knowledge? Why would he include that information?

One possible reason for Jephthah to be identified that way might be to show us that God doesn't choose only beautiful, whole, good people to do His work. The background matters little. It's what is in the heart that counts.

Paul urges the Corinthians to consider their calling. They were not very wise, nor were they mighty or noble (I Corinthians 1:26). God often seems to choose those of less than noble background and to make them into useful instruments.

What is it about your background that you'd like to forget? Maybe you are a child of an adulterous relationship, or a result of a broken or alcoholic home? Probably all of us have something we'd like to forget—or, at least, change—so that, in our opinion, God would be better able to use us.

I have good news for you! He'll use you as you are, with all the blotches and blemishes you have or think you have. What He wants is a surrendered, obedient heart. That's all! Would you give Him yours today to do with as *He* chooses?

Direction for today: Give thanks, for you are fearfully and wonderfully made.

Prayer for today: "Father, use me and all I am to build up Your kingdom."

September 11: Read Judges 12,13

Key verse: ". . . then they would say to him, 'Say now, Shibboleth!' But he said 'Sibboleth', for he could not pronounce it correctly. . ." (Judges 12:6 NAS).

Children sometimes have make-believe clubs and clubhouses. Only certain close friends who may belong to the club may gain entry to the clubhouse. Entry is by saying "the password."

In our home, when we were trying to teach our children "please" and "thank you," we used to ask them what the magic word was. When the proper response was forthcoming, they received what they had asked for. Call "please" and "thank you" passwords, if you will.

In a similar way, the Gileadites had a password designed to help them to ferret out Ephraimites. Their word was "Shibboleth." Knowing that the people of Ephraim couldn't pronounce the "sh," this was the word decided on by the people of Gilead.

Each of us must also know the password to gain access to heaven. Many people don't know it, and it's our responsibility to tell them. Our password—". . . if you confess with your mouth Jesus as Lord, and believe in your heart that God raised Him from the dead, you shall be saved" (Romans 10:9)—is more than a word. But it is the key to heaven!

Know Jesus and believe, and pass on the good word so that many more may have access to the King.

Direction for today: Jesus is Lord!

Prayer for today: "Father, make me aware of all who don't know, and awaken in me the desire to tell them the password to eternal life."

September 12: Read Judges 14,15

Key verse: "However she wept before him seven days while their feast lasted. And it came about on the seventh day that he told her because she pressed him so hard . . " (Judges 14:17 NAS).

As I read these chapters, and particularly this verse, I was reminded of another instance in Samson's life when his giving in to those around him was much more tragic than the occasion described above. You will recall that, later in his life, he gave the secret of his strength to his wife Delilah. She, in turn, told her countrymen who, when they cut off Samson's hair, were able to overcome him. He eventually lost his life because of that.

I'm reminded of the various places in Scripture in which we are commanded to be careful of the kinds of people we choose as our friends. I'm further reminded from the story of Daniel how he purposed in his heart not to defile himself with the rich Babylonian food. I believe the story of Daniel teaches us the need, often, to stand alone.

We need to be so careful of the influence of people and things around us. Peer pressure in our society is so great. It's especially tension-causing for our youth. But it's also dangerous for adults. It's an interesting exercise to stand back and examine why we do what we do. Often, it's because somebody expects it of us.

God would have us live for Him. We need always to beware of the influences around us, influences which may be good or bad. We need to try to turn them for good, not to be turned by them to evil.

Direction for today: Be careful of the influences around you.

Prayer for today: "Lord, make me as wise as a serpent and as gentle as a dove."

Memory Verse

"For thus says the Lord God, 'Indeed I Myself will search for My sheep and seek them out' " (Ezekiel 34:11 NKJV).

September 13: Read Judges 16

Key verse: "He did not know that the Lord had left him" (Judges 16:20c NIV).

There is probably no sadder verse in the Old Testament than verse 20 of this chapter. Here is a tragedy of a man who is unaware of the fact that the Lord was no longer with him. In such a situation, shame and defeat are inevitable.

The weakened Samson was now easily captured by the Philistines. With his eyes put out, he was brought to Gaza, the scene of one of his earlier feats of strength, and put to work at the tedious task of grinding corn.

This task was not only menial but humiliating. It is surprising that his captors, having ascertained the secret of his great strength, did not take steps to see that he was shaved regularly; perhaps they thought they had little to fear from this sightless, shambling wreck. Although it is not specifically stated, the inference is that Samson's strength returned as his hair grew. It may also be that, during his confinement in prison, contemplating the shame and failure of his life, some spark of repentance was kindled.

Direction for today: Remember, "God keeps His promise, and He will not allow you to be tested beyond your power to remain firm" (1 Corinthians 10:13b TEV).

Prayer for today: "Father, thank You for Your promise of strength during times of testing."

September 14: Read Judges 17,18

Key verse: "There was no king in Israel at that time; everyone did whatever he wanted" (Judges 17:6 TEV).

Direction for today: The last five chapters of Judges are among the most depressing in the entire Bible. They contain horrible stories of man's inhumanity to man, all rooted in the cause stated in our key verse: "everyone did whatever he wanted." When human beings abandon morality and trade obedience to God for obedience to their own desires, devastation will be the result.

Read these stories with one eye on the Bible and the other on the daily newspaper, which often echoes similar tales from our own day. Allow the Holy Spirit to use this shocking truth to spur you to intercessory prayer.

Direction for today: Pray for our nation, that we may be delivered from "everyone doing what they want."

Prayer for today: "Lord, deliver us from the evils that are attacking our society."

September 15: Read Judges 19

Key verse: "While they were enjoying themselves, some wicked men of the city surrounded the house" (Judges 19:22a NIV).

As the nation continues in its ignorance of God, the stories do not get any better! Again today, we read an appalling account of sin and depravity.

Our key verse gives us a picture of an important spiritual truth. The traveller, his concubine and their hosts were all sinful people. The earlier verses indicate the state of their homes; the fact that the host was willing to surrender his daughter indicates the depths to which he had fallen.

Their sin only led to greater and more disastrous sin—perversion, rape and murder.

The verse gives us a picture of the people enjoying "small sins" inside the house, whereupon they were invaded by more dramatic sin from the outside.

Sin is always like that. We may think we can handle our situations, sinning only occasionally and in secret. Many Christians deal with sinful habits in just that way.

The truth is, sin invites more sin; we cannot be "only a little disobedient." When we practice small, secret sins, we soon find our lives invaded by sins more public, more ugly, and more devastating.

Direction for today: Seek to avoid all sin!

Prayer for today: "Lord, forgive me for my sin and deliver me from the sins that would seek to invade my life."

September 16: Read Judges 20

Key verse: "And the men of Israel went out to battle against Benjamin" (Judges 20:20a NKJV).

It is God's will that His people be one in the unity of the Holy Spirit. When we are walking in the Spirit, serving the Lord, we will know that communion which exists between all who truly believe in Christ.

In fact, in John 17:23, Jesus said that the world will be able to judge whether the Father has sent the Son when it sees love shown between believers!

In this chapter, we are presented with stark evidence of what happens when God's people abandon obedience and seek after the false attractions of sin. Not only do we become estranged from God—we also begin to fight with our brothers and sisters. Benjamin was a tribe of Israel, yet sin had caused enmity between that tribe and its brothers.

When Christians sin and begin to fight with one another, Satan wins a major battle against the kingdom! If you have been contributing to dissension between believers, do all you can to make the situation right and to allow the Spirit to rebuild the unity to which God has called His people.

Direction for today: Live in fellowship and unity with other Christians.

Prayer for today: "May we be one, that the world will know the Father has sent the Son."

September 17: Read Judges 21

Key verse: " 'O Lord, the God of Israel,' they cried, 'why has this happened to Israel?' " (Judges 21:3a NIV).

It is gratifying to find that, after the stormy outburst of the previous chapter, there came a return of tender feelings—like gentle rain after lightning and thunder. Human tears, as they well forth on behalf of others, reveal underlying fountains in the strongest natures and the existence of those tender feelings of compassion.

Those who act in haste repent at leisure. Already there were symptoms that a sweeter and purer spirit was about to rise up in Israel. At least one star shone in the black night; truth began to be revered and the people would not go back on their solemn vow.

Direction for today: Recognize God's purposes in everything through which He allows you to go.

Prayer for today: "Search me, oh Lord, and cleanse me from every sin."

I and II Corinthians

The two letters from Paul to the church at Corinth are vitally important to our understanding of the functioning of the Christian church. They also provide some valuable insights of the great missionary apostle himself, especially as we read the highly autobiographical second letter.

The letters contain teachings essential to the faith and practice of the church. There is a detailed account of church discipline, an impassioned plea for growth toward Christian maturity, and invaluable instructions concerning the Lord's Supper (I Corinthians 11), as well as the gifts of the Spirit (I Corinthians 12 and 14), and, of course, the key to the whole Christian life, the "love chapter" (I Corinthians 13), echoed in the calls to love and forgiveness that recur throughout the second letter.

These two letters are apparently part of a continuing correspondence between Paul and his Corinthian converts. Throughout the letters, there is evidence that Paul is answering specific questions concerning which the Corinthian Christians have written to him (I Corinthians 7:1, for example).

Here we have 29 chapters of vital spiritual correspondence, inspired by the Holy Spirit, from the apostle Paul to an early church struggling with perennial problems. Paul founded this church along with Aquila and Priscilla (see Acts 18), and had a deep love for his people even when he knew them to be in error. We can learn much from these two dynamic letters.

September 18: Read I Corinthians 1,2

Key verse: "But God hath chosen the foolish things of the world to confound the wise; and God hath chosen the weak things of the world to confound the things which are mighty" (I Corinthians 1:27 KJV).

In this verse, we are reminded of the Word of the Lord writtern by Isaiah: "For My thoughts are not your thoughts, neither are your ways My ways, saith the Lord. For as the heavens are higher than the earth, so are My ways higher than your ways, My thoughts than your thoughts" (Isaiah 55:8-9).

God's ways are definitely not our ways. His plans are often in conflict with ours because we don't clearly hear His plans for us. The people we would choose for a certain task are often not those chosen by God. The specific approach we would take to accomplish a task may be set aside by Him. His timing is often completely different from ours. Truly, God's ways are not our ways, nor His thoughts our thoughts.

Why not? Because, as 1 Corinthians 1:20 and 2:5 tells us, if God accomplishes something, we cannot glory in man's ability but only in God's. And that's why God loves to take that which is unspectacular or simple or different and make it into something special.

And so we never dare minimize what the Lord may do with us or through us. We may see ourselves as totally unfitted for the task at hand, but God can take us and make us into something beautiful for Him.

Direction for today: Allow the Lord to use you in the way He sees fit.

Prayer for today: "Lord, make me into the type of Christian who will bring honour to Your name."

September 19: Read I Corinthians 3,4

Key verse: "And I, brethren, could not speak to you as to spiritual men, but as to men of flesh, as to babes in Christ. I gave you milk to drink, not solid food; for you were not yet able to receive it" (I Corinthians 3:1,2a NAS).

Campbell McAlpine, in his excellent book, Alone With God, writes: ". . . our spiritual maturity is determined by the answer to the question, 'How well do I know God?' Too many Christians are living in unnecessary stages of immaturity." He goes on to ask, "Do you believe your spiritual growth is commensurate with the time you have known God? Have you neglected the means of growth? What adjustments do you believe are necessary in your life to correct this?"

These are interesting questions. For Paul, the issue of spiritual maturity was connected to the matter of the unity of the Body of Christ. Paul says the people are immature because they have a party spirit: "I'm for Paul, I'm for Apollos." The 'super-spiritual' were "for Christ."

How is it with you and your maturing as God's person? Are you more mature today than you were when you first came to Jesus? How do you judge your maturity? If McAlpine is right and spiritual maturity is contingent on how well one knows God, do you know God better today than you did when you first met Him?

Knowing the Father is crucial if we are to be people of the Kingdom. The world needs people of the Kingdom who are eager to live out Kingdom principles. In Daniel 11:32-33, we read: ". . . the people that know their God shall be strong and do exploits, and they that understand among the people shall instruct many." God needs a people who know Him so that men will come to know Him.

Direction for today: Commit Yourself to grow up to know God.

Prayer for today: "Father, I long to know You better so I can grow up. Please teach me more about You."

Memory Verse

"He has delivered us from the power of darkness and translated us into the kingdom of the Son of His love" (Colossians 1:13 NKJV).

September 20: Read I Corinthians 5,6

Key verse: "Do you not know that a little leaven leavens the whole lump of dough?" (I Corinthians 5:6b NAS).

When I stop to think about it, I'm intrigued by the action of yeast in a hunk of dough. My wife sometimes bakes bread; for bread to rise, you need to use yeast or leaven, as Paul calls it. If one tries to watch yeast work, it is almost impossible to see the process taking place; only results are observable. After some time, if baking doesn't halt the action, the yeast may cause the loaf of bread to rise well over the edge of the pan, making it seem almost out of control.

Paul is pointing out that sin, if allowed to remain unchecked, will eventually corrupt the whole loaf, whatever the whole loaf may be. It may be our body, our family, our church. We can see the results of unchecked sin in many areas of our nation's life.

It's the "rotten apple" principle. Left to itself, one rotten apple will eventually spoil the whole bushel or bag or basket. Whatever the rotten apple in our lives may be, if unchecked, it will eventually affect the whole.

Paul, inspired by the Spirit of God, urges us to "clean out the old leaven and to become a new lump" (verse 7). Good advice. We all are tempted to trifle with sin, to cuddle it a bit. And yet, we need to take radical measures to clean out the old so the new may enter. The old man needs to be crucified daily in order for the new man to arise to new life in Christ. Let's be new people, leavening the whole lump for God.

Direction for today: Be radical in your elimination of old leaven.

Prayer for today: "Lord, cause me to be willing to be leavened only by Your Holy Spirit."

September 21: Read I Corinthians 7

Key verse: "Ye are bought with a price; be not ye the servants of men" (I Corinthians 7:23 KJV).

It's so easy for us to forget to whom we are indebted. Stated another way, it's difficult for us to remember whom we serve. Differently still, whom do we try to please?

We could say that Paul's writing about peer pressure. It's a bad thing for all of us, but an especially devastating thing for our youth. The clothes we wear, the movies we watch, the style of our hair, the area in which we live, the number of times we have travelled to certain places—all are important, or seem to be important, to acceptance.

Yet we *must* learn that we are accepted in the beloved (Ephesians 1:7). Nothing less and nothing more—we are acceptred because of God's love for us in Jesus.

Often we live as though the opinion of the God we cannot see—and who bought us with the price of Jesus' blood—is of less importance than the opinion of those whom we can see. Our God desires us to be His servants: to love and serve Him above everything and everybody else.

Direction for today: Be a faithful servant of God.

Prayer for today: "Lord, make me mindful of my roots and grateful that I belong to You."

September 22: Read I Corinthians 8,9

Key verse: "Know ye not that they which run in a race run all, but one receiveth the prize? So run, that ye may obtain" (I Corinthians 9:24 KJV).

Paul was very familiar with athletic events, particularly running. He used examples from those things with which people were acquainted in order to teach spiritual truths.

We, too, can identify with his picture of a race. There is only one winner; all the rest of the contestants finish second and beyond, but there's only one winner. All run, and run hard, but only the best wins.

Although there is certainly more than one winner on the pathway to heaven, we, too are daily involved in a race. Paul encourages us to run so that we may win the prize.

This, of course, has nothing to do with earning our way to heaven by good works. It has everything to do with commitment to God's working out His purposes in our lives according to His will and direction and believing in Him, no matter what.

We need, day by day, to commit ourselves to the running of the race by faithfully following our Lord.

Direction for today: Run the race to obtain the prize.

Prayer for today: "Father, by Your Holy Spirit help me to exercise the discipline I need to honour You in my life each day."

September 23: Read I Corinthians 10

Key verse: "So whether you eat or drink or whatever you do, do it all for the glory of God" (I Corinthians 10:31 NIV).

St. Augustine summed up the Christian life in these few words: "Love God, and do what you will." At first glance, that may seem like an invitation to hedonism but, after we consider the implication of the first two words, the real meaning becomes clear.

If we truly love God, then what we choose to do will honour Him. Love begets obedience; obedience begets glory to God.

Paul and Augustine were saying exactly the same thing. Both gave a wonderful summation of the goal of every Christian life: to bring glory to God.

How much would your life change if, before you did anything at all, you asked, "Will this bring glory to God?" Most of us would have to confess this would radically change our approach to living. These changes would be very much for the better.

Direction for today: Do everything for the glory of God!

Prayer for today: "Lord, help me to weigh every decision in the light of Your will and Your glory."

September 24: Read I Corinthians 11

Key verse: "For whenever you eat this bread and drink this cup, you proclaim the Lord's death until He comes" (I Corinthians 11:26 NIV).

In many churches, the communion service has become ritualistic and boring. This is more than sad—it is calamitous! The Lord's Supper has always been central to the community worship of the church. In communion, we celebrate several truths that are central to the existence of the body of Christ.

First, as Paul tells us, we proclaim the death and resurrection of Jesus. Without His death, there is no forgiveness; without His resurrection, there is no victory! For this reason alone, communion should be a time of sober thanksgiving and joyous celebration!

But there is more: in communion, we celebrate "until He comes." We eat and drink with the awareness that one day we will sup with the Lord at the marriage supper of the Lamb. In communion, we anticipate eternity with Christ and eternal residence in heaven. This is still more reason to celebrate!

And even beyond this: when we eat and drink, we do so together as a clear sign of our unity one with another. It is "comm-union"—the community is one.

One of these truths is enough to cause a lot of joy; all of them together should make the Lord's Supper a meaningful, triumphant act of worship.

Direction for today: The next time you celebrate communion, truly celebrate!

Prayer for today: "Thank you, Jesus, that You died, rose again, and are coming back."

September 25: Read I Corinthians 12,13

Key verse: "But eagerly desire the greater gifts. And now I will show you the most excellent way" (I Corinthians 12:31 NIV).

It is wonderfully appropriate that today's reading includes both of these chapters, for they are usually read in exclusion one from the other and often in opposition one to the other!

Some Christians—even entire denominations—have come to emphasize one half of the truth of these chapters while ignoring the other. Some stress the gifts of chapter 12 while ignoring the element of Christian love in chapter 13. Others stress love while arguing that the gifts are no longer important.

As you read these two great chapters, you will realize that neither position could possibly be correct. God has given the gifts of His Spirit to His people and He expects them to be used to win the lost and to build up the church.

But the Lord insists that the gifts be exercised within an environment of love, the love that is possible only through the work of the Holy Spirit.

The Spirit is given to us to produce fruit—including love—and to give gifts, from wisdom to the interpretation of tongues. We should seek to love and to know and employ the gifts of the Spirit!

Direction for today: "Follow the way of love and eagerly desire spiritual gifts" (I Corinthians 14:1).

Prayer for today: "Lord, may I always seek to know You in all Your fullness."

September 26: Read I Corinthians 14

Key verse: "I thank God that I speak in tongues more than all of you" (I Corinthians 14:18 NIV).

In emphasizing this passage as the key verse, we must not lose sight of Paul's overall argument in this chapter: that the most important gifts are those that build up the church, and that all things must be done properly: in spiritual order.

But it is also good to note this short verse, which tells us something very important in a day when "speaking in tongues" continues to be a controversial issue.

Paul certainly is concerned that tongues be used correctly in private or in corporate worship. However, he makes it very plain that he speaks in tongues, that he does so frequently and thanks the Lord for this gift.

Many Christians have put tongues aside to avoid stirring up controversy. Paul did no such thing; he boldly declared that the Holy Spirit had given him this gift and, because of this, he used it!

Earlier, Paul says, "He who speaks in a tongue edifies himself." To edify means to build up—the gift of tongues will build you up spiritually.

Direction for today: Do not be afraid to ask the Lord for the gifts of the Spirit.

Prayer for today: "Father, build me up spiritually in whatever ways You choose."

Memory Verse

"Now to Him who is able to keep you from stumbling, and to present you faultless before the presence of His glory with exceeding joy, to God our Saviour, who alone is wise, be glory and majesty, dominion and power, both now and forever. Amen" " (Jude 24,25 NKJV).

September 27: Read I Corinthians 15

Key verse: "For as in Adam all die, so in Christ all will be made alive. But each in his own turn: Christ, the firstfruits; then, when He comes, those who belong to Him" (I Corinthians 15:22,23 NIV).

This chapter is a commentary on the glorious promise of resurrection and eternal life. Paul celebrates the truth that all believers who die will be raised again to eternal life, their corrupt bodies changed into incorruptible, eternal bodies.

For Paul, Christ's resurrection was not only the ultimate victory over death; it was also the first of many resurrections to follow, including Paul's own!

The chapter is filled with hope—hope for ourselves, and especially for our loved ones who have died in the Lord. Millions of believers who have died in years and centuries past will spend eternity in full, abundant life with us because all who believe will be raised in Christ!

This portion of Scripture should also spur us to the work of evangelism, for those who die denying Christ will also be raised, but only to be sent to their second, eternal death in hell.

Direction for today: Take hope in the resurrection to come!

Prayer for today: "Praise You, Jesus, for Your victory over death."

September 28: Read I Corinthians 16

Key verse: "On the first day of the week let each one of you lay something aside, storing up as he may prosper, that there be no collections when I come" (I Corinthians 16:2 NKJV).

In our day, ministers and evangelists are often criticized for asking for financial support. But the critics are wrong, for here we see that Paul felt perfectly free to instruct the churches to which he wrote to give money, both to him and for other needs.

When he wrote to the Philippians, he commended them for being partners in his work. And here, in the first letter to the Corinthians, Paul instructs them to prepare to help support needy brothers and sisters in the Jerusalem church.

In neither case is Paul ashamed. Instead, he assumes that generous, cheerful giving is a normal part of the Christian life. He also speaks against giving only in immediate crises, declaring that the act of giving should be habitual!

Like many other aspects of Christian life, until we discover the blessing of giving financially, we will never know the full blessing of the Lord!

Direction for today: As a believer, make giving a habit.

Prayer for today: "Lord, direct me in my giving to Your work."

September 29: Read II Corinthians 1

Key verse: "For as the sufferings of Christ abound in us, so our consolation also abounds through Christ" (II Corinthians 1:5 NKJV).

God never leaves His people wanting. He has promised to meet our needs and He will always do so.

This does not mean, however, that everything we perceive to be a need is genuinely necessary! God certainly knows better than you or I do what we need or do not need.

For example, those who are suffering usually believe they need to be delivered. But Paul, who knew suffering in many forms, tells persecuted believers that, if they suffer, the consolation of the Holy Spirit—the Comforter—will abound to uphold them during that difficult circumstance.

God can deliver you from whatever trouble you are in, but He may also use those trials to strengthen you, all the while ministering to you by the the Holy Spirit. Allow Him to do what is best.

Direction for today: Trust God in every situation.

Prayer for today: "Lord, use my circumstances to strengthen my faith in You."

September 30: Read II Corinthians 2,3

Key verse: ". . . on the contrary, you ought rather to forgive and comfort him, lest perhaps such a one be swallowed up with too much sorrow" (II Corinthians 2:7 NKJV).

There are two great lacks among believers today: a lack of discipline and a lack of forgiveness. Both discipline and forgiveness must be based in Christ's love. Paul had much to say about each.

In I Corinthians 5, he is sharply critical of the Corinthians for tolerating sexual immorality in their midst. He commands them to deal quickly in disciplining the offending brother, a command that many churches today would do well to heed.

However, in II Corinthians 2, we encounter the contrasting command. Most scholars believe Paul is writing about the same situation, but that, this time, he is commanding the Corinthians to forgive and accept their repentant brother.

As Christians, we must be prepared to submit to the discipline of our churches, but we must also be eager to forgive anyone who repents of his or her sin. Too often, Christians seem to be far less forgiving than is our Lord.

Direction for today: Be eager to forgive.

Prayer for today: "Lord, show me if there is someone whom I have failed to forgive so that I may put that right. Help me to understand the completeness of Your mercy and grace."

10

Healing

*He walks in my heart garden
among flowers, wet with dew,
Withdraws weeds
Sows seeds of faith.*

*Comforted by His presence
Tranquility reigns.
His sacrifice
has released me.*

*Daily He tends the garden
Blossoms flourish,
His grace abounds—
My joy is to share His word.*

— *Kathleen Preston*

October 1: Read II Corinthians 4,5

Key verse: "Therefore, if anyone is in Christ, he is a new creation; old things have passed away; behold, all things have become new" (II Corinthians 5:17 NKJV).

This is a glorious promise!

Satan is a liar and a deceiver; he will continually attempt to convince the Christian that nothing has changed in his or her life. The devil would love to have us believe we are caught in all the old bondages, enslaved to all the same sins and trapped in the same wicked nature.

But he's lying! The Bible says that you are a new creation; none of the old remains! There is no need to continue in bondage: in Christ, you are free!

Act on the basis of God's word today. Turn from the enslaving habits of drugs, alcohol, tobacco, lust or greed that are, in reality, dead in Christ. Walk in your newness of life. Live like a new creation, for you are one, created anew by the one great Creator!

Direction for today: Live like a new creation!

Prayer for today: "Praise You, Jesus, that all things have become new. Help me to see situations and circumstances as You see them."

October 2: Read II Corinthians 6,7

Key verse: "Do not be unequally yoked together with unbelievers. For what fellowship has righteousness with lawlessness? And what communion has light with darkness?" (II Corinthians 6:14 NKJV).

The Bible has much to say about the Christian's relationships with unbelievers. Jesus made it plain that we are to be a light in our world, yet we are not to be "of the world". We are to take the message of Christ to unbelievers, but must be separate from their unbelief and sin.

Here Paul states that latter principle in very clear terms: Christians are not to be "yoked", or joined together, with those who do not share their faith. This applies to romantic attachments, business arrangements and any other circumstances which might compromise the Christian's ethics or integrity.

Far too many Christian young people have left their first love for Jesus because they have "fallen in love" with a non-Christian. Far too many Christian business people have found their honesty compromised through partnership with non-believers.

This passage does not imply that a Christian who is already married to a non-Christian should leave; it warns, instead, of initiating such relationships. Too often, the enemy has damaged a believer by laying such traps.

Direction for today: Obey the Lord and follow His principles in your relationships.

Prayer for today: "Lord, may my relationships always honour You".

October 3: Read II Corinthians 8

Key verse: *"For you know the grace of our Lord Jesus Christ, that though He was rich, yet for your sakes He became poor, that you through His poverty might become rich" (II Corinthians 8:9 NKJV).*

Jesus is not only our Saviour and Lord; He is also our great example. We are to strive to live like Christ as imitators of Him (Ephesians 5:11). That imitation has some very practical applications, as Paul points out to the Corinthians in this passage. Jesus willingly gave up all He had—and that is far more than all of us together will ever have—and became absolutely poor for us.

What is Jesus asking us to give up for Him? Too often, Christians strive to have all of the blessings of Christianity as well as those of our secular society. Sometimes, to be spiritually rich may mean that we must surrender our worldly wealth.

If the Lord has shown you His will for your possessions, be sure to obey Him. If, in disobedience to Him, you cling to earthly possessions, you will endanger your eternal inheritance.

Jesus became poor for you; in return, He asks that you be obedient to Him.

Direction for today: Do not risk the loss of eternal life by clinging to that which is temporal.

Prayer for today: "Lord, help me to follow You in all things."

Memory Verse

"The Lord is my rock and my fortress and my deliverer; my God, my strength, in whom I will trust; my shield and the horn of my salvation, my stronghold" " (Psalm 18:2 NKJV).

October 4: Read II Corinthians 9,10

Key verse: *"For the weapons of our warfare are not carnal but mighty in God for pulling down strongholds" (II Corinthians 10:4 NKJV).*

What strongholds do you face today? What problems and situations seem to be insurmountable? Claim this promise from the Lord right now: "the weapons of our warfare are . . . mighty in God for pulling down strongholds."

The Lord is eager to work in your life, in the midst of your problems and circumstances, to destroy the strongholds of the enemy and set you free! Perhaps you battle against strongholds in your own flesh—perhaps you need deliverance from habits or new healing. The weapons of our warfare are mighty in God.

Do you face strongholds in your family or among your co-workers? Are there people close to you who do not know the Lord, but to whom you cannot seem to break through for Jesus? Give those circumstances to the Lord, for the weapons of our warfare are mighty in God.

It may be that you sense strong spiritual attack against you, in your personal life or in your ministry. The weapons of our warfare are mighty in God!

Praise the Lord for the reality of this promise. Praise Him for the victory He has won for us. Praise Him for the difference it will make in your life when you claim this mighty promise!

Direction for today: Praise God for being your champion.

Prayer for today: "Lord, by Your Spirit, bring Your weapons of spiritual warfare to bear against the strongholds I face. Thank You."

October 5: Read II Corinthians 11

Key verse: "For Satan himself transforms himself into an angel of light. Therefore it is no great thing if his ministers also transform themselves into ministers of righteousness, whose end will be according to their works" (II Corinthians 11:14b,15 NKJV).

This is a strong, clear warning. Throughout this chapter, Paul is building walls of spiritual protection around his friends and fellow believers in Corinth. He is deeply concerned that they not be deceived and led into false teaching by a devilish "minister of light".

We need to be equally aware of these dangers today. If Satan cannot lure us from believing, he will try to trap us in false belief. The newspapers frequently carry stories about sincere people who have been lured to death and destruction by a false prophet who claimed to speak in the name of Jesus or even *as* Jesus Himself.

How can we be safe? The Lord is our protection. If we put our faith in Him, and not in any attractive leader, we will be protected. If we remain obedient to the Lord and to the promptings of the Holy Spirit; if we are faithful in the Word and in prayer and loyal to the body of believers that Jesus has placed us in, we will be protected.

As Jesus Himself said, beware of those who try to lure you with new revelations of Jesus.

Direction for today: Beware of the false teachers that abound.

Prayer for today: "Lord, by Your Spirit and through Your Word, keep me safe and strong, believing only in the gospel of Jesus Christ."

October 6: Read II Corinthians 12,13

Key verse: "And He said to me, 'My grace is sufficient for you, for My strength is made perfect in weakness.' Therefore most gladly I will rather boast in my infirmities, that the power of Christ may rest upon me" (II Corinthians 12:9 NKJV).

The Sunday school teacher was a humble man. He knew that he was not terribly intelligent, did not speak eloquently, and might not even be able to interest a class of young boys. In an earthly sense, he was the wrong person for the job. But God often works in exact contradiction to the systems of this world. How many times has that same situation occurred, and yet the blessing of the Lord has rested upon hundreds and thousands of inadequate, poorly trained Sunday school teachers.

All over the world, there are hundreds of thousands of believers who were led to the Lord by a teacher who was "wrong" for the job. But God doesn't worry about those things—if He has called you to a responsibility, His strength will be made perfect in your weakness.

Paul, who was a strong, powerful man, had to be made weak—blinded and confused on the road to Damascus—before the Lord could use him. Peter, who was impetuous and often egotistical, had to have his weaknesses exposed in his denial of Christ before he could be charged with the responsibility to "feed Christ's sheep". The strength of Jesus will be shown in your weakness if you are willing to let Him work through you.

Direction for today: Remember that your weaknesses are never a barrier to God.

Prayer for today: "Lord, may Your strength be shown through my weakness."

Ruth

In the midst of the time of the Judges comes this beautiful love story. The book of Ruth is an account of one of the most moving acts of loyalty and of the way the Lord honoured that loyalty and love. The pledge of Ruth is a truly blessed promise (1:16,17).

Even in the midst of the evil and corruption in Israel at this time there are those who love the Lord God. That number includes this one Moabite woman, who leaves her own people and religion for the people and religion of the Lord. In a time of apostasy, Ruth stands as a bright and shining light pointing to the way of faith, a way that was to be completed in her descendant, born over 1,000 years later, in Ruth's adopted hometown of Bethlehem. For, from the lineage of Ruth comes the Messiah, Jesus Christ!

October 7: Read Ruth 1,2

Key verse: "But Ruth said, 'Entreat me not to leave you, or to turn back from following after you; for wherever you go, I will go; and wherever you lodge, I will lodge; your people shall be my people, and your God, my God" (Ruth 1:16 NKJV).

What a beautiful example of loyalty and faithfulness! Ruth was a foreigner to Israel, a girl who had been raised to worship other gods, yet her love for Naomi prompted her completely to change her life in order to be with her.

This is a wonderful picture of the love that we, as believers, should have for the Lord Jesus. Our pledge to Him should echo those words: we will follow wherever He takes us; we will abide faithfully with Him; His people will be our new family and friends and His Father will be our Father.

You may read these words with a hint of sadness. Perhaps you have made these promises to Jesus, but realize today that you really have not kept them. Your first love and loyalty have grown cold.

What a wonderful opportunity to renew those vows of faithfulness and love for Christ. Right now, renew these promises to Him and, in the power of the Spirit, begin to live them out.

Direction for today: Renew your promise of faithful love to Christ.

Prayer for today: "Lord, I will follow You always, abide in You and love Your family, the church."

October 8: Read Ruth 3,4

Key verse: "And they called his name Obed. He is the father of Jesse, the father of David" (Ruth 4:17b NKJV).

God's blessings are always overwhelming! He gives and gives and gives far beyond anything we could imagine! If we are faithful to Him, we will never cease to receive from the fullness of the storehouses of heaven.

Ruth had little reason to expect anything from life. As a young widow she travelled with her mother-in-law to a land that was completely foreign to her. There, the two widows could expect only a harsh, hand-to-mouth existence; they would glean some grain and live on the occasional generosity of others.

Instead, Ruth is redeemed from her status by a wealthy kinsman, Boaz. That act of redemption is a picture of what our divine Redeemer does for us. Ruth is elevated to the status of honoured wife. In addition, she gives birth to a son and is not only a wife again but, for the first time, a mother. Naomi, who had lost her entire family, now has a precious grandson. What more could they ask?

Just this: Ruth, the Gentile newcomer to Israel, the woman raised under false gods, who accepted Naomi's God as her own, became the ancestor of our Lord Jesus. She was David's great-grandmother and from her direct line came Jesus Christ, born to another humble young woman.

Direction for today: Remember that God can do astounding things through a simple life that is yielded to Him.

Prayer for today: "Lord, give me a heart like that of Ruth."

I and II Samuel

The next two books tell of the "life and times" of three of the most interesting figures in the Bible—Samuel the prophet, Saul, the first king of Israel, and David, king, warrior, song-writer, musician, and "man after God's own heart."

They also tell how God acts regarding His people. These books, while written as history, are far more than that. For, while we see men interacting with men, the Holy Spirit has also granted us a far grander view. We see how God interacts with men, to bless, to warn and, if necessary, to condemn.

Samuel is a powerful man of God, a prophet who also seems to have the responsibilities of a priest. He is the last of the judges and the first of the prophets who are to have a key role in the next centuries of Israel. As we see his close relationship to God, we should ask that we, too, might hear God's voice and know Him.

Saul is a tragic case, a man initially anointed by the Spirit, who turned from God in rebellion and lost his contact with the Lord. Let us pray that God may keep us from a fate like that of Saul.

David, God's man, is shown, sins and all. We learn of his faith and great victories, both political and spiritual, but we also read of tragic failure and sin. David's heart was soft. He was open to rebuke and chastening and desired, most of all, to serve his God. Let us ask God for a heart like David's, open to the promptings of the Holy Spirit.

October 9: Read I Samuel 1

Key verse: "In bitterness of soul Hannah wept much and prayed to the Lord" (I Samuel 1:10 NIV).

Hannah—like Sarah and Rebekah in the Old Testament, and Elizabeth in the New—experienced the bitterness of being childless. For a time, Hannah could not bear the sorrow of her anguish and "wept and could not eat." Like many of us, with a fretful spirit, she took too much to heart the provocations of Peninnah and deprived herself of the comforts of her husband and God.

But then, like our blessed Saviour who, on the Mount of Olives, "being in anguish, prayed more earnestly" (Luke 22:44), she appealed to God. In fervent prayer, she committed her case to Him and "was no longer downcast".

Let us not be excessively concerned with the crosses we bear and thus miss the comfort of God through earnest prayer. Prayer can and does ease pain.

October 10: Read I Samuel 2

Key verse: "But now the Lord declares: 'Far be it from me! Those who honour Me I will honour, but those who despise Me will be disdained' " (I Samuel 2:30b NIV).

In this chapter, we see the dishonouring of God by the sons of Eli. While the priests were entitled to a share in the sacrificial offerings, they were seizing the best part of the meat before the offering had even been given to God. To make matters worse, they were debauching the women who came to worship at the door of the tabernacle.

The honour of the high priestly office was bestowed upon Eli's family provided they served faithfully. Walking continually before God was the condition of this covenant (see Genesis 17:1).

We are reminded of Jesus' words in John 12:26, "Whoever serves Me must follow Me; and where I am, my servant also will be. My Father will honour the one who serves Me." If we humble ourselves and keep our eyes on Jesus, we can depend on Him to honour us.

Direction for today: Be faithful in your service to God.

Prayer for today: "Help us, Father, to be like Jesus."

Memory Verse

"Now may the God of peace Himself sanctify you completely; and may your whole spirit, soul and body be preserved blameless at the coming of our Lord Jesus Christ" (I Thessalonians 5:23 NKJV).

October 11: Read I Samuel 3,4

Key verse: "Therefore, I swore to the house of Eli, 'The guilt of Eli's house will never be atoned for by sacrifice or offering' " (I Samuel 3:14 NIV).

In chapter 3, Samuel is directed by God to declare judgment on the house of Eli because he failed to discipline his sons for their contemptible behaviour. In chapter 4, we have the fulfillment of that judgment as Hophni and Phinehas die at the hands of the Philistines, together with 34,000 of their countrymen. To make matters worse, the ark of the covenant falls into enemy hands.

Our key verse points out the imperfection of the legal sacrifices which could not purge the iniquity of Eli's house. Praise God that today "the blood of Jesus, His Son, purifies us from all sin" (I John 1:7). We are saved from eternal death, which is the wages of sin.

Direction for today: "If we confess our sins, He is faithful and just and will forgive us our sins and purify us from all unrighteousness" (I John 1:9 NIV).

Prayer for today: "Thank you, Father, for the blood of Your Son Jesus Christ, which covers all our sins."

October 12: Read I Samuel 5,6

Key verse: "And the men of Beth Shemesh asked, 'Who can stand in the presence of the Lord, this holy God? To whom will the ark go up from here?' " (I Samuel 6:20 NIV).

In these chapters, we have a contrast of the handling of the ark in the hands of the Philistines and, subsequently, by the men of Beth Shemesh on its return to Israel. When the Philistines placed the ark in the temple beside their god, Dagon, they intended to do honour to the God of Israel; instead, they abused Him. They did not understand that the God of Israel did not share worship with an idol.

On the other hand, the men of Beth Shemesh offended God by looking into the ark. Even Israel had to learn not to overstep the mark and treat God as an object of idle curiosity.

Today we are invited, encouraged and enabled, through Jesus Christ, to stand before God and worship Him. Let us do it with reverence, not presuming upon His goodness or seeking to get all we can out of Him.

Direction for today: Acknowledge God in all things. Serve Him with wholehearted devotion and a willing mind.

Prayer for today: "Father, teach me never to take You for granted."

October 13: Read I Samuel 7,8

Key verse: "They said to him, 'You are old, and your sons do not walk in your ways; now appoint a king to lead us, such as all the other nations have' " (I Samnuel 8:5 NIV).

As Samuel grew older and his sons perverted their priestly office, the elders of Israel requested a king to rule over them "like all other nations have." While God had intimated to Israel that, in due time, they would have a king (Deuteronomy 17:14,15), He knew their motives were wrong at that point, and that they would suffer devastating consequences. In fact, they would face conscription, forced labour, and taxation, as well as loss of property and personal liberty. In effect, they would become slaves to the king. But even this did not deter them.

If Israel had waited ten or twelve years longer, they would have had as their king, David, a man after God's own heart, and would have avoided all the calamaties which befell them under Saul.

In making our requests to God, we should check our motives and seriously consider what might happen if God does answer our prayer. Perhaps God has something better for us if only we will wait for His timing; but we are often so impatient, aren't we? We don't want to wait at all.

Direction for today: When you pray, be sure that your requests are for God's glory and not your own. Be patient—wait for God's perfect timing.

Prayer for today: "Holy Spirit, teach us to pray according to our Father's will."

October 14: Read I Samuel 9

Key verse: "Now the day before Saul came, the Lord had revealed to Samuel; Tomorrow about this time I will send to you a man from the land of Benjamin, and you shall anoint him to be prince over My people Israel" (I Samuel 9:15,16a RSV).

Isn't it great to have the assurance that God knows your tomorrow? Oh, for the ability to relax and trust God implicitly. He loves you and is leading you! He doesn't make mistakes!

Each of us must learn to come before the Lord in all honesty; we must learn to confess our sins as soon as we sin. We must learn to repent and make things right with others. We do not know when we will start off looking for lost donkeys and end up being anointed by God for service.

Praise God! His ways are exciting and challenging. He brings deep satisfaction to the trusting, obedient heart.

Direction for today: Do what must be done. Don't worry. Keep watching for the evidence of God's presence.

Prayer for today: "Lord, keep me close to You. Cause me always to trust You rather than to demand from You *my* way."

October 15: Read I Samuel 10

Key verse: "When he turned his back to leave Samuel, God gave him another heart . . ." (I Samuel 10:9a RSV).

It is God's will to give His people a new heart. Jeremiah declares God will give His people a new heart and a right spirit. Have you been born from above? Are you filled with the Holy Spirit? Are you a member of the Kingdom of heaven? Is this Kingdom in your heart?

Jesus promised that all these things shall be "added unto" the one who seeks first His Kingdom. Many Christians today are longing for all the added unto things, but are failing to seek first the Kingdom.

Anyone who reads the Bible thoughtfully can see that God's people are a supernatural people. They have a new heart and a right mind; they are filled with the Holy Spirit and power, and are given specific direc-

tions—preach the kingdom of heaven, heal the sick, cast out demons, demonstrate the love of God to all people. Christians are God's people. Everything they do or say should glorify God.

Direction for today: Go forth in the name of Jesus and demonstrate to one and all that you have a new heart.

Prayer for today: "Lord, let my life be so under the blood of Jesus that others will see only Him in me."

October 16: Read I Samuel 11,12

Key verse: "Moreover as for me, far be it from me that I should sin against the Lord by ceasing to pray for you; and I will instruct you in the good and right way" (I Samual 12:23 RSV).

Saul passed his first test as king by leading the people in victory over the Ammonites; Samuel was praying for him. Saul's kingship was reestablished; Samuel was praying for him.

Do you have someone on whom you can count to pray for you? John Wesley was a proud, selfish, stubborn boy who loved the sinful crowd and turned his back on God, but his mother was praying for him. He became a worldwide evangelist and reformer; still his mother was praying for him.

For whom are you praying? Has God laid on your heart someone to hold up in prayer? You will enter into their work and their reward from

God by praying for them. Prayer changes things. Which things are you changing? Praise God for the privilege and power of prayer!

Direction for today: Take time to move God's hand in prayer.

Prayer for today: "God, I lift up (name that person) before You today. Give (him or her) victory over every testing and temptation, and make (him or her) fruitful in Your kingdom."

October 17: Read I Samuel 13

Key verse: "Samuel said to Saul, you have done foolishly; you have not kept the commandment of the Lord your God, which He commanded you; for now the Lord would have established your kingdom over Israel forever" (I Samuel 13:13 RSV).

How important is God's Word? We read, in Psalm 107:20, "He sent His Word and healed them" (KJV). The Word is light and truth. God's words last forever. His words have power to do good, heal, and to bring judgment. If we break God's Word and His eternal principles, then we must suffer the consequences. If we believe His Word and keep it, the blessings of His eternal principles are ours.

Saul broke God's Word and lost his kingdom. David kept His Word and became the first of an eternal dynasty through Jesus Christ.

Direction for today: Feed on God's Word. Meditate on it, memorize it and enjoy it.

Prayer for today: "Let Your Word, oh God, motivate me to work for Your honour and glory."

Memory Verse

"Therefore be mercviful, just as your Father also is merciful" (Luke 6:36 NKJV).

October 18: Read I Samuel 14

Key verse: ". . . for nothing can hinder the Lord from saving by many or by few" (1 Samuel 14:6b RSV).

Jonathan knew the power of God in Samuel's life. He had learned to believe in God and knew what God could do, so he acted on his faith and put God to the test. God had said he would deliver Israel from all of her enemies; Jonathan chose to believe God. God had said that one would put a thousand to flight; is God's Word true or not? Can we trust His promises or can't we? Jonathan found that one can depend on God's Word: he and his armour-bearer gained a great victory over the Philistines.

Do you know God's Word? Can you claim His promises? Will they work? You, too, can walk in victory even if by faith you claim God's promises.

Direction for today: Read God's Word in its context. Believe what it declares and act upon its direction.

Prayer for today: "Lord, let Your Word move mightily in and through my life."

October 19: Read I Samuel 15

Key verse: "But Samuel replied: Does the Lord delight in burnt offerings and sacrifices as much as in obeying the voice of the Lord? To obey is better than sacrifice, and to heed is better than the fat of rams" (I Samuel 15:22 NIV).

What a waste it is when one filled with great potential comes to nothing; when a life that started well ends so badly. Saul, a mighty man, chosen to be ruler of the nation of God, became rejected. Saul's biggest problem was himself: he wanted to build a kingdom for himself rather than for God.

Later, we see that David, Saul's successor, also sinned; but David did not lose his throne, nor did he lose God's love. What was the difference? Though David sinned horribly, he repented. When Saul sinned, he tried to blame it on others and to justify his mistakes. Saul's sin was an act of disobedience, a direct violation of what God had commanded him. His rebellion against God was immediately followed by building a monument to himself.

Upon hearing God's verdict, Saul's concern was with how he was looked upon by the nation. He wanted Samuel to make him look good before the elders and before Israel.

We all make mistakes, but honest repentance brings God's forgiveness. God hates rebellion. More than anything else He desires our obedience, and obedience earns His blessing.

Direction for today: Obey God always.

Prayer for today: "Lord, help me so to live that I may always be pleasing to You."

October 20: Read I Samuel 16

Key verse: ". . . The Lord does not look at the things man looks at. Man looks at the outward appearance, but the Lord looks at the heart" (I Samuel 16:7b NIV).

There are two key words in today's Scripture; these apply to all who would truly be children of God. They describe characteristics of all who have been used of God. Down through the annals of history, these characteristics have been predominant in all great church leaders. The words are: "chosen" and "served."

Samuel had to go all the way to the fields to find a shepherd boy whom God had chosen to be king. Surely, Samuel thought, God would choose a handsome man with great stature; but He did not. When God looks for a man or a woman, He looks at the heart.

If you belong to God's family, you, too, are "chosen." John 15:16 says, "You did not choose Me, but I chose you . . ." I Peter 2:9, 10 reads: "But you are a chosen people, a royal priesthood, a holy nation, a people belonging to God, that you may declare the praises of Him who called you out of darkness into His wonderful light. Once you were not a people, but now you are the people of God; once you had not received mercy, but now you have received mercy."

Isn't that exciting? We are chosen by God to belong to His royal family.

We are also called to serve. Samuel anointed David for service a number of years before he became king; David served humbly and he served well.

Direction for today: Remember that it is God who provides promotion. He doesn't need our help.

Prayer for today: "Thank you, Lord, for choosing me to serve You."

October 21: Read I Samuel 17

Key verse: "David said to the Philistine, 'You come against me with sword and spear and javelin, but I come against you in the name of the Lord Almighty, the God of the armies of Israel, whom you have defied' " (I Samuel 17:45 NIV).

The Philistine champion gave the challenge, "I defy the ranks of Israel." There were two responses to this daring challenge. Saul and all the Israelites were terrified, but David, the mere youth, had the heart of a brave man.

While tending the sheep, David used his hands to slay the lion and the bear, for the Lord was with him. He knew this nine-foot giant would fare no differently.

When David faced Goliath, there was a frightened, defeated army behind him, but with him were all the forces of heaven, doing battle in the name of the Lord. There is no such thing as defeat when God is with us. Goliath was big in stature, but David was big in faith.

David could not bear to hear anyone defy God. He rose to the challenge, not to defend his brothers, his country or his king, but to defend his God. David knew the battle was already won; that is why he could say to Goliath: "I come against you in the name of the Lord Almighty . . . This day the Lord will hand you over to me."

Direction for today: Face every problem and every situation in the name of the Lord.

Prayer for today: "Lord, in Your name help me to defeat the giants in my life."

October 22: Read I Samuel 18

Key verse: "In everything he did he had great success, because the Lord was with Him" (I Samuel 18:14 NIV).

When the Lord is in something, it cannot fail. Whatever David did, he met with great success. His key to success was his relationship with God.

Saul's successes had caused him to become arrogant; David's successes brought him closer to God. Motives determine relationships. Saul lived for self; David lived for God. As Cal Bombay once said, "Our greatness is in our humility. Our service to God is what counts; for the Christians all true success brings glory to Jesus."

Because Saul was living for himself, he became paranoid when David achieved success. He believed David was trying to gain leadership of the kingdom.

In today's reading, David teaches us three lessons. First, if we walk with God, He fights our battles, and God doesn't lose. Second, we don't have to do anything to further our own cause. Third, we must serve wholeheartedly. Even if those in authority do not know God or do what is right, my responsibility is to serve them "as unto the Lord."

Direction for today: Do not be selfish; selfishness has no place in leadership.

Prayer for today: "Lord, keep me so close to You that I may never notice when others do me wrong."

October 23: Read I Samuel 19

Key verse: "Jonathan spoke well of David to Saul his father and said to him, 'Let not the king do wrong to his servant David; he has not wronged you, and what he has done has benefited you greatly' " (I Samuel 19:4 NIV).

We all need friends. God graciously supplied this need in David's life through Jonathan. A true friend stands by us through all adversity. He will even put his life in danger in defense of the one he loves. Jonathan was such a friend.

As Christians, we, too, need friends in whom we can trust. Jesus is such a friend, but each of us also needs someone who will encourage us along the way. If you do not have such a friend, ask God to provide one. Also, you should be such a friend. The way to gain friendship is to offer friendship, but the motive must be to give, not to receive. It is in the giving that we receive.

Direction for today: Cultivate true friendship.

Prayer for today: "Lord, help me to be a friend to others, that I might encourage them."

October 24: Read I Samuel 20

Key verse: "And Jonathan again caused David to vow, because he loved him; for he loved him as he loved his own soul" (I Samuel 20:17 NKJV).

The key theme in this story is love. Jonathan and David understood what it meant to love ·with a godly love—their affection was shown in commitment, in the keeping of promises and the willingness of each to sacrifice himself for the good of the other.

We often think of David as a picture of the coming King of kings, Jesus Christ. Jonathan also serves as a prophetic example for, although he was heir to the crown, he was willing to give up all of his rights because of his love for his friend. Jesus "emptied Himself" (Philippians 2:7) for you because He loved you before you ever came to love Him; like Jonathan, He was willing to die for His loved ones.

Too often, God's people fail to act in love toward their brothers and sisters in Christ. To the watching, hostile world, the church is frequently a terrible example of love, showing instead strife, bickering and bitterness.

We can learn much from the love between these two godly men, David and Jonathan.

Direction for today: Be sure your love for Christ and for fellow believers is a godly example of commitment and self-sacrifice.

Prayer for today: "Lord, may I learn to love as You love."

Memory Verse

"The fear of man brings a snare, but whoever trusts in the Lord shall be safe" (Proverbs 29:25 NKJV)

October 25: Read I Samuel 21,22

Key verse: "And everyone that was in distress, and everyone that was in debt, and everyone that was discontented, gathered themselves unto him; and he became a captain over them: and there were with him about four hundred men" (I Samuel 22:2 KJV).

This key verse shows the kinds of people who followed David to seek refuge from Saul.

Later, David was also joined by the priest Abiathar, who gave spiritual leadership to his fledgling kingdom. Thus, David was equipped with a small, but powerful and faithful group of followers who shared a common situation. Each had suffered at the hands of Saul and his governments; each one may have seen an opportunity to improve conditions if David were to be made king. All were fugitives whose lives were in constant danger from their enemies—but they gave their allegiance to David.

We have given our allegiance to Christ. When He is crowned King, we shall reign with Him and the world will be full of righteousness.

Direction for today: Live today as though you will reign with Christ tomorrow.

Prayer for today: "Lord, help me to encourage others to follow You."

October 26: Read I Samuel 23

Key verse: "David stayed in strongholds in the wilderness, and remained in the mountains in the wilderness of Ziph. Saul sought him every day, but God did not deliver him into his hand" (I Samuel 23:14 NKJV).

Like David, each Christian is pursued by an enemy: "Your adversary the devil walks about like a roaring lion, seeking whom he may devour" (I Peter 5:8b). But, like David, Christians have nothing to fear from that enemy as long as we remain safe within our stronghold.

David had many hiding places in the wilderness where he could safely rest in rocks and caves, but he knew who his true "Stronghold" was— "The Lord is my rock, and my fortress, and my deliverer" (Psalm 18:2a). David was not saved from Saul because he was clever and adept at covering his tracks, nor because he was physically stronger or faster than the king. He was saved because God kept him safe.

Just like David, we can rely on our God, our Stronghold, to keep us safe when the enemy attacks. Our Lord is a sure safety, an omnipotent protector.

Direction for today: Be sure that you are safely hidden in the stronghold—the arms of the Lord.

Prayer for today: "Lord, thank You for protection, safety and deliverance."

October 27: Read I Samuel 24

Key verse: "The Lord judge between me and thee, and the Lord avenge me of thee: but mine hand shall not be upon thee" (I Samuel 24:12 KJV).

David was determined that he would not kill Saul although Saul was determined to kill him. He believed that God Himself would deal with Saul in His own good time. David also knew that God was merciful and might have a plan whereby Saul could be spared the embarrassment of losing his kingdom. He did not covet Saul's crown; because he knew God had chosen him for that position, David was content to wait for God's timing in allowing him to rule over Israel.

David wanted to be like the Lord, and he revealed his godly character when he showed mercy to Saul in the cave.

Jesus said, "Love your enemies, bless tham that curse you, do good to them that hate you, and pray for them which despitefully use you . . . That ye may be the children of your Father which is in heaven" (Matthew 5:44-45a).

We may find it difficult not to retaliate when others do us wrong, but God can and will deal with them in a far wiser way than we would.

Direction for today: Let God deal with your enemies.

Prayer for today: "Lord, help me to follow Your example of mercy and love."

October 28: Read I Samuel 25

Key verse: "And blessed be thy advice, and blessed be thou, which hast kept me this day from coming to shed blood, and from avenging myself with mine own hand" (I Samuel 25:33 KJV).

Nabal was wrong in refusing to help David, but David was also wrong in his decision to take revenge against him. Sometimes, in our anger and frustration, we make decisions we would never consider in calmer moments. Hasty decisions can be dangerous; when they are accompanied by rash, irresponsible actions, they can cause irreparable harm.

David was about to do something for which he would forever be sorry. He had judged Nabal guilty and had decided on the punishment, a task which truly was not his. However, God had some wise counsel for him if only he would be sensitive enough to realize that it was coming from the Lord.

Finally, as he listened to the advice given to him through Abigail, David did realize that God was speaking to him. God speaks to us today in a number of ways: it may be through passages in His Word, through a sermon or a word of prophecy, or by an impression in our spirit (through a God-given inner sense) that we are being directed to take a certain action.

Perhaps you have never experienced God's guidance. Today, simply expect that He will make His way clear to you and then be open to receive it in whichever way He chooses to give it.

Direction for today: Listen for the advice of the Lord.

Prayer for today: "Lord, help me to be a sensitive listener."

October 29: Read I Samuel 26,27

Key verse: "And the Lord will repay each man for his righteousness and his faithfulness" (I Samuel 26:23a NAS).

David and Abner had an excellent opportunity to rid Israel—and themselves—of the rule of Saul; having entered Saul's camp at night, they could easily have killed him. Abner wanted to kill Saul, but David refused to harm the Lord's anointed.

David then declared to his men that the Lord would repay each man for his righteousness and his faithfulness. Though David must have wondered if he would ever indeed rule as king of Israel, he needed to remind himself that God was in control.

All of us need to ask that from time to time. Is God really in charge? David asked that question and so did Job. Doubtless Joseph and Daniel also asked it. When all seems lost and it seems that nothing more can go wrong, it's easy to complain to God.

That's the time during which we need to remind ourselves of God's faithfulness. As they were about to be thrown into a fiery furnace, Shadrach, Meshach and Abednego asked themselves the same question. They were able to say that, no matter what, they would trust God.

That's the place to which each of us must come—to acknowledge that God is in control, and that He will reward our total trust and faithfulness.

Direction for today: Trust the Lord—He is in control.

Prayer for today: "Father, teach me to recognize Your love and care for me, no matter what my circumstance may be."

October 30: Read I Samuel 28,29

Key verse: "When Saul inquired of the Lord, the Lord did not answer him, either by dreams or by Urim or by prophets" (I Samuel 28:6 NAS).

This must be a horrible state to be in—when the Lord no longer speaks to one who had been chosen by Him. That was now Saul's situation. It was because of Saul's disobedience that God had become silent. What Samuel had told Saul earlier is exactly what was coming to pass.

Saul was desperate. Surrounded by the Philistines, he knew he was in big trouble; he needed help, and he needed it fast. Though he undoubtedly remembered Samuel's earlier warning (I Samuel 14:23) about rebellion being equal to divination, he felt he desperately needed help. Although he knew that, in obedience to God, mediums had been driven out of the land, he thought he had to find one, for that was how he would obtain the direction he needed.

How sad! Saul, chosen by God to lead Israel, was now set aside. When he really needed God, he looked to another form of help.

What about you? To what or to whom do you turn when your back is against the wall? What is your reaction to a God who seems quiet? Do you, perhaps, "conjure up" your own form of help?

God is "Emmanuel"—"God with us"! That does not ever change. Perhaps today you need to confess that God reigns and *is* trustworthy.

Direction for today: Believe the Word of the Lord.

Prayer for today: "Father, into Your hands I commit myself."

October 31: Read I Samuel 30,31

Key verse: "Moreover David was greatly distressed because the people spoke of stoning him, for all the people were embittered, each one because of his sons and his daughters. But David strengthened himself in the Lord his God" (I Samuel 30:6 NAS).

These devotional thoughts are like yesterday's in that both deal with our reaction when under pressure. But that's the only similarity. Saul's and David's reactions are as different as night and day.

David and his men had returned to camp to discover that their families had been taken captive, and their possessions wiped out by the Amalekites. Not only was David grieving his personal loss, he was also concerned by the bitterness of his men, who had lost their wives and children.

Once again, we catch a glimpse of the greatness of David. He could have pleaded innocence and claimed it wasn't his fault. He could have pointed out that he had lost two wives, not just one.

And David himself could have become bitter towards God; instead, he "strengthened himself in the Lord his God."

What is your first reaction when you are unjustly accused, when you have lost something or someone precious to you? Because David knew that the Lord was his strength, he could lean on God and endure.

Direction for today: Strengthen yourself in the Lord.

Prayer for today: "Thank you, Father, that You are my Strength."

11

Fortress

It is as I crumble,
Having glimpsed the real me
and recoiling in horror,

that I understand why
You had to die for my sin—

As sobs wrack my body and tears stream
down my face,

I realize how much more
You have grieved for me

Time and time again;

Your unfailing, unconditonal love
compels the eyes of my spirit

To look up,
beyond my faltering steps
and gross weakness,

To Your indomintable strength

— Hilda Schnell

"Therefore, having been justified by faith, we have peace with God through our Lord Jesus Christ" (Romans 5:1 NKJV).

November 1: Read II Samuel 1

Key verse: *"Then David said to him, 'How is it you were not afraid to stretch out your hand to destroy the Lord's anointed?' " (II Samuel 1:14 NAS).*

Again, we notice David's utmost respect for the Lord's anointed. He knew that he himself had been anointed by God to succeed Saul. Indeed, there were those in David's camp who wanted him to exercise his right and wipe out Saul. If he had taken a poll, he would surely have found that the people wanted a change and, given his popularity, David would certainly have defeated Saul.

But his goal was always and only to please the Lord and to act in a godly way and in God's time, so David chose to honour the Lord's anointed.

What of us today? Do we honor the Lord's anointed servants as we ought? Those placed in positions of authority over us are, in effect, the Lord's anointed. We are commanded to pray for them and to honour them as anointed of God and placed in those positions by God Himself.

Direction for today: Honour the Lord's anointed: that is what He requires you to do.

Prayer for today: "Father, teach me to see Your hand for my good in those whom You place over me."

November 2: Read II Samuel 2

Key verse: *"And David sent messengers to the men of Jabesh-gilead, and said to them, 'May you be blessed of the Lord because you have shown this kindness to Saul your lord, and have buried him' " (II Samuel 2:5 NAS).*

May you be blessed of the Lord.

The men of Jabesh-gilead had shown kindness to Saul's body by taking it and burying it. David remembered that and thanked them for what they had done. I don't believe he was looking for any favours from them; rather he was the kind of person who took time to remember to thank others.

"May you be blessed of the Lord . . ." We can all add our own greeting to those few words, yet we do this so infrequently.

The story is told of a man who was moved to remember a school teacher who had given of her time and care to make something of him when he had no ambition in life. That man wrote a note to the teacher, thanking her for every effort she had made. She, now an elderly lady, told how meaningful that note was and how it had blessed her.

I'd like to encourage you today to have the Lord show you someone whom you can encourage. Write that person a note expressing appreciation—and call on the telephone, or pay a visit. Maybe it'll be an elderly parent whose sleepless nights and prayer vigils on your behalf you might consider. Maybe it'll be a pastor or teacher, a thoughtful child, a friendly neighbour, an employer or an employee. Thank that one today for what he or she has done for you. You will be glad you did!

Direction for today: Thank someone today—and be blessed!

Prayer for today: "Lord, I thank You for those whom You have placed in my life. Help me always to express my appreciation to them—never to take them for granted."

November 3: Read II Samuel 3

Key verse: "Now there was a long war between the house of Saul and the house of David. But David grew stronger and stronger, and the house of Saul grew weaker and weaker" (II Samuel 3:1 NKJV).

There is nothing more foolish than to stand against the will of the Lord. Yet that is exactly what a huge majority of people spend their lives doing. Even Christians often decide that in certain circumstances they want to go their own way rather than God's way.

Today's key verse should be a warning to all. Saul's family and supporters continued his enmity with David. In doing so, they were not only opposing an earthly king, but were fighting against the plan of God. Nobody wins in that situation!

Sure enough, "the house of Saul grew weaker and weaker." That is the inevitable fate of any who oppose the will of the Lord. Unbelievers who live in rebellion will see their lives dwindle and end. Christians who foolishly ignore God's will soon find that their spiritual strength and blessings have disappeared.

Far better to stand with David in the will of God—for His will will be done!

Direction for today: It is difficult, foolish and, ultimately, fatal to stand against the will of the Lord.

Prayer for today: "Lord, show me Your will and I will do it!"

November 4: Read II Samuel 4,5

Key verse: "David was thirty years old when he began to reign, and he reigned forty years" (II Samuel 5:4 NKJV).

Those first three decades of David's life must have seemed like an eternity to the young man. Early in his life, he was anointed by the prophet Samuel as king. For many years, he carried that unfulfilled promise in his heart.

But David always knew that God is faithful to His Word. He knew that the Lord would fulfill all that had been prophesied and refused to try to find a shortcut to the throne. When he had opportunities to kill Saul, David refused to do so. He was willing to wait during all of those years of running and hiding in the wilderness.

God kept His promises. David was crowned king by his people and reigned for a much longer time than his waiting period had been!

Often, we would like to hurry God along—to bring about His plans sooner than He wills it. We need to learn to have the patience and trust of David, knowing that God will keep His promises in His time.

Direction for today: Trust God to keep His Word.

Prayer for today: "Lord, give me the patience of the Spirit to wait on You."

November 5: Read II Samuel 6

Key verse: "They brought the ark of the Lord and set it in the place" (II Samuel 6:17a NIV).

Psalm 68 was probably written when the ark was brought to Jerusalem. Its opening words remind us of what Moses used to say whenever the ark set out: "Arise, O Lord . . ." (Numbers 10:35). As Jerusalem was built on land elevated far above most of the surrounding countryside, the psalmist records (in reference to bringing the ark up to Jerusalem): "Thou didst ascend the high mount" (Psalm 68:18).

Paul was later to apply this to Christ's ascension into heaven when writing to the Ephesians (4:8). Just as the joyful entrance into Jerusalem with the ark symbolized God's seating Himself on His throne, so the ascension into heaven further revealed the kingship of Jesus our Lord.

Not everyone was happy on this occasion. Saul's daughter Michal, who had been restored as David's wife, watched. She loved the famous hero, not the simple believer. No one in Saul's house had been concerned about the ark. To her, it was a mystery that everyone was so happy.

Because of Michal's scoffing, she became childless. The house of David was not to be built through her. She did not share David's faith nor his attitude toward the people. When we fear the Lord, we are one with God's people.

Direction for today: Like David, be wholehearted in your worship of the Lord.

Prayer for today: "Thank You, O Lord, for Your ever-abiding presence in my life."

November 6: Read II Samuel 7

Key verse: "*Your house and your kingdom will endure forever before Me; Your throne will be established forever*" *(II Samuel 7:16 NIV).*

The Lord had indeed given David the victory over his enemies but, because of those wars, David's reign was filled with conflict. His son would reap the fruits of the victories and would be a king of peace. The Lord would build David's house forever, and David's son would build a house for the Lord.

This was the Lord's covenant with David. The Lord gave David that great promise not because of any merit on David's part, but out of free grace. The promise could only be truly fulfilled through Christ—David's great son. He would build the real temple.

The Lord fulfilled this in a marvelous way, building His people as a temple when He poured out His Holy Spirit. When Christ returns, He will make the entire earth a house of God.

Direction for today: Remember that the words of the Lord are trustworthy.

Prayer for today: "Thy kingdom come, Thy will be done in earth, as it is in heaven."

November 7: Read II Samuel 8-10

Key verse: "*. . . I will surely show you kindness for the sake of your father Jonathan . . . and you will always eat at my table*" *(II Samuel 9:7 NIV).*

In chapter nine, we see the Lord's lovingkindness toward Saul's descendants. His family was not wiped out from among the people of Israel. Mephibosheth already had a little son, thus preserving the family name and inheritance.

David had shown his faithfulness to the covenant he had once made with his friend Jonathan (I Samuel 20:14-16). If a covenant between two people can be upheld—as we see from David's loyalty to his vow with Jonathan—how much more faithful will Jesus be to the covenant He has made with us, His bride.

Though he deemed himself unworthy, Mephibosheth received again Saul's family estate, was admitted to the royal table and treated as one of the king's sons. All this was due to the unmerited favour of the king; it is a picture of all those spiritual blessings with which the God and Father of our Lord Jesus Christ has blessed us in heavenly places in Him (Ephesians 1:3).

Direction for today: Seek ways today to show unmerited favour to someone. There is special blessing and strength for this from God.

Prayer for today: "Father, may we tap into Your capacity to show grace in a greater way. Teach us, Lord!"

"Add to your faith virtue, to virtue knowledge, to knowledge self-control, to self-control perseverance, to perseverance godliness, to godliness brotherly kindness, and to brotherly kindness love" (II Peter 1:5b-7 NKJV).

November 8: Read II Samuel 11-12

Key verse: *"In the spring, at the time when kings go off to war, David sent Joab out with the king's men and the whole Israelite army. They destroyed the Ammonites and beseiged Rabbah. But David remained in Jerusalem" (II Samuel 11:1 NIV).*

Our key verse describes how David sets himself up for temptation and disaster by idling around the palace when he should have been with his army in the field. Had he been at his post at the head of his forces, he would have avoided this temptation, which led to adultery with Bathsheba and the murder of Uriah.

Scripture is faithful in relating the faults of even those it holds in high regard. Idleness gives great opportunity to the tempter; this story is recorded so that we can take warning from the sins of David.

Let us heed Paul's admonition to the Corinthians: "I want you to be wise about what is good, and innocent about what is evil" (Romans 16:19b).

Direction for today: Do not let temptation give root to sin.

Prayer for today: "Father in Heaven, lead us not into temptation, but deliver us from evil."

November 9: Read II Samuel 13

Key verse: *"Then Amnon hated her with intense hatred. In fact, he hated her more than he had loved her. Amnon said to her, 'Get up and get out!' " (II Samuel 13:15 NIV).*

In the previous chapter, we read that Nathan chastised David for his sin with respect to the murder of Uriah and told him that the sword would never depart from his house (II Samuel 12:10). In chapter 13, we find this prophecy beginning to unfold as David is beset with one trouble after another. Adultery and murder were David's sins, and were repeated among his children. Amnon defiled his sister Tamar, and Absolom murdered his brother Amnon. This was all part of David's punishment.

In our key verse, we see the devil, as tormentor and betrayer, immediately turning Amnon's love for Tamar into hatred. We can learn from this the terrible consequences of sin. Sin may be temporarily sweet but, afterwards, it becomes painful.

Direction for today: Do not desire forbidden fruit.

Prayer for today: "Help me, Lord, to put aside evil desires."

November 10: Read II Samuel 14

Key verse: "Like water spilled on the ground, which cannot be recovered, so we must die. But God does not take away life; instead, He devises ways so that a banished person may not remain estranged from Him" (II Samuel 14:14 NIV).

In this chapter, we read of the devious way in which Joab brought about a reconciliation between David and his son Absolom. He brings a widow before the king to present a fake issue on which David is asked to waive the next of kin's obligation to avenge her murdered relative. The application to David is obvious, Joab wins his point and Absolom is returned from exile.

In her appeal, the widow pleads God's mercy and His clemency to guilty sinners. While the case she presented was false, the two instances of God's mercy cited by her were true.

First, we see the patience He displays towards those who break His law, for He does not immediately take away the lives of those who break it. Secondly, He has made provision for their restoration to His favour, for "He is not willing that any should perish" (II Peter 3:9).

Direction for today: Remember the words of the Apostle Peter: "Bear in mind that our Lord's patience means salvation" (II Peter 3:15a NIV).

Prayer for today: "Father, I pray that lost loved ones will heed Your call."

November 11: Read II Samuel 15

Key verse: "Now David had been told, 'Ahithophel is among the conspirators with Absalom! So David prayed, 'O Lord, turn Ahithophel's counsel into foolishness' " (II Samuel 15:31 NIV).

From Chapter 12, the saga of David's family reads like a horror story, with incest, murder, intrigue and rebellion. Now his favourite son, Absalom, after four years of planning, tries to usurp his father's throne.

To David, nothing seemed more threatening in Absalom's plot than that Ahithophel, his counselor, was involved. David reasoned that, if he could outwit Ahithophel's farsighted counsel, Absolom's conspiracy was doomed to failure. But take note how David sets out to accomplish this.

First, he prays, not against Ahithophel personally, but against his counsel. Secondly, he writes the third Psalm, a song of worship to the Lord.

What a testimony to David's faith and total dependence on God to deliver him from his enemies!

Direction for today: Like David, learn to put your trust completely in the Lord and to worship Him even when you don't feel like doing so.

Prayer for today: "Help us, Lord, to back up our prayers with obedience."

November 12: Read II Samuel 16

Key verse: "Now in those days the advice Ahithophel gave was like that of one who inquires of God. That was how both David and Absalom regarded all of Ahithophel's advice" (II Samuel 16:23 NIV).

As Absalom makes his triumphant entry into Jerusalem, he brings with him his political advisor, Ahithophel. While Ahithophel is noted for his political wisdom, the advice he gives to Absalom is far from wise. Finding that David had left his concubines to take care of the palace, he advises Absalom to sin by taking over his father's harem. No king could forgive such a public insult.

It is interesting to note that, by Absalom's compliance with this wicked advice, the Word of God was fulfilled. God had told David, through Nathan the prophet, that, because he had committed adultery with Bathsheba, his own wives would be publicly defiled (II Samuel 12:11,12).

Today, we ought to be very careful of those who excel in worldly wisdom and set themselves up as oracles of God but are, in truth, completely devoid of God's grace.

Direction for today: Beware that anyone who encourages you to act outside of the will of God is a tool of Satan.

Prayer for today: "Protect me, Father, from those who would cause me to stumble."

November 13: Read II Samuel 17

Key verse: "And Absalom and all the men of Israel said, 'Counsel of Hushai the Arkite is better than the counsel of Ahithophel. For the Lord has ordained to defeat the good counsel of Ahithophel, so that the Lord might bring evil upon Absalom" (II Samuel 17:14 RSV).

Our God is in control of everything. He permits certain things to happen as we exercise our free will, but His great plan for the ages—as well as His plan for our lives—will not be altered by someone else.

Absalom had exercised his free will. He had rebelled against his father, and, therefore, against God. Ahithophel had given sound advice that could have led to David's defeat and Absalom's becoming king.

God anointed Hushai to speak more forcefully and persuasively to convince Absalom and all Israel to do differently. This led directly to Absalom's defeat.

God confutes the wise and exalts those of low account. Be sure your life is totally given over to Jesus and His will for you.

Direction for today: Seek the kingdom first, and you will find God's wisdom and direction.

Prayer for today: "Lord, I seek You and Your purpose for me."

November 14: Read II Samuel 18

Key verse: "Then the king was deeply moved, and went up to the chamber over the gate, and wept. And as he went, he said thus: 'O my son Absalom—my son, my son Absalom—if only I had died in your place! O Absalom my son, my son!' " (II Samuel 18:33 NKJV).

David's son had led a rebellion against him. Absalom had conspired to destroy his father and to wrest the kingdom from him. But, even though his son had become his declared enemy, David had attempted to guard his life in battle; when his command was ignored, he wept and mourned the death of his rebellious son.

He went so far as to declare that he would have been willing to die in Absalom's place. This of course, he could not do.

God's children have rebelled against Him, as well. Each of us, in our sin, has conspired to war against God and to be lord of our own lives in His place. But, even though we are enemies of God, the Father has declared Himself willing to be our Protector, our Deliverer, and our Saviour. God does not delight in the death of the wicked, but is willing that all should come to repentance.

Unlike David, God did not only wish to die in our place; He did so! Jesus died so that enemies of God could become sons and daughters of God.

What love has been shown to us!

Direction for today: Remember that, while you were still a sinner—an enemy of God—Christ died for you!

Prayer for today: "Thank You, Lord, for such overwhelming love!"

Memory Verse

"The Spirit of the Lord shall rest upon Him, the Spirit of wisdom and understanding, the Spirit of knowledge and of the fear of the Lord" (Isaiah 11:2 NKJV).

November 15: Read II Samuel 19

Key verse: "But the king covered his face, and the king cried out with a loud voice, 'O my son Absalom! O Absalom, my son, my son!' " (II Samuel 19:4 NKJV).

Paul tells us, in Galatians 6:7, that God will not be mocked by our actions: whatever we sow, that we will reap. Here, we see an element of David's bitter harvest.

He had sinned in comitting murder, adultery and in lying. In response to Nathan's parable (II Samuel 12:6), David had pronounced a four-fold judgment, little realizing that he was issuing his own penalty. He reaped that judgment: the baby died, Amnon seduced his sister Tamar, Absalom killed Amnon, and Absalom lost his life in battle against his father.

But, even though David was broken by those circumstances, his followers were right in urging him to go on in victory. As long as we live, it is never too late to claim the victory the Lord has for us.

Direction for today: Press on by faith. Meet the challenge in the power of the Holy Spirit.

Prayer for today: "Lord, thank You for forgiveness, restoration and revitalization."

November 16: Read II Samuel 20,21

Key verse: "Now there was a famine in the days of David for three years, year after year, and David inquired of the Lord" (II Samuel 21:1a NKJV).

These two chapters reveal a land in which a lot of housecleaning was

still necessary. There were rebellions, and there was unfinished business for David to complete.

He was faithful to the Lord in cleansing the land. He put down the rebellions and righted wrongs that were pointed out to him by the Lord.

We need to inquire of the Lord, as well. Often, there are problems in our lives of which we are not even aware, but the Lord is willing to reveal them to us and enable us to clean our house.

If we do not come to the Lord regularly, it may take a major crisis—perhaps an illness or other major trauma—before we listen to Him and obey Him.

Direction for today: Keep in touch with God—and in tune with His will.

Prayer for today: "Lord, show me any housecleaning that needs to be done in my life."

November 17: Read II Samuel 22

Key verse: *"And he said, 'The Lord is my rock, my fortress and my deliverer" (II Samuel 22:2 NKJV).*

These words take on much more significance since we have just read chapter after chapter from the life of David. The king has lived a perilous life fleeing first from Saul and later from his own son. From the earliest days as a shepherd boy among the wild beasts to the rebellions that threatened his life in the latter years of his reign, David knew the need for a hiding place in a time of crisis.

David had hidden in the cleft of a rock; he had known the protection of a fortress, but he experiences no confusion about how he had been saved each time—he was never protected only by a physical rock or a fortress made of stone. He knew that his true deliverer in every case was the Lord God.

David had no doubt that, throughout every moment of his life, the Lord was with Him. For this he offered great praise.

Is this any less true for you?

Direction for today: The Lord is your rock, your fortress and your deliverer.

Prayer for today: "Praise You, Lord, that You are always there: my fortress and my deliverer."

November 18: Read II Samuel 23

Key verse: *". . . When one rules over men in righteousness, when he rules in the fear of God, he is like the light of morning at sunrise on a cloudless morning, like the brightness after rain that brings the grass from the earth." (II Samuel 23:3b, 4 NIV).*

In this, David's last sermon, he relates the results of a fruitful life and ministry. When the ungodly rule a nation, its people tremble in fear. On the other hand, when the righteous rule, the nation flourishes and rejoices. Here David says that righteous rulership is like the light in the morning, bursting forth to usher in a new and glorious day. It is like the fresh, fragrant air that comes after the rain. David had a good reign, although not without its struggles. Righteousness ruled and reigned, and the nation flourished.

David had a successful reign because the Lord was with him, but also because he had good men around him. Today's leaders also need good people to support. When Jesus walked the dusty roads, He had people to help Him. Our pastors need the support of God's people; they need our loyalty, our efforts and prayers. They cannot stand alone.

The men around David appear to have been extremely loyal. We, too, need to be loyal to God, to those who have spiritual oversight over us and to those in civil authority.

Direction for today: Pray for those whom the Lord has placed over you.

Prayer for today: "Lord, teach me to be truly loyal."

November 19: Read II Samuel 24

Key verse: "David built an altar to the Lord there and sacrificed burnt offerings and fellowship offerings. Then the Lord answered prayer in behalf of the land, and the plague on Israel was stopped" (II Samuel 24:25 NIV).

Sin is a violation against God. It stirs the wrath of God and must be dealt with.

Obviously, the children of Israel were committing national sins. Comparing today's Scripture with I Chronicles 21:1, which records the same event, it appears God decided to test His people by allowing Satan to tempt them with sin. The Chronicles' account says Satan provoked David to number Israel.

The numbering of the armed forces by David was an act of pride and self-gratification, but he gave in to sin. One tragedy of sin is its widespread effect. Our sins do not affect only us, but others around us. The higher the position, the greater the influence.

We are constantly influencing others. We influence by our words, actions and attitude; even a smile or a frown influences others. We can influence for good or bad.

David's sin led to the death of 70,000 people. Although he repented, sacrificed and gained God's mercy, others were still adversely affected. Will you spread good or evil?

Direction for today: Remember that your life affects others. Live accordingly.

Prayer for today: "Lord, may my life draw others to You."

Galatians

When Paul wrote to the Christians in the district of Asia Minor (now Turkey) known as Galatia, he wrote from the heart at once angry and concerned. He loved the Galatian Christians, and expressed that love, but he was also very upset that they had abandoned the freedom of the Holy Spirit for a religious life bound in legalism.

Teachers had come to Galatia and had convinced the Christians that faith in Jesus was not enough to save them: they must also obey the Old Testament law.

Paul argued that the law has fulfilled its purpose, that of showing men and women that they are hopelessly bound in sin. Now, he said, Christ has come to set us free from sin.

As you read, allow God to show you any areas in which you may be bound in legalism, and then celebrate the truth that Jesus has made you free indeed!

November 20: Read Galatians 1,2

Key verse: "I marvel that you are turning away so soon from Him who called you in the grace of Christ, to a different gospel" (Galatians 1:6 NKJV).

Do you remember the first days of your life as a Christian—days of enormous joy and peace? Can you recall the immense freedom you felt and the wonderful realization that Jesus loved you just as you are?

Is your life still full of that joy, peace, freedom and sense of acceptance? Perhaps not. For many Christians, these important things quickly fade as the enemy sneaks in like a thief and robs them of these precious gifts from God.

This is what happened to the Galatian Christians. They had discovered the freedom that is available in Christ, but soon turned to "another gospel," which was really no gospel (good news) at all. They began to try to please God, to live a good life through obeying a set of rules but, instead, became joyless legalists.

Paul had very hard words for these brothers and sisters in Christ. He told them, clearly and directly, that they were wrong and that they had been stupid. He called them back to the freedom that was theirs in Christ, to the joy of serving Jesus because of love and the power of the Spirit, not because of bondage to duty.

Direction for today: Call on the Lord to restore His joy and freedom to your life!

Prayer for today: "Father, may I again know my first love for You; restore to me Your joy!"

November 21: Read Galatians 3,4

Key verse: "And because you are sons, God has sent forth the Spirit of His Son into your hearts, crying out, 'Abba, Father!' " (- Galatians 4:6 NKJV).

What a tremendous change! We were enemies of God, but have become His friends—and more than friends, we have become children of God. As His enemies, we deserved His wrath. Instead, He has shown us His infinite love. We deserved to be punished; instead, we are welcomed into the kingdom of God as members of His family.

In these chapters, the Apostle Paul explains the astounding change of status to his Galatian friends. He tells them that they have come from being slaves—slaves to sin, to obedience out of duty and to inevitable death—to being heirs, members of the family of God.

In keeping with the earlier chapters, Paul chastises them for continuing to live as slaves when, in reality, they have the rights, privileges and freedoms of sons and daughters of the King.

And, for those who doubted his words, Paul added our key verse: we know we are children of God, not only because the Word tells us so, but because the Lord has sent His Spirit into our hearts, bringing a witness of our status as children of God.

If you are a child of God, the Holy Spirit bears witness in you to that reality. If you do not sense such a testimony by the Spirit, then simply tell that to the Lord and ask Him to confirm in you that you are indeed a "King's kid."

Direction for today: One of our sources of strength and confidence is the inner witness of the Holy Spirit.

Prayer for today: "Thank you, Father, that You are my Father, and that I am Your child!"

Memory Verse

"Beloved, do not imitate what is evil, but what is good. He who does good is of God, but he who does evil has not seen God" (III John 11 NKJV).

November 22: Read Galatians 5,6

Key verse: "But the fruit of the Spirit is love, joy, peace, longsuffering, kindness, goodness, faithfulness, gentleness, self-control. Against such there is no law" (Galatians 5:22,23 NKJV).

Our key verses give us an excellent description of the maturing Christian life. These elements of the fruit of the Spirit are to be seen in us as we walk in the Spirit of the Lord.

The Christian alone cannot produce any of these things. We may struggle and strive to be loving, gentle or self-controlled, but we are bound to fail, just as the Galatian Christians did.

But, on the other hand, the Holy Spirit will not produce these things in us without our cooperation. The Scriptures teach, very plainly, that we can stifle the work of the Spirit in our lives. In his first letter to the Thessalonians, Paul says: "Do not quench the Spirit" (I Thessalonians 5:19); and to the Ephesians, he wrote "Do not grieve the Holy Spirit of God" (Ephesians 4:30).

The fruit of the Spirit—which is also the key to a fulfilled life and an effective witness—grows only as we allow the Holy Spirit to work in us, conforming us to the image of Jesus Christ.

Direction for today: Be sure you are allowing the Holy Spirit to work freely in your life, accomplishing all that God intends.

Prayer for today: "Father, I am willing for the fruit of the Spirit to be produced in me. Work in me to make me loving, joyful, peaceful, longsuffering, kind, good, faithful, gentle and self-controlled."

I and II Kings

These books might well be termed "The Decline and Fall of the Israelite Empire". David had led the kingdom to a point of peace and prosperity. As we begin I Kings, David is old and about to die; already his kingdom is rife with conflict—his sons are conspiring against one another as to whom should succeed him.

Eventually, Solomon, the man of God's choosing, gains control. Under him, Israel reaches the peak of its importance. It truly approaches the level of an empire, with wide-spread influence. But this situation does not last. Solomon disobeys God, introduces idol worship into his very houshold, and sets a pattern that will destroy the nation he loved.

There is much good during Solomon's reign; this includes the construction of the beautiful temple. B ut the moment he dies, the nation is split in two and the history of the divided kingdoms begins—a story of decline, apostasy and, ultimately, defeat.

I Kings covers the first years of this decline, from 970 to 852 B.C. II Kings takes us to the fall of the southern kingdom in 586 B.C.

The second volume confronts us with the stark reality that disobedience brings destruction. The northern kingdom suffers under a succession of wicked kings and is eventually defeated and carried into exile by Assyria. The southern kingdom is ruled by David's heirs but many of these men are also wicked, and the kingdom is ultimately defeated and forced into exile in Babylon.

November 23: Read I Kings 1

Key verse: "Praise be to the Lord, the God of Israel, who has allowed my eyes to see a successor on my throne today." (I Kings 1:48 NIV).

In this Scripture, we see a potential family feud and the possibility of a civil war being brought to a peaceful conclusion.

No precedent had been established in Israel to determine succession to the throne. Saul and David, although chosen and anointed by God, had been elected by the people.

Though it may not have been public knowledge, David had earlier chosen Solomon to succeed him. David's handling of the problem defused what could have been a national tragedy.

Within our own homes and families, tragedy strikes when struggles of leadership and authority arise. Blessed and peaceful is the home that allows God to rule and reign. Solomon set a beautiful example by allowing his brother to escape punishment for his presumptuous actions.

Direction for today: Remember that, to whom much is given, much is required. Do not seek after a lofty position without first counting the cost.

Prayer for today: "Lord, please direct the leaders of our nation; give them wisdom and understanding."

November 24: Read I Kings 2

Key verse: "And observe what the Lord your God requires: Walk in His ways, and keep His decrees and commands, His laws and requirements, as written in the Law of Moses, so that you may prosper in all you do and wherever you go" (I Kings 2:3 NIV).

Before David died, he had a talk with Solomon. The charge David gave to his son sounds much like the book of Deuteronomy. In fact, it is very similar to God's charge to Moses.

David realized Solomon would need all the wisdom and favour of God to have a successful reign over such an unruly people.

To be in close communion with God, we need to walk in harmony with Him and keep His laws. David's charge was: be strong, observe, walk and keep God's ways so you may prosper. To violate God's way is to court disaster. It has been said, "God's love cannot embrace what His holiness abhors."

Though we may not rule kingdoms, David's advice is still appropriate. "Walk in God's ways, and keep His decrees and commands."

Direction for today: Walk the straight and narrow way, that you may arrive at your destination.

Prayer for today: "Lord, help me to walk in Your wisdom."

November 25: Read I Kings 3,4

Key verse: *"So give Your servant a discerning heart to govern Your people and to distinguish between right and wrong. For who is able to govern this great people of Yours?" (I Kings 3:9 NIV).*

One of the most precious and meaningful requests ever made to God was made by Solomon. When God offered him anything he desired, Solomon could have chosen wealth, fame or long life; instead, he asked for wisdom.

Solomon had a deep love for God. He appreciated God's blessings upon his father David and the throne given him by God. Solomon desired, above all else, to serve well both God and his great nation. He wanted to administer justice. How would you respond to a similar opportunity? Would you seek blessings for yourself or for God and others? Are you motivated for God or for self?

Because Solomon asked selflessly, God was not only pleased to fulfill his request but abundantly gave additional blessings he had not requested.

Direction for today: Serve God out of a pure heart of service, not out of selfishness.

Prayer for today: "Lord, give me wisdom so I might better serve You."

November 26: Read I Kings 5,6

Key verse: *"Concerning this house which thou art in building, if thou wilt walk in My statutes, and execute My judgments, and keep all My commandments to walk in them; then will I perform My word with thee, which I spake unto David thy father" (I Kings 6:12 KJV).*

Solomon had almost finished building the temple in Jerusalem when the Word of the Lord came to him. God knew how Solomon would turn out; therefore, He gave him some instructions which, if followed, would keep him from harm and assure him of God's promise to establish him and his children upon the throne of Israel.

God loves those who are His and longs to provide for them. Because He wants nothing but the best for us, He has provided His Word to establish us in His kingdom. It is very interesting to note that His Word to us is closely connected to His house, the church. It's a fact that not all who attend a church are true Christians, but all true Christians *should* attend the house of the Lord.

Direction for today: Be faithful in attending a place of worship, and seek fellowship with God's people.,

Prayer for today: "Lord, bless our churches and grace them with Your presence."

November 27: Read I Kings 7

Key verse: "Thus all the work that King Solomon had done for the house of the Lord was finished; and Solomon brought in the things which his father David had dedicated: the silver and the gold and the furnishings. And he put them in the treasuries of the house of the Lord" (I Kings 7:51 NKJV).

Paul wrote, "I planted, Apollos watered, but God gave the increase. So then neither he who plants is anything, nor he who waters, but God who gives the increase" (I Corinthians 3:6,7). It is very hard for us to see things from God's perspective, to realize that our timing may not be His timing, or that our plans may not fit His planning.

David very much wanted to build the temple in Jerusalem, but God had specifically told him that such was not his task; it was appointed to Solomon.

Yet, when the temple was completed, furnishings which David had set aside for a day he knew he would never see, were carefully placed in the new temple by his son. David did not live to see the completion of the project, but he played an important role in it. Paul knew that he would not see the completion of the work he had begun, but he was prepared to leave the results to the Lord.

That is all God asks of us: to be faithful and to leave the results to Him. At times, we will see the completion of a specific task; other times, we will know nothing of the results until eternity.

We must trust the Lord to give the increase.

Direction for today: Obey, and leave the rest to God.

Prayer for today: "May I always be faithful to You, Lord."

November 28: Read I Kings 8

Key verse: "So that the priests could not stand to minister because of the cloud: for the glory of the Lord had filled the house of the Lord" (I Kings 8:11 KJV).

Solomon's Temple was undoubtedly one of the wonders of the world. For four centuries, it was to stand in awe-inspiring splendor as the epitome of Solomon's great works.

But the glory of this temple made by human hands faded to insignificance when the people of Israel were confronted by the One who is worthy of all glory and honour and power. The glory of the Lord so filled the temple that those in the building could not even stand before it.

As God manifested Himself in this way, He was indicating His blessing on this great building dedicated to Him, but He was also revealing the fact that the greatest works of man pale to insignificance next to the reality of God Himself.

Pray that the Lord will reveal Himself to you in glory and power and majesty. Worship this great God of all creation!

Direction for today: Know that the Lord is God, and that nothing in all creation can rival His glorious beauty.

Prayer for today: "Thou art worthy, O Lord, to receive glory and honour and power."

"Then they will see the Son of Man coming in the clouds with great power and glory" (Mark 13:26 NKJV).

November 29: Read I Kings 9, 10

Key verse: "Now if you walk before Me as your father David walked, in integrity of heart and in uprightness, to do according to all that I have commanded you, and if you keep My statutes and My judgments, then I will establish the throne of your kingdom over Israel forever, as I promised David your father . . . " (I Kings 9:4,5a NKJV).

Obedience is the key to a right relationship with God. It was the key in Old Testament days, and it is the key today.

The writer here records God's response to Solomon's prayer. God appears to Solomon a second time and again speaks to him. You will recall the first momentous occasion on which God appeared to Solomon. "Ask anything of Me," said the Lord. Solomon responded by asking for wisdom, but God also gave him riches and honour. Then God said the same words as those contained in our key verse (compare I Kings 3:14). God, knowing what would happen to Solomon, was driving home the necessity of obedience.

This is the key for our lives too. Solomon, according to I Kings 3:3, loved the Lord; his actions proved this, but there still remained the issue of obedience.

We do not obey to gain admission to heaven; rather, we obey because our admission to heaven is secure. Jesus said that those who love Him are the ones who obey Him, and those who obey are like those who have their houses built on rock. Integrity and uprightness of heart should result in obedience.

Direction for today: Walk with integrity and uprightness of heart, and be obedient to the Lord.

Prayer for today: "Father, help me to show my love for You by my obedience."

November 30: Read I Kings 11

Key verse: "For it came about when Solomon was old, his wives turned his heart away after other gods, and his heart was not wholly devoted to the Lord his God, as the heart of David his father had been" (I Kings 11:4 NAS).

This is one of those verses which we wish the Bible did not have to record. It's a verse that tells of disobedience and defeat and spells the end for King Solomon. The wisest man who ever lived, one of the richest men who ever lived—the one who asked God for wisdom when he could have asked for anything else—fell into worshipping false gods!

We notice a progression of sin in Solomon's life. First, he had made an alliance with Pharaoh and, as part of that alliance, married Pharaoh's daughter. Then, in the first two verses of today's reading, we discover that Solomon loved many foreign women and "held fast to them in love," though he very likely knew God's command about such associations. Finally, in verse five, he began to worship the idols of his wives. Such was Solomon's downfall.

Has there been, or is there currently, a progression of sin in your life? If so, repent and turn from it. We often tend to think that what has happened to others will never happen to us. Some of us even feel that it's okay to dabble in sin without getting hurt. But that which happened to Solomon teaches us we need to be so careful not to fall into a similar trap. It's not too late to change the direction in which you are going. God's grace is always greater than our sin.

Direction for today: In your daily life, watch for the "caution" and "danger" signs.

Prayer for today: "Father, give me the grace to see where I need to repent and turn from sin, and to do so now."

12

Why Did You Choose This Birth?

Why did You choose this birth?
Why did You come to earth at such a time,
And such a place?
Amazing love, infinite grace
Is all complete in You.

God is in Bethlehem.
His great and eternal plan is now fulfilled
In time and space.
A baby born, we see God's face.
He is complete in You.

The focus of history,
The meaning of mystery is found in You.
A child is born.
A broken world, corrupt and torn,
Will be complete in You.

— Paul Knowles

December 1: Read I Kings 12

Key verse: *"And the king answered the people harshly, for he forsook the advice of the elders which they had given him" (I Kings 12:13 NAS).*

There is a proverb concerning the wisdom of many counselors. The idea is that, the more counsel we have, the more accurate a decision we should be able to make. As we see from today's reading, this is not always the case.

Jeroboam and the people confronted Rehoboam about the government's heavy involvement in the lives of the people. Rehoboam, seeking to make his mark as the new king, consulted with those who were trusted advisors to his father. Not willing to take their gentle and bridge-building advice, he consulted with some of the young men. Their advice was totally opposite to that of the elders. What was he to do?

Rehoboam came down harshly on the people. He did not listen to the counsel given him by godly men, and that foolsih decision caused political disaster. The nation of Israel was divided in two as a result.

This is another case of disobedience and dishonour toward the elders God has provided. Each of us can easily fall into an "I'll-do-it-my-way" mentality but, when we go in that direction, we do so to our own hurt. The wisdom of the generations which have gone before needs to be heeded. If we are to pass on accurately the truths learned by those who have preceded us, we must also heed them in our own lives.

Direction for today: Heed the advice of elders in the Lord.

Prayer for today: "Lord, help me not to despise the wisdom of those godly people who have gone before me."

December 2: Read I Kings 13,14

Key verse: *"And Judah did evil in the sight of the Lord, and they provoked Him to jealousy more than all that their fathers had done, with the sins which they committed" (I kings 14:22 NAS).*

The history of Israel—from the division of the kingdom and, indeed, from its very beginning as a nation—is marred by disobedience to God. Round and round the cycle goes: Israel has a good relationship with God and then becomes involved with other gods; God sends other nations to confront Israel to bring her to repentance, Israel can't handle the other nations by herself and so cries out to God in repentance and God delivers her. The whole history of Israel repeats this cycle over and over and over.

Our key verse is a terrible indictment on the nation as she opens yet another cycle of her history: "Judah did evil . . . worse than her forefathers."

God constantly calls each generation to Himself. He sends prophets, opens the Word in new ways, and sends renewals and revivals—all designed to turn people to Himself. He never forsakes His own, but He requires us to walk in obedience. He desires, as He leads us to a newer and deeper understanding of His Word, that we walk in the wisdom He gives. This is the essence of the obedience which needs to be the goal of every believer.

Direction for today: Determine to follow the Lord, no matter what He calls you to do.

Prayer for today: "Lord, help me always to have a submissive heart."

December 3: Read I Kings 15,16

Key verse: "Now Ahab the son of Omri did evil in the sight of the Lord, more than all who were before him" (I Kings 16:30 NKJV).

Ahab was one of the worst kings who ever ruled over God's people. His life was filled with idolatry, immorality, rebellion and every kind of sin; he was utterly rebellious against God.

The Lord raised up the prophet Elijah to stand against Ahab; he was constantly a thorn in the flesh of the evil king. Even in the face of danger and threats to his life, Elijah stood against the wickedness of the king, and the Lord spoke to His people through him.

In our day, too, the Lord has need of men and women who will stand against overpowering evil. We must be open to His call to take such a stand.

Whatever it is you are hearing from the Lord, be sure to be obedient.

Direction for today: When God calls, obey.

Prayer for today: "Lord, I am willing to stand for You. Guide me, I pray."

December 4: Read I Kings 17,18

Key verse: "Then Elijah said to the people, 'I alone am left a prophet of the Lord; but Baal's prophets are four hundred and fifty men' " (I Kings 18:22 NKJV).

Who would have guessed that the odds favoured the one against the 450? Who would have predicted that Elijah could win a contest against so many formidable opponents? Yet that is precisely what happened and this dramatic confrontation has frequently drawn the comment, "One person with God is always a majority."

The Scriptures are full of examples which prove that numerical superiority never guarantees that the majority is right. Noah, Gideon and almost all of the Old Testament prophets stood alone at one time or another—and all stood with the Lord. Jesus, at the most critical point in his life, was left entirely alone. Paul, writing his second letter to Timothy, said that most of his friends had left him and he felt as though he was alone.

But we need never worry about being in the majority or about having the favour of people. Instead, we should concern ourselves solely with being in the will of God. That was the key to victory for Elijah and these other heroes of the Bible. They knew that a mere 450 men had no chance against one man of God!

Direction for today: One who stands with the Lord always stands in victory.

Prayer for today: "Lord, may I always be in Your will, and not swayed by the opinions of those around me in the world."

December 5: Read I Kings 19

Key verse: *"After the earthquake came a fire, but the Lord was not in the fire. And after the fire came a gentle whisper" (I Kings 19:12 NIV).*

Here we are brought to a standstill as we catch a glimpse of the stillness there is in God, in the changelessness of His grace and redemption. He knows how His grace will finally be vistorious in the lives of His people. By faith, we learn to understand this and to rest in Him; then we come to His stillness. This stillness has nothing to do with mystical speculations about silence.

The revelation of God to Elijah was preceded by violent signs. Immediately afterward, he was again thrown into the middle of the struggle. Those who engage in the struggle must possess the assurance of the victory of God's grace. From that certainty, our faith must continually be fed. Only as that happens will we live in stillness while engaged in the struggle.

Direction for today: Remember always to allow the Lord to reveal the stillness during times of struggle.

Prayer for today: "Father, in spite of the wind, the earthquake and the fire, let me hear your still, small voice."

Memory Verse

"Before the mountains were brought forth, or ever You had formed the earth and the world, even from everlasting to everlasting, You are God" (Psalm 90:2 NKJV).

December 6: Read I Kings 20

Key verse: *"Then he said to him, 'Thus says the Lord: "Because you have let slip out of your hand a man whom I appointed to utter destruction, therefore your life shall go for his life, and your people for his people' " (I Kings 20:42 NKJV).*

"But, God, I've got a better idea!"

We may not say it that way, but how often do we act just like this? The Lord has shown us His way, but we are convinced we know more than He does that it would best be handled *our* way.

It can happen in marriage: a young Christian is in love with an unbeliever and disregards God's command against being unequally yoked. Saying, "It will work out," is the same as declaring, "God, I know better than You."

It can happen in ministry: the Lord sends a pastor to a small congregation, but he chooses instead to accept an offer from a larger, more financially stable church. His ministry does not prosper and he wonders why.

It can happen in child-raising: we do not take the time to train our children in the ways of the Lord, yet we wonder why they run wild. We should not have known better than God!

That lesson is learned by two characters in today's reading: the man who refused to strike the prophet (and thus disobeyed God's command) and Ahab himself, as he spared Ben-Hadad. Both men thought they knew more than the Lord; their error cost them dearly.

Direction for today: Our Father always knows best!

Prayer for today: "Lord, help me humbly to obey."

December 7: Read I Kings 21

Key verse: "And he lay down on his bed, and turned away his face, and would eat no food" (I Kings 21:4b NKJV).

In our family, we call this "sulking". A perpetual sulker becomes known as a "spoiled brat".

In the kingdom of God, it is not rare to run into "spoiled brats", people who, by their sulking, are casting a pall over the fellowship of which they are a part. This usually happens when we do not get our own way over some issue we think is important. We are convinced we are right and, when the decision goes against us, withdraw in a sulk from involvement in our congregation.

This can happen over small things—like the colour of paint to be used in the church kitchen—or large things, such as the proper pastor to call to your congregation. But, whatever the reason, sulking is damaging to the Christian and to his or her church.

In Ahab, sulking (which occurred frequently, you will note) was the sign of a self-centred, immature, shallow person. The same may be true in us.

If we withdraw in bitterness, we will never grow. If we withold our support, everyone will suffer. Ther Lord is never pleased when the body is suffering and disunited.

Direction for today: If you are withdrawn in bitterness, confess and be restored. Remember that sulking withers your spirit and damages your church.

Prayer for today: "Lord, help me to become mature in Christ."

December 8: Read I Kings 22

Key verse: *"And Micaiah said, 'As the Lord lives, whatever the Lord says to me, that I will speak' " (I Kings 22:15 NKJV).*

Micaiah has set an example that Christians would do well to follow. Here was a brave man for whom nothing was more important than serving the Lord.

He knew that he might suffer because of his proclamation of the word of the Lord, but went ahead anyway. For Micaiah, obedience to God was more important than pleasing any other person or maintaining his personal safety. His proclamation resulted in physical suffering and in being sent to prison, but he remained faithful.

Around our world today, there are many who stand just where Micaiah stood. In communist countries, preachers and evangelists are preaching the word of the Lord despite the knowledge that they may be sent to prison or to "psychiatric" institutions. Christians are risking the wrath of state authorities in Moslem countries. In some Asian nations, one can be imprisoned for publicly admitting to being a Christian. In some African nations, families expel any members who convert to Christianity.

We in the west must be deeply grateful for the lack of persecution. But we must also be ready to face it if it comes during our lifetime—for, some day, it surely will. Then let us stand, with Micaiah, in open confession of the Lord.

Direction for today: Let nothing be more important than your obedience to God.

Prayer for today: "Lord, strengthen and deliver my brothers and sisters who suffer and are imprisoned for the gospel."

December 9: Read II Kings 1,2

Key verse: *"Is it because there is no God in Israel that you are sending to inquire of Baal-zebub, the god of Ekron?" (II Kings 1:6b NKJV).*

Today, thousands of Christians will lean back in their easy chairs, sip a cup of tea or coffee and read their horoscope in the newspaper. Others may have tea leaves read or their fortune told—"just for fun", they'll say.

This week, in thousands of Christian homes, children will be allowed to play with ouija boards or games involving sorcery and witchcraft. It may be that you, as a Christian parent, have just decided to buy your child such a game or toy for Christmas. All of these things, and many others common to our day, from water-witching to palmreading, are elements of the occult. They are all attempts to know the future through non-biblical means.

Sadly, many Christians have become ensnared in these things, especially in horoscopes. If they don't read it in the newspaper or a magazine with astrological predictions, they hear it on the radio or television.

Seeking such illicit knowledge brought the curse of death from the Lord upon Ahaziah. Obviously, God takes these things seriously and He has ordered His people to have nothing to do with them. Heed the warning of Elijah.

Direction for today: Cleanse your life and your house of any involvement with the occult.

Prayer for today: "Lord, show me any evil thing in my life, that I might be cleansed."

December 10: Read II Kings 3

Key verse: *"Now bring me a musician.' And it happened, when the musician played, that the hand of the Lord came upon him" (II Kings 3:15 NKJV).*

What in the world was Elisha doing? He wanted to hear the word of the Lord, so he asked for a musician—does this make any sense?

For anyone who has experienced the wonderful, uplifting impact of worship through music, it certainly does. God has given music as much more than an art form or entertainment. Over and over in Scripture, music is portrayed as a key method of worship.

The psalms continually urge us to sing and to make music in joyful praise and worship to God; the Apostle Paul echoes that instruction when he urges Christians to sing and make music with all our hearts unto the Lord!

Worship in song brings us into the presence of the Lord, whether we are singing corporately with other members of the body of Christ or individually before the Lord.

God delights in our musical worship. And He does not ask us to be great musicians—only to be great worshippers!

Direction for today: Sing to the Lord a new song!

Prayer for today: "Lord, place a song of worship in my spirit."

December 11: Read II Kings 4,5

Key verse: *"Now it came to pass, when the vessels were full, that she said to her son, 'Bring me another vessel.' And he said to her, 'There is not another vessel.' So the oil ceased" (II Kings 4:6 NKJV).*

How much are you ready to receive from the Lord? Are you prepared to be blessed by God in His fullness, to receive everything that He has for you? Or are you content to live on the fringes of His kingdom?

This story of a miracle performed through Elisha is a good example of how God works through our faith. Elisha told the woman to gather many vessels from her neighbours so that she would have a large quantity of oil to sell.

As we see in our key verse, God multiplied the oil to the exact volume of the vessels she had collected. Now, the woman had obviously shown great faith, for the sale of the oil provided enough for her and her family to live on. However, had she collected only two or three vessels, that would have been the limit of the oil which was miraculously provided. Had she supplied more vessels, God would have provided more oil.

How many vessels have you gathered to receive the blessings of the Lord? Do you have vessels enough to receive the miracles God can do in your life? Are there enough to contain the gifts of the Spirit the Lord wants to give you? Are there enough for healings, financial miracles or opportunities to minister? Or do you have only one small vessel labelled "salvation" with which you are content?

Direction for today: Be prepared to receive the great blessings of God.

Prayer for today: "Pour out Your oil on me, Lord."

December 12: Read II Kings 6,7

Key verse: "And Elisha prayed, and said, 'Lord, I pray, open his eyes that he may see.' Then the Lord opened the eyes of the young man, and he saw. And behold, the mountain was full of horses and chariots of fire all around Elisha" (II Kings 6:17 NKJV).

It is good to be reminded that most of us really have very poor vision. While we may have 20/20 vision in this world, we cannot see many of the important and exciting things that are happening around us.

Occasionally, the Lord allows a brief glimpse of the eternal realities that surround us, as He did for Elisha and his servant. For a moment, they saw things as they really are: there were crowds of angelic warriors surrounding them, ready to protect them.

God has not changed. He still charges his angels with the responsibility of guarding and protecting His people. We do not often see them, but that doesn't mean they do not exist.

When we reach eternity, our resurrection bodies will surely include eyes capable of seeing all of reality, not just the small segment we can now grasp. We may look forward in anticipation to that day.

And we can rejoice that the Lord our God has provided all of the protection and help we need through His angels, His Spirit and His people.

Direction for today: You are precious to the Lord, and He cares for you.

Prayer for today: "Thank You, Father, that in Your Word You have revealed true reality."

"Whoever does the will of My Father in heaven is My brother and sister and mother" (Matthew 12:50 NKJV).

December 13: Read II Kings 8

Key verse: "Yet the Lord would not destroy Judah, for the sake of His servant David, as He promised to give a lamp to him and his sons forever" (II Kings 8:19 NKJV).

Oh, the faithfulness of God! He always keeps His promises. No matter how often we fail Him, His Word is absolutely sure.

The writer of this chapter must have caught a faint glimpse of the glory that we know intimately, the glory of Jesus Christ. He spoke prophetically when he wrote that God had promised David a lamp, for the son of David, Jesus of Nazareth, became the light of the world, a lamp far brighter than this Old Testament writer could ever have imagined.

God must have been deeply hurt by the unfaithfulness of His people, Judah. The Lord must have wept at their sin and depravity. Although judgment fell on the disobedient ones, still God protected His people so that His promise would be fulfilled.

From the darkness of the sin and rebellion that encompassed the people of God came a light that shines eternally.

Direction for today: Remember that the Word of the Lord is sure.

Prayer for today: "Thank You, Father, for giving us the Light of the world, Your Son."

December 14: Read II Kings 9

Key verse: "And he poured the oil on his head, and said to him, 'Thus says the Lord God of Israel: "I have anointed you king over the people of the Lord, over Israel' " (II Kings 9:6b NKJV).

Jehu was anointed king of Israel. God had appointed him to replace the wicked king Ahab. Yet Jehu, while he accepted the will of the Lord in this, immediately began to sin against God.

There is a lesson here for all of us. Each believer is gifted through the Holy Spirit to minister for the Lord. God will place each of us in the right role in His church.

Just because we are gifted and placed in ministry does not mean we "have it made" spiritually. Too often, God's leaders have fallen into sin because they assumed that their high position guaranteed a high level of spirituality.

Like Jehu, we are always in danger of relying on a past blessing while heading into deep spiritual difficulty.

We can never rely on a previous experience with God as a guarantee that we are right with Him now. Unlike Jehu, we must continue to walk with the Lord, communing with Him and obeying Him daily.

Direction for today: Be sure you have not fallen away from your first love for Christ.

Prayer for today: "Lord, may I know I know Your anointing and blessing each moment of the day."

December 15: Read II Kings 10

Key verse: "However Jehu did not turn away from the sins of Jeroboam the son of Nebat, who had made Israel sin, that is, from the golden calves that were at Bethel and Dan" (II Kings 10:29 NKJV).

Jehu must have felt very spiritual. In obedience to God, he had destroyed all of the places of Baal worship. This false religion was—for the time being, at least—eradicated from the land of Israel.

But all of Jehu's efforts were useless because he continued to follow another false religion—the worship of the golden calves that had been established by Jeroboam, the first king of the northern kingdom. He was just as much an idolator as he had been when every altar to Baal was still standing.

We ourselves must beware of such evils. Oh, we probably don't have sacred groves in our backyards, but don't we often come to the Lord, confess sin and disobedience to Him and yet secretly hang on to one or two favourite sins?

If we make a show of obeying God—even going so far as to confess and cease a number of sins—it really does no good when we continue to harbour a couple of golden calves in our lives.

Unless everything is cleansed, we aren't really cleansed at all. Jehu's calves were a barrier between him and God; so are our "secret" sins.

Direction for today: If you want to be clean, clean *everything*!

Prayer for today: "Lord, search me and see if there be any wicked way in me; I will confess it and trust You to cleanse it."

December 16: Read II Kings 11,12

Key verse: "Jehoash did what was right in the sight of the Lord all the days in which Jehoiada the priest instructed him" (II Kings 12:2 NKJV).

What a difference a godly ruler can make to the fate of a nation! Both Judah and Israel had fallen far from the days of prosperity and unity they

had enjoyed under David and Solomon. Since the death of Solomon, the northern kingdom of Israel had had no righteous kings. Every man who ruled that land—many taking the throne by murder and intrigue—rejected God and followed after idolatry and immorality. But, in the southern kingdom of Judah, there were occasionally rulers—like young Jehoash—who turned back to serve the Lord.

Because of the faithfulness of those few men, interspersed among evil southern kings, the nation of Judah was allowed to stand for a century and a half longer than the northern kingdom. Their intercession prolonged the life of their nation.

Christians in our country can have the same kind of impact. Our intercession on behalf of our leaders, our neighbours and our land will cause the Lord to extend His mercy.

Direction for today: Be an intercessor for your family and your country.

Prayer for today: "God, keep our land."

December 17: Read II Kings 13,14

Key verse: "So it was, as they were burying a man, that suddenly they spied a band of raiders; and they put the man in the tomb of Elisha; and when the man was let down and touched the bones of Elisha, he revived and stood on his feet" (II Kings 13:21 NKJV).

This is an astounding story. It is also an amusing picture: a group of men abandon their efforts to bury a dead friend's body because enemies have come over the hill. They shove the body into an occupied tomb and immediately run away. Can you imagine their surprise as they hear a voice and turn to find the dead man running after them, also seeking to escape the Moabite raiders?

This is also a miraculous picture of the impact that a truly holy life will have on others. Elisha's power from God was so great that he performed one final miracle long after he was dead!

Do we who are alive and breathing have that kind of impact for good on those around us? Does the touch of our life on others point them to Jesus?

If the answer is "no", you can change that now by yielding your life in obedience to Jesus Christ.

Direction for today: Live a life that offers life to others.

Prayer for today: "Lord, may others be pointed to life in You whenever they touch my life."

December 18: Read II Kings 15,16

Key verse: ". . . he killed him and reigned in his place" (II Kings 15:30 NKJV).

What a horrible litany of evil and destruction! How far from the will of God the nation of Israel had fallen!

The first kings of Israel, Saul, David and Solomon, had been appointed by God and anointed by His prophet. But now the northern kingdom had fallen so far into sin that few kings died a natural death; instead, they were cut down by some conspiracy which placed another ruler on the throne.

The northern kingdom had continued to ignore God and now they were reaping their reward. There was internal strife and external danger. Foreign kings were exhorting money from the nation and Israel was too weakened to stop it.

How far they had fallen from the days when a few men led by the Lord were enough to storm a city or defeat an enemy. How far they were from the days when the Lord won battles for them without a single sword being unsheathed.

The nation had surrendered its relationship with God. It now bore the horrible consequences.

Direction for today: Never forsake the Lord.

Prayer for today: "Father, keep me close to You."

December 19: Read II Kings 17

Key verse: "Therefore the Lord was very angry with Israel, and removed them from His sight; there was none left but the tribe of Judah alone" (II Kings 17:18 NKJV).

The dreaded moment had come upon the northern kingdom. God's judgment was finally poured out upon his disobedient and rebellious people. He had given the ten tribes of Israel many opportunities to repent. He had sent them prophets and had given guidance to their leaders, but neither leader nor people ever chose to listen.

Unlike the southern nation, the northern tribes did not turn to the Lord even briefly; their pagan worship was continuous and their disregard for the Lord and His laws, complete.

God does not always strive with us. There comes a time of judgment, a time when our choices are locked in. We often think this happens only at death, but there are examples in the Bible of such a time coming during one's lifetime after continued rejection of the Lord.

The northern tribes were conquered and carried into exile, never to return. The people who eventually came back from captivity to rebuild Israel were only those from the southern kingdom of Judah. The northern tribes simply wrote themselves out of God's plans.

Direction for today: Remember that God is not blindly merciful; He is also the Judge.

Prayer for today: "Lord, may I remain faithful to Christ, who took upon Himself my penalty."

Memory Verse

"The eternal God is your refuge, and underneath are the everlasting arms" (Deuteronomy 33:27 NKJV).

December 20: Read II Kings 18

Key verse: "He trusted in the Lord God of Israel, so that after him was none like him among all the kings of Judah, nor any who were before him" (II Kings 18:5 NKJV).

Today's thought is especially directed to Sunday school teachers. That doesn't mean everyone else should stop reading, but this is especially for those who have responsibility for the spiritual teaching of children and young people.

Many of the children in our Sunday school classes come from seemingly impossible situations. Their parents may be separated or divorced; there may be rampant immorality in their homes and they may have been exposed to all manner of sin. Their background seems so bad that we could easily despair of accomplishing anything with them. But look for a minute at Hezekiah. Among all the good and evil kings of Judah, he stands as a shining light. He served the Lord completely, destroyed false religion in the land and was blessed by God to the point of accomplishing some military victories—a rare feat in those failing days.

Hezekiah's father, Ahaz, had been one of the most evil of the kings of Judah. The writer compared him with the vile kings of the northern nation! He practised child sacrifice and all manner of abominations. Yet, somehow, his son, Hezekiah, was a holy and devout worshipper of God who brought much blessing and peace to the land.

As long as the Lord lives, there is always hope that children can be turned from the wicked ways of their fathers unto righteousness.

Direction for today: Never give up hope: God still does miracles in the most unlikely lives.

Prayer for today: "Lord, use me to turn some back to righteousness."

December 21: Read II Kings 19

Key verse: "Now therefore, O Lord our God, I pray, save us from his hand, that all the kingdoms of the earth may know that You are the Lord God, You alone" (II Kings 19:19 NKJV).

Oh, how easy it is to steal some of the glory from God. How quickly the temptation comes to take some of the credit or the attention for ourselves.

Perhaps the Lord has done a great miracle in our lives and we have begun to tell others about it. How soon it is that our testimony is given so we can receive some of the attention that comes from hearing a good story. Perhaps we have been gifted with leadership abilities and are often in front of people in our church. How soon it is that we begin to enjoy those opportunities not for the chance to worship God, but for the chance to receive the attention of our friends.

How much we need to read the words of Hezekiah, who knew that, if the Lord delivered them, all glory and honour would go to Him and Him alone. Remember this—to God alone be the glory.

Direction for today: Be very sure you are not stealing glory from the Lord.

Prayer for today: "Father, I give You all the glory for all that You have accomplished in me and through me. Praise Your holy name."

December 22: Read II Luke 1:5-25

Key verse: "And he will turn many of the children of Israel to the Lord their God" (Luke 1:16 NKJV).

The time was fulfilled. God had set in motion events that would lead to the most important moments in the history of creation. This miraculous announcement to an elderly couple was a key scene in the triumphant drama of God's grace.

Zacharias and Elizabeth were to have a son! Once again, the Lord was healing a barren woman and giving her the answer to years of prayer. They would call him John, and he would be a prophet in a land that had heard no voice of a prophet for hundreds of years.

More than that—this son would be the voice crying in the wilderness, preaching repentance, awakening the hearts of the people, and most importantly, preparing the way of the Lord.

The people who had lived in darkness would soon see a very great light!

Direction for today: Praise God for the fulfillment of His great plan of salvation!

Prayer for today: "Thank You, Lord, that You use simple people to accomplish Your wonderful purposes!"

December 23: Read II Luke 1:26-45

Key verse: "He will be great, and will be called the Son of the Highest; and the Lord God will give Him the throne of His father David. And He will reign over the house of Jacob forever, and of His kingdom there will be no end" (Luke 1:32,33 NKJV).

Until yesterday, our readers have been in the final chapters of II Kings. There, we are reading about the decline and fall of the once-great nation of Israel. The northern kingdom has been carried off into permanent exile; the southern kingdom will soon be conquered.

From a human perspective, the Israelites in those centuries before Christ would have had every reason to think that God's chosen people had reached the end of their history.

Little did they know that they had not yet come to the real beginning! God worked miracle after miracle, restoring them to their land, bringing the nation back together again, and now, as we read, providing the Great King to sit on the long-vacant throne of David.

The Messiah was coming, to be born to—impossible, wonderful truth—a virgin. He would be the sinless one, the great High Priest, the sacrifice, Jesus the Lord! God was about to fulfill every promise that seemed to be lost in the ruts of the roads to Assyria and Babylon. God is the great Promise-Keeper!

Direction for today: God never fails.

Prayer for today: "Praise to the King, who sits on the throne and who will reign forever and ever."

December 24: Read Matthew 1

Key verse: "And she shall bring forth a son, and thou shalt call His name Jesus: for He shall save His people from their sins," (Matthew 1:21 KJV).

This is the greatest proclamation ever made to the world!

No other religion claims that sins may be forgiven. There is always a constant striving and searching but, outside of the Lord Jesus Christ, there is no assurance of the forgiveness of sins. Man, wherever he is found in the world, has a deep longing in his heart to find God, to have fellowship with Him and to know the assurance of eternal life. However, he finds the guilt of sin only reminds him that his search is not over.

When God announced the birth of His Son Jesus, He was proclaiming to the world that whoever put their trust in Jesus would have the forgiveness of sins, an assurance of peace with God and everlasting life. All those who believe in Christ are His, and God says He shall save His people from their sins.

Direction for today: Let Christ be your Saviour.

Prayer for today: "Grant me peace with God, through Jesus Christ our Lord."

December 25: Read Luke 2:1-20

Key verse: "And when they had seen it, they made known abroad the saying which was told them concerning this child" (Luke 2:17 KJV).

When Jesus was born in Bethlehem, God sent a message by His angels to the shepherds, who were tending their sheep on the hills outside the town.

God could have sent His messengers to the nobility or to the religious leaders, but He chose shepherds who were probably very poor in this world's goods, but rich in faith toward God. Their hearts were ready to accept the message and believe this was a fulfillment of prophecy that Israel's Messiah had really come.

Christ will always be revealed where there are hearts willing to receive Him—and not only to receive Him but, like the shepherds, to proclaim Him. Christ was born in Bethlehem that night; He was also born in the hearts of those shepherds.

Direction for today: On this anniversary of the birth of our Saviour, give God thanks for sending Him.

Prayer for today: "Lord, help me to proclaim the Lord Jesus Christ."

December 26: Read Matthew 2:1-15

Key verse: "And having been warned by God in a dream not to return to Herod, they departed for their own country by another way" (Matthew 2:12 NAS).

In this section of the Word, there are several examples which talk about God leading His people. The wise men were following the star, the priests and scribes found the answer to the magi's questions about the

Christ in the writing of the prophet, God spoke to the magi in a dream and, again, an angel appeared to Joseph in a dream.

Today, we sometimes wonder if God leads us and, if so, how does he do it? We may not have experienced dreams or visions or followed a star, but God just as surely guides today as He did then.

God leads most surely by His Word. Timothy is told by Paul that all (note, *all*) Scripture is "inspired by God and profitable for teaching . . . for training in righteousness." God's most certain revelation of His will is found in His Word.

God also leads by circumstances. These are often called "open doors" or "closed doors." By whatever name we call them, being in the right place at the right time or the wrong place at the wrong time can all work to our good in God's sovereign plan.

A third way God leads is by what one Bible teacher has called "sanctified common sense": that wisdom which God has placed within us. It's a combination of circumstances and acting on the knowledge which God has, by His Spirit, deposited in us.

Truly God does lead today, often in ways of which we're not aware, but He *does* lead. Count on it. He's the sovereign God.

Direction for today: Know that God is in control.

Prayer for today: "Father, lead me in the way *You* would have me go."

Memory Verse

"A little while longer and the world will see Me no more, but you will see Me. Because I live, you will live also" (John 14:19 NKJV).

December 27: Read II Kings 20,21

Key verse: "The word of the Lord came to him, saying, 'Return and tell Hezekiah the leader of My people, "Thus says the Lord, the God of David your father: 'I have heard your prayer, I have seen your tears; surely I will heal you' " ' " (II Kings 20:4b,5 NKJV).

God hears and answers prayer. What a marvellous truth this is! We have been granted permission—indeed, authority—to enter into the presence of God through prayer, and we are assured that, if we are right before Him, He will hear and answer.

In Hezekiah's case, God's answer meant healing and longer life.

What are your areas of need? God will hear and answer. That doesn't mean He will always do as you ask; He often knows better than we do! But, if we are obedient to Him, we are assured of His attention and intervention.

Come to the Lord today in the confidence that, whatever you ask in

prayer, believe the Lord hears and responds, just as He did to Hezekiah.
Be prepared for mighty miracles of God!

Direction for today: Remember, God hears and answers prayer.

Prayer for today: Bring an urgent need before the Lord, expecting His perfect answer for you.

December 28: Read II Kings 22

Key verse: "Now it happened, when the king heard the words of the Book of the Law, that he tore his clothes" (II Kings 22:11 NKJV).

If you have been using this Bible Reading guide regularly, you have been reading the Bible daily for at least a year. You are nearing the end of this year's readings and are half-way through the Bible (If you started with Volume 1, you have read through the entire Bible except for three chapters).

I trust your daily time in the Scriptures has not become an empty habit, but that, as you read the Word of God, you are allowing it to move you as it moved Josiah. When he heard the words of the Book, Josiah was so moved that he tore his clothes in repentance. Obviously, he learned of sin in his life and in the life of his nation.

May the Scriptures always have such an impact on our lives. May we be open to teaching, to correction and reproof. May we sense conviction when we are wrong and glory when we are right with the Lord.

May the Word always be a mirror in which we see ourselves; a sword which can cut out the areas of continuing sin; a light to guide us in the way of truth.

May reading the Word of God never be a boring daily exercise. If it has become such, repent and ask the Lord to revitalize your time in His Word.

Direction for today: Allow the Bible to speak to your spirit.

Prayer for today: "Lord, speak to me, today and every day, through Your Word."

December 29: Read II Kings 23

Key verse: "And he did evil in the sight of the Lord, according to all that his fathers had done" (II Kings 23:32 NKJV).

A few days ago, we read about Hezekiah, a righteous king whose father had been an evil man. We took hope that children can, through the love and the power of God, be delivered from an evil heritage.

Today, we see the dark side: the opposite can also be true. Josiah was a king who served the Lord and brought the Word of the Lord to the people of Judah. He had made very effort to return his land to service unto their God. Yet Josiah's son, Jehoahaz, was an evil king. He did not follow in his father's footsteps, but returned to the evil ways of the former kings of Judah.

What can we learn from this? We must understand that a person's relationship with Christ is his own responsibility. It is never enough to have Christian parents, a good church or a fine pastor. Each person must make the individual choice to follow Jesus.

Parents need to take note of this: it is not enough to be Christian and to raise our children well. We must attempt to lead them to personal faith in Christ and must continually intercede in prayer on their behalf.

Environment is never enough; each of us must personally encounter the Lord.

Direction for today: Be an intercessor for someone near to you who needs Jesus.

Prayer for today: "Lord, please bring *(name your loved one)* to Yourself."

December 30: Read II Kings 24

Key verse: "And the Lord sent against him raiding bands of Chaldeans, bands of Syrians, bands of Moabites, and bands of the people of Ammon; He sent them against Judah to destroy it, according to the word of the Lord which He had spoken by His servants the prophets" (II Kings 24:2 NKJV).

God is patient, but He will not forever endure disobedience in His people and the flagrant misuse of His name. The nations of Israel and Judah had continued to be known as the people of God, but neither acted in a manner honouring to God.

The Lord gave both nations much opportunity to change, but they never learned that key lesson. Israel is gone, and Judah's king—in the last days of the nation—refuse to turn to the Lord.

God finally refused to see evil done in His name any longer. He hurled enemy after enemy against Judah until the nation was a mere puppet of foreign rulers.

This principle is also true today. If we claim to be people of God, we must act to bring honour and glory to our Lord. If we carry the name of Jesus, let us never bring shame to Him.

If we sin, He will forgive; but if we blatantly continue to sin, He will bring judgment into our lives to stop our sin or to bring us to a painful repentance.

Direction for today: You bear the name of Christ; live to honour Him.

Prayer for today: "Lord, may You never be ashamed of me."

December 31: Read II Kings 25

Key verse: "And all the army of the Chaldeans who were with the captain of the guard broke down the walls of Jerusalem all around" (II Kings 25:10 NKJV).

What a terrible day! The capital city, the symbol of the nation of Israel, was destroyed. Jerusalem was laid waste. The leaders of the people were carried off in captivity to Babylon. Worst of all, the temple was destroyed.

Things had never looked worse for the nation of Israel. God's chosen people were forced out of the Promised Land. What of God's promises now? What of the Messiah, the Son of David?

Have you encountered circumstances when things looked as bad as they did to the captive Israelites—when everything good in your life seemed to be destroyed and all of God's promises sounded empty?

Look ahead: the nation is restored under leaders like Nehemiah and Ezra. The temple and the city walls of Jerusalem are rebuilt. The nation comes to know a time of peace and prosperity during the rule of the Maccabees. And, greatest of all, of course, in the City of David, the Messiah is born, a Deliverer greater than all the prophets had imagined!

Look ahead to the year which will begin tomorrow and know that God can turn around your circumstances.

No situation is so dark that God cannot break in, bringing the light of the world!

Direction for today: In every situation, look to the Light.

Prayer for today: "Thank You, Lord, that from despair You bring great joy!"

Notes